Taste of Home

201
RECIPES
YOU'LL MAKE
FOREVER

CLASSIC RECIPES FOR TODAY'S HOME COOKS

TASTE OF HOME BOOKS • RDA ENTHUSIAST BRANDS, LLC • MILWAUKEE, WI

© 2019 RDA Enthusiast Brands, LLC.
1610 N. 2nd St., Suite 102, Milwaukee WI 53212-3906
All rights reserved. Taste of Home is a registered
trademark of RDA Enthusiast Brands, LLC.
Visit us at **tasteofhome.com** for other Taste of Home
books and products.

International Standard Book Numbers:
978-1-61765-856-3 (Hardcover)
978-1-61765-792-4 (Paperback)
LOCC: 2018951860

Deputy Editor: Mark Hagen
Senior Art Director: Raeann Thompson
Editor: Hazel Wheaton
Art Director: Maggie Conners
Senior Designer: Courtney Lovetere
Designer: Arielle Jardine, Jazmin Delgado
Copy Editor: Chris McLaughlin

Cover Photography: Taste of Home Photo Studio

Printed in China
7 9 10 8

TABLE OF CONTENTS

All the must-have recipes every home cook should know.

From kitchens across the country, home cooks share their heirloom recipes with you!

Exploring the recipes in this book is just like coming home—with familiar, well-loved favorites on every page to welcome you. Would you like biscuits & gravy for breakfast, or a fresh-baked blueberry muffin with your coffee? For lunch, how about the best grilled cheese sandwich ever and some tomato-basil soup? And for dinner…can you smell the pot roast simmering on the stove? Of course, you'll want some buttermilk biscuits to soak up that rich gravy. And finish off your meal with a slice of cherry pie, or maybe some peach cobbler.

We've collected the essential recipes of American home cooking in one incredible volume. Each one was submitted by a talented home cook and tested and approved in our Test Kitchen, so you can be sure you have the best versions of the very best recipes.

These are the crowd-pleasers, the greatest hits, the sure-fire winners. They are the tried-and-true dishes that are certain to please family and friends, the recipes that every home cook should know how to make.

Best of all, each one of the 201 featured recipes includes a color photo and nutrition facts, so you know exactly what you're making.

As an added benefit, look for the more than 30 bonus recipes scattered through this book—recipes that provide a variation or an add-on to a well-loved classic. So in addition to beloved buttermilk pancakes, you'll get a recipe for pumpkin pancakes. As an alternative to a classic bacon cheeseburger, we'll give you the recipe for turkey burgers. As well as presenting a recipe for homemade bagels, we'll share a special honey-cinnamon butter to spread on top. And you can choose between two different varieties of stuffing for Thanksgiving! Plus, there are tips from our experts in every chapter to guarantee your success.

Handy icons throughout the book identify recipes that will save money and time. Recipes with the **SLOW COOKER** icon are all made using that most convenient kitchen tool. The **5 INGREDIENTS** icon notes recipes that call for five items or fewer (not including water; optional extras; and pantry staples like salt, pepper, and oil). To help you plan ahead, the **FREEZE IT** icon identifies recipes that can be prepped and frozen to use at a moment's notice.

If you are a new cook looking for a perfect place to start exploring the kitchen, this book is for you. And if you're an experienced cook simply in need of a colorful collection of the best versions of your all-time favorites—this book is for you, too! Dig in and enjoy, knowing that family and friends are waiting with thumbs-up approval!

BREAKFAST & BRUNCH

RISE AND SHINE WITH ONE OF THESE TIMELESS BREAKFAST DISHES.

COFFEE-GLAZED DOUGHNUTS

There's no treat like hot doughnuts! The coffee-flavored glaze on these makes them a perfect day starter.
—Pat Siebenaler, Random Lake, WI

PREP: 25 min. + rising • **COOK:** 5 min./batch
MAKES: about 4 dozen

- 2 pkg. (¼ oz. each) active dry yeast
- ¼ cup warm water (110° to 115°)
- 2 cups warm 2% milk (110° to 115°)
- ½ cup butter, softened
- 1 cup hot mashed potatoes (without added milk and butter)
- 3 large eggs
- ½ tsp. lemon extract, optional
- 1 cup sugar
- 1½ tsp. salt
- ½ tsp. ground cinnamon
- 9¼ to 9¾ cups all-purpose flour

COFFEE GLAZE
- 6 to 8 Tbsp. cold 2% milk
- 1 Tbsp. instant coffee granules
- 2 tsp. vanilla extract
- ¾ cup butter, softened
- 6 cups confectioners' sugar
- ½ tsp. ground cinnamon
  Dash salt
  Oil for deep-fat frying

1. In a large bowl, dissolve yeast in warm water. Add milk, butter, potatoes, eggs and, if desired, extract. Add sugar, salt, cinnamon and 3 cups flour. Beat until smooth. Stir in enough remaining flour to form a soft dough. Cover and let rise in a warm place until doubled, about 1 hour.

2. Stir down dough. On a well-floured surface, roll out to ½-in. thickness. Cut with a floured 2½-in. doughnut cutter. Place on greased baking sheets; cover and let rise for 45 minutes.

3. Meanwhile, for glaze, combine 6 Tbsp. milk, coffee and vanilla; stir to dissolve the coffee. In a large bowl, beat butter, sugar, cinnamon and salt. Gradually add milk mixture; beat until smooth, adding more milk as necessary to reach the desired dipping consistency.

4. In an electric skillet or deep-fat fryer, heat oil to 375°. Fry doughnuts, a few at a time, about 1½ minutes per side or until golden. Drain on paper towels. Dip tops in glaze while warm.

1 doughnut: 231 cal., 7g fat (3 sat. fat), 17mg chol., 121mg sod., 39g carb. (19g sugars, 1g fiber), 4g pro.

AUNT BETTY'S BLUEBERRY MUFFINS

My Aunt Betty creates a mouthwatering array of baked goods each Christmas, but I especially look forward to these!
—Sheila Raleigh, Kechi, KS

PREP: 15 min. • **BAKE:** 20 min.
MAKES: about 1 dozen

- ½ cup old-fashioned oats
- ½ cup orange juice
- 1 large egg
- ½ cup canola oil
- ½ cup sugar
- 1½ cups all-purpose flour
- 1¼ tsp. baking powder
- ½ tsp. salt
- ¼ tsp. baking soda
- 1 cup fresh or frozen blueberries

TOPPING
- 2 Tbsp. sugar
- ½ tsp. ground cinnamon

1. Preheat oven to 400°. In a large bowl, combine oats and orange juice; let stand for 5 minutes. Beat in the egg, oil and sugar until blended. Combine flour, baking powder, salt and baking soda; stir into the oat mixture just until moistened. Fold in the blueberries.

2. Fill greased or paper-lined muffin cups two-thirds full of batter. Combine topping ingredients; sprinkle over the batter. Bake muffins for 20-25 minutes or until a toothpick inserted in the center comes out clean. Cool 5 minutes; remove from pan to a wire rack. Serve warm.

Note: If using frozen blueberries, use without thawing to avoid discoloring the batter.

1 muffin: 208 cal., 10g fat (1g sat. fat), 18mg chol., 172mg sod., 28g carb. (13g sugars, 1g fiber), 3g pro.

CHEESY ZUCCHINI QUICHE

Put your pie dough together the night before and stash it in the fridge until morning. That rest time will give your quiche a more tender crust.
—Karen Howard, Lakeville, MA

PREP: 25 min. • **BAKE:** 35 min. + standing
MAKES: 8 servings

Pastry for single-crust pie (9 in.)
3 Tbsp. butter
4 cups thinly sliced zucchini (about 3 medium)
1 large onion, thinly sliced
2 large eggs
2 tsp. dried parsley flakes
½ tsp. salt
½ tsp. garlic powder
½ tsp. dried basil
½ tsp. dried oregano
¼ tsp. pepper
2 cups shredded part-skim mozzarella cheese
2 tsp. prepared mustard

1. Preheat the oven to 400°. On a lightly floured surface, roll dough to a ⅛-in.-thick circle; transfer to a 9-in. pie plate. Trim pastry to ½ in. beyond rim of plate; flute edge. Refrigerate while preparing filling.
2. In a large skillet, heat the butter over medium heat. Add zucchini and onion; cook and stir until vegetables are tender. Drain and cool slightly.
3. Whisk the eggs and seasonings until blended. Stir in the cheese and zucchini mixture. Spread mustard over the pastry shell; add filling.
4. Bake on a lower oven rack until a knife inserted in the center comes out clean and the crust is golden brown, 35-40 minutes. If needed, cover edge loosely with foil during the last 15 minutes to prevent overbrowning. Let quiche stand for 10 minutes before cutting.

Pastry for single-crust pie (9 in.): Combine 1¼ cups all-purpose flour and ¼ tsp. salt; cut in ½ cup cold butter until crumbly. Gradually add 3-5 Tbsp. ice water, tossing with a fork until dough holds together when pressed. Wrap in plastic wrap and refrigerate 1 hour.

1 piece: 332 cal., 23g fat (13g sat. fat), 103mg chol., 559mg sod., 20g carb. (3g sugars, 2g fiber), 12g pro.

TOP TIP

Test dishes that contain beaten eggs—quiches, stratas or custards—for doneness by inserting a knife in the center of the dish. If the knife comes out clean, the eggs are cooked.

OVERNIGHT CHERRY DANISH

These pastries will melt in your mouth. Leave a few unfrosted and store them in the freezer for another day.
—Leann Sauder, Tremont, IL

PREP: 1½ hours + chilling
BAKE: 15 min. + cooling • **MAKES:** 3 dozen

- 2 pkg. (¼ oz. each) active dry yeast
- ½ cup warm 2% milk (110° to 115°)
- 6 cups all-purpose flour
- ⅓ cup sugar
- 2 tsp. salt
- 1 cup cold butter, cubed
- 1½ cups warm half-and-half cream (70° to 80°)
- 6 large egg yolks
- 1 can (21 oz.) cherry pie filling

ICING
- 3 cups confectioners' sugar
- 2 Tbsp. butter, softened
- ¼ tsp. vanilla extract
  Dash salt
- 4 to 5 Tbsp. half-and-half cream

1. In a small bowl, dissolve the yeast in warm milk. In a large bowl, combine flour, sugar and salt. Cut in butter until crumbly. Add the yeast mixture, cream and egg yolks; stir until the mixture forms a soft dough (dough will be sticky). Refrigerate, covered, overnight.

2. Punch down dough. Turn onto a lightly floured surface; divide into four portions. Roll each portion of dough into an 18x4-in. rectangle; cut into 4x1-in. strips.

3. Place two strips side by side; twist together. Shape into a ring and pinch the ends together. Place rings 2 in. apart on greased baking sheets. Repeat with the remaining strips. Cover the rings with kitchen towels; let rise in a warm place until doubled, about 45 minutes.

4. Preheat oven to 350°. Using the end of a wooden spoon handle, make a ½-in.-deep indentation in the center of each Danish. Fill each with about 1 Tbsp. pie filling. Bake for 14-16 minutes or until lightly browned. Remove from pans to wire racks to cool.

5. For icing, in a bowl, beat confectioners' sugar, butter, vanilla, salt and enough cream to reach the desired consistency. Drizzle over Danish.

1 Danish: 218 cal., 8g fat (5g sat. fat), 55mg chol., 188mg sod., 33g carb. (16g sugars, 1g fiber), 3g pro.

HOMEMADE BISCUITS & MAPLE SAUSAGE GRAVY

I remember digging into flaky, gravy-smothered biscuits on Christmas morning and other special occasions when I was a child. What a satisfying way to start the day!
—Jenn Tidwell, Fair Oaks, CA

PREP: 30 min. • **BAKE:** 15 min.
MAKES: 8 servings

- 2 cups all-purpose flour
- 3 tsp. baking powder
- 1 Tbsp. sugar
- 1 tsp. salt
- ¼ tsp. pepper, optional
- 3 Tbsp. cold butter, cubed
- 1 Tbsp. shortening
- ¾ cup 2% milk

SAUSAGE GRAVY

- 1 lb. bulk maple pork sausage
- ¼ cup all-purpose flour
- 3 cups 2% milk
- 2 Tbsp. maple syrup
- ½ tsp. salt
- ¼ tsp. ground sage
- ¼ tsp. coarsely ground pepper

1. Preheat oven to 400°. In a large bowl, whisk flour, baking powder, sugar, salt and, if desired, pepper. Cut in butter and shortening until the mixture resembles coarse crumbs. Add milk; stir just until moistened. Turn onto a lightly floured surface; knead gently 8-10 times.
2. Pat or roll dough to 1-in. thickness; cut with a floured 2-in. biscuit cutter. Place 1 in. apart on an ungreased baking sheet. Bake 15-17 minutes or until golden brown.
3. Meanwhile, in a large skillet, cook the sausage over medium heat 6-8 minutes or until no longer pink, breaking meat into crumbles. Stir in the flour until blended; gradually stir in milk. Bring mixture to a boil, stirring constantly; cook and stir for

4-6 minutes or until sauce is thickened. Stir in the remaining ingredients. Serve with warm biscuits.

1 biscuit with ½ cup gravy: 371 cal., 19g fat (8g sat. fat), 41mg chol., 915mg sod., 38g carb. (11g sugars, 1g fiber), 11g pro

DELECTABLE GRANOLA

Here's a great make-ahead recipe. Be sure to remove the granola from the cookie sheets within 20 minutes, or it may stick to the pans.
—Lori Stevens, Riverton, UT

PREP: 20 min. • **BAKE:** 25 min. + cooling
MAKES: 11 cups

- 8 cups old-fashioned oats
- 1 cup finely chopped almonds
- 1 cup finely chopped pecans
- ½ cup sweetened shredded coconut
- ½ cup packed brown sugar
- ½ cup canola oil
- ½ cup honey
- ¼ cup maple syrup
- 2 tsp. ground cinnamon
- 1½ tsp. salt
- 2 tsp. vanilla extract
  Plain yogurt, optional

1. Preheat oven to 350°. In a large bowl, combine the oats, almonds, pecans and coconut. In a small saucepan, combine the brown sugar, oil, honey, maple syrup, cinnamon and salt. Heat for 3-4 minutes over medium heat until the sugar is dissolved. Remove mixture from the heat; stir in vanilla. Pour over the oat mixture; stir to coat.
2. Transfer to two 15x10x1-in. baking pans coated with cooking spray. Bake for 25-30 minutes or until crisp, stirring every 10 minutes. Cool in pans on wire racks. Store in an airtight container. Serve with yogurt if desired.

½ cup: 288 cal., 15g fat (2g sat. fat), 0 chol., 170mg sod., 36g carb. (15g sugars, 4g fiber), 6g pro. **Diabetic exchanges:** 2½ starch, 2 fat.

BRUNCH BURRITOS

I like to use a second slow cooker to keep the tortillas warm and pliable when I serve these yummy burritos. Just place a clean wet cloth in the bottom, then cover it with foil and add your tortillas.
—Beth Osburn, Levelland, TX

PREP: 30 min. • **COOK:** 4 hours
MAKES: 10 servings

- 1 lb. bulk pork sausage, cooked and drained
- ½ lb. bacon strips, cooked and crumbled
- 18 large eggs, lightly beaten
- 2 cups frozen shredded hash brown potatoes, thawed
- 1 large onion, chopped
- 1 can (10¾ oz.) condensed cheddar cheese soup, undiluted
- 1 can (4 oz.) chopped green chilies
- 1 tsp. garlic powder
- ½ tsp. pepper
- 2 cups shredded cheddar cheese
- 10 flour tortillas (10 in.), warmed
  Optional toppings: jalapeno peppers, salsa or hot pepper sauce

1. In a large bowl, combine the first nine ingredients. Pour half of the egg mixture into a 4- or 5-qt. slow cooker coated with cooking spray. Top with half of the cheese. Repeat layers.

2. Cook, covered, on low for 4-5 hours or until center is set and a thermometer reads 160°.

3. Spoon ¾ cup of the egg mixture across center of each tortilla. Fold the bottom and sides of the tortilla over the filling and roll up. Add toppings of your choice.

1 burrito: 683 cal., 38g fat (15g sat. fat), 449mg chol., 1650mg sod., 41g carb. (3g sugars, 7g fiber), 35g pro.

"This is a great recipe for those busy weekends. It has been a hit with my family, and I'll keep using it for years to come!"
—RANDCBRUNS, TASTEOFHOME.COM

FLUFFY WAFFLES

A friend shared the recipe for these light and delicious waffles. The cinnamon cream syrup is a nice change from maple syrup, and it keeps quite well in the fridge. Our two children also like it on toast.

—Amy Gilles, Ellsworth, WI

PREP: 25 min. • **COOK:** 20 min.
MAKES: 10 waffles (6½ in.) and 1⅔ cups syrup

2	**cups all-purpose flour**
1	**Tbsp. sugar**
2	**tsp. baking powder**
½	**tsp. salt**
3	**large eggs, separated**
2	**cups milk**
¼	**cup canola oil**

CINNAMON CREAM SYRUP

1	**cup sugar**
½	**cup light corn syrup**
¼	**cup water**
1	**can (5 oz.) evaporated milk**
1	**tsp. vanilla extract**
½	**tsp. ground cinnamon**

1. In a bowl, combine the flour, sugar, baking powder and salt. Combine the egg yolks, milk and oil; stir into dry ingredients just until moistened. In a small bowl, beat egg whites until stiff peaks form; fold into batter. Bake in a preheated waffle iron according to manufacturer's directions.

2. Meanwhile, for syrup, combine sugar, corn syrup and water in a saucepan. Bring to a boil over medium heat; cook and stir for 2 minutes or until thickened. Remove from the heat; stir in the milk, vanilla and cinnamon. Serve with waffles.

Freeze option: Cool waffles on wire racks. Freeze between layers of waxed paper in a resealable plastic freezer bag. Reheat waffles in a toaster on medium setting. Or microwave each waffle on high for 30-60 seconds or until heated through.

1 waffle with 2½ Tbsp. syrup: 424 cal., 12g fat (4g sat. fat), 94mg chol., 344mg sod., 71g carb. (41g sugars, 1g fiber), 9g pro.

Ham & Cheese Waffles: Omit sugar and Cinnamon Cream Syrup. Increase flour to 2½ cups. Fold in 1½ cups shredded mozzarella cheese and ½ cup cubed fully cooked ham.

Tropical Waffles: Omit Cinnamon Cream Syrup. Increase baking powder to 4 tsp.. Before adding egg whites, stir in 1 can (8 oz.) well-drained crushed pineapple, ¼ cup flaked coconut and ¼ cup chopped macadamia nuts.

Blueberry Waffles: Increase baking powder to 2½ tsp.. Before adding egg whites, fold in 1½ cups fresh or frozen blueberries.

Cinnamon Waffles: Substitute brown sugar for sugar. With flour, stir in ½ tsp. ground cinnamon. With egg yolk, stir in ¾ tsp. vanilla.

BONUS: RAISED YEAST WAFFLES

These terrific waffles are crispy on the outside and tender on the inside. Never too filling, they leave room for sampling the rest of the brunch buffet!
—Helen Knapp, North Pole, AK

PREP: 15 min. + rising • **BAKE:** 5 min./batch
MAKES: 10 waffles

- 1 pkg. (¼ oz.) active dry yeast
- 1 tsp. sugar
- ½ cup warm water (110° to 115°)
- 2 cups warm 2% milk (110° to 115°)
- 2 large eggs
- ½ cup butter, melted
- 2¼ cups all-purpose flour
- 1 tsp. salt
- ⅛ tsp. baking soda

Dissolve yeast and sugar in warm water; let stand 5 minutes. Beat in milk, eggs and butter. In another bowl, combine flour, salt and baking soda; stir into the yeast mixture just until combined. Cover and let rise in a warm place until doubled, about 45 minutes. Stir the batter. Bake in a preheated waffle iron according to manufacturer's directions until golden brown.

2 waffles: 453 cal., 23g fat (14g sat. fat), 131mg chol., 726mg sod., 49g carb. (6g sugars, 2g fiber), 12g pro.

CORNED BEEF HASH & EGGS

Sunday breakfasts have always been special in our house. It's fun to get in the kitchen and cook with the kids. No matter how many new recipes we try, everyone always rates this one No. 1!
—Rick Skildum, Maple Grove, MN

PREP: 15 min. • **BAKE:** 20 min.
MAKES: 8 servings

- 1 pkg. (32 oz.) frozen cubed hash browns
- 1½ cups chopped onion
- ½ cup canola oil
- 4 to 5 cups chopped cooked corned beef
- ½ tsp. salt
- 8 large eggs
  Salt and pepper to taste
- 2 Tbsp. minced fresh parsley

1. Preheat the oven to 325°. In a large ovenproof skillet, cook hash browns and onion in oil until the potatoes are browned and the onion is tender. Remove from the heat; stir in corned beef and salt.
2. Make eight wells in the hash browns. Break one egg into each well. Sprinkle with salt and pepper. Cover and bake for 20 25 minutes or until the eggs reach desired doneness. Garnish with parsley.
1 serving: 442 cal., 30g fat (6g sat. fat), 242mg chol., 895mg sod., 24g carb. (3g sugars, 2 fiber), 20g pro.

5 INGREDIENTS
FLUFFY SCRAMBLED EGGS

When our son wants something other than cereal in the morning, he whips up these eggs. Cheese and evaporated milk make them especially good.
—Chris Pfleghaar, Elk River, MN

TAKES: 15 min. • **MAKES:** 3 servings

- 6 large eggs
- ¼ cup evaporated milk or half-and-half cream
- ¼ tsp. salt
- ⅛ tsp. pepper
- 1 Tbsp. canola oil
- 2 Tbsp. process cheese sauce

In a bowl, whisk the eggs, milk, salt and pepper. In a large skillet, heat oil over medium heat. Pour in egg mixture; stir in cheese sauce. Cook and stir until eggs are thickened and no liquid egg remains.
½ cup: 246 cal., 18g fat (6g sat. fat), 438mg chol., 523mg sod., 4g carb. (4g sugars, 0 fiber), 15g pro.

EGGS BENEDICT WITH HOMEMADE HOLLANDAISE

Legend has it that poached eggs on an English muffin started at Delmonico's in New York. Here's my take on this brunch classic—and don't spare the hollandaise!
—Barbara Pletzke, Herndon, VA

TAKES: 30 min. • **MAKES:** 8 servings

- 4   **large egg yolks**
- 2   **Tbsp. water**
- 2   **Tbsp. lemon juice**
- ¾   **cup butter, melted**
     Dash white pepper

ASSEMBLY

- 8   **large eggs**
- 4   **English muffins, split and toasted**
- 8   **slices Canadian bacon, warmed**
     Paprika

1. For hollandaise sauce, in top of a double boiler or a metal bowl over simmering water, whisk egg yolks, water and lemon juice until blended; cook until the mixture is just thick enough to coat a metal spoon and the temperature reaches 160°, whisking constantly. Remove from heat. Very slowly drizzle in warm melted butter, whisking constantly. Whisk in pepper. Transfer to a small bowl if necessary. Place bowl in a larger bowl of warm water. Keep warm, stirring occasionally, until ready to serve, up to 30 minutes.

2. Place 2-3 in. of water in a large saucepan or a skillet with high sides. Bring to a boil; adjust heat to maintain a gentle simmer. Break one egg into a small bowl; holding the bowl close to the surface of water, slip the egg into the water. Repeat with three more eggs.

3. Cook, uncovered, 2-4 minutes or until whites are completely set and the yolks begin to thicken but are not hard. Using a slotted spoon, lift eggs out of the water. Repeat with the remaining four eggs.

4. Top each muffin half with a slice of bacon, a poached egg and 2 Tbsp. sauce; sprinkle with paprika. Serve immediately.

1 serving: 345 cal., 26g fat (14g sat. fat), 331mg chol., 522mg sod., 15g carb. (1g sugars, 1g fiber), 13g pro.

TOP TIP

Hollandaise sauce is best served as soon as possible after it's done, although it can be held for up to an hour as long as it's kept warm. The sauce is famous for "breaking," or separating, if it gets too cold or too hot. To attempt a rescue, whisk some hot water into cold sauce, or cold water into hot sauce, to recombine and smooth it out.

BUTTERMILK PANCAKES

You just can't beat a basic buttermilk pancake for a down-home hearty breakfast. Pair it with sausage and fresh fruit for mouthwatering morning meal.
—Betty Abrey, Imperial, , SK

PREP: 10 min. • **COOK:** 5 min./batch
MAKES: 2½ dozen

4	cups all-purpose flour
¼	cup sugar
2	tsp. baking soda
2	tsp. salt
1½	tsp. baking powder
4	large eggs
4	cups buttermilk

1. In a large bowl, combine the flour, sugar, baking soda, salt and baking powder. In another bowl, whisk eggs and buttermilk until blended; stir into dry ingredients just until moistened.

2. Pour batter by ¼ cupfuls onto a lightly greased hot griddle; turn when bubbles form on top. Cook until second side is golden brown.

3 pancakes: 270 cal., 3g fat (1g sat. fat), 89mg chol., 913mg sod., 48g carb. (11g sugars, 1g fiber), 11g pro.

BONUS: PUMPKIN PANCAKES

For a sweet and satisfying fall breakfast, these pancakes are just the thing. The pumpkin and cinnamon are perfect together.
—Nancy Horsburgh, Everett, ON

TAKES: 25 min. • **MAKES:** 12 pancakes

1	cup all-purpose flour	1⅔	cups whole milk
1	cup quick-cooking oats	1	large egg, lightly beaten
2	Tbsp. toasted wheat germ	¾	cup canned pumpkin
2	tsp. sugar	2	Tbsp. canola oil
2	tsp. baking powder		Chocolate chips or raisins,
½	tsp. salt		optional
	Pinch ground cinnamon		

1. In a large bowl, combine flour, oats, wheat germ, sugar, baking powder, salt and cinnamon. In a small bowl, whisk milk, egg, pumpkin and oil; stir into the dry ingredients just until moistened.

2. Pour batter by ¼ cupfuls onto a hot greased griddle; turn when bubbles form on top of the pancakes. Cook until the second side is golden brown. Decorate with chocolate chips and raisins if desired.

2 pancakes: 274 cal., 10g fat (2g sat. fat), 49mg chol., 435mg sod., 38g carb. (6g sugars, 4g fiber), 9g pro.

TOP TIP

Once you have classic buttermilk pancakes down, you can start playing! To make blueberry pancakes, fold 1 cup of fresh or frozen blueberries into the batter. To make banana-nut pancakes, fold in two finely chopped ripe bananas and ⅔ cups finely chopped walnuts. Add spices, such as cinnamon, ginger, and cloves to the flour mixture, too!

BEEFY HUEVOS RANCHEROS

This recipe is quick and easy, and it helps use the eggs from our chickens. It works for breakfast, lunch or dinner and is great served with fruit or salad and some flour tortillas. Guests can add lots of toppings or just a little, however they like.
—Sandra Leonard, Peculiar, MO

PREP: 15 min. • **COOK:** 20 min.
MAKES: 6 servings

- 1   lb. lean ground beef (90% lean)
- 1   small onion, finely chopped
- 2   cans (14½ oz. each) diced tomatoes
- 1   cup frozen corn
- 1   can (4 oz.) chopped green chilies
- ½   tsp. salt
- 6   large eggs
- ¼   tsp. pepper
- 6   Tbsp. shredded cheddar cheese
- 6   flour tortillas (8 in.), warmed
      Optional toppings: reduced-fat sour cream, guacamole, salsa and chopped green onions

1. In a large skillet, cook beef and onion over medium heat 6-8 minutes or until beef is no longer pink and onion is tender, breaking up beef into crumbles; drain and return to pan.
2. Drain tomatoes, reserving ½ cup liquid. Stir tomatoes, reserved liquid, corn, chilies and salt into the beef mixture; bring to a simmer. With the back of a spoon, make six wells in the beef mixture; add an egg to each well. Sprinkle with pepper. Cover and cook for 5-7 minutes or until egg whites are completely set.
3. Sprinkle with cheddar cheese. Serve with tortillas and toppings as desired.
1 serving: 434 cal., 17g fat (6g sat. fat), 241mg chol., 879mg sod., 41g carb. (6g sugars, 5g fiber), 29g pro.

CROQUE MADAME

My son and I prefer a fried egg atop our grilled ham and cheese, but you can make the sandwich without it (that's a Croque Monsieur).
—Carolyn Turner, Reno, NV

TAKES: 30 min. • **MAKES:** 8 servings

- 1   lb. thinly sliced Gruyere cheese, divided
- 16 slices sourdough bread
- 1½ lbs. thinly sliced deli ham
- ½   cup butter, softened
- 4   to 6 Tbsp. mayonnaise
  EGGS
- 2   Tbsp. butter
- 8   large eggs
- ½   tsp. salt
- ½   tsp. pepper

1. Preheat oven to 400°. Place half of the cheese on eight bread slices; top with ham and the remaining bread. Spread outsides of sandwiches with softened butter.
2. On a griddle, toast sandwiches over medium heat 2-3 minutes on each side or until golden brown. Spread tops with mayonnaise; top with remaining cheese. Transfer to an ungreased baking sheet; bake 4-5 minutes or until cheese is melted.
3. Meanwhile, for eggs, heat 1 Tbsp. butter on griddle over medium-high heat. Break four eggs, one at a time, onto griddle. Reduce heat to low. Cook to desired doneness, turning after whites are set if desired. Sprinkle with salt and pepper. Place eggs over four sandwiches. Repeat with remaining ingredients.
1 sandwich: 758 cal., 47g fat (24g sat. fat), 344mg chol., 1691mg sod., 40g carb. (2g sugars, 2g fiber), 46g pro.

STICKY CINNAMON-SUGAR MONKEY BREAD

I prepare the dough pieces and put the sauce ingredients in the pan the night before so it's ready for the morning. For a bit of crunch, sprinkle chopped nuts in with the dough pieces before pouring on the sauce and baking.
—Diana Kunselman, Rimersburg, PA

PREP: 20 min. + rising • **BAKE:** 20 min.
MAKES: 16 servings

- 2 loaves (1 lb. each) frozen bread dough, thawed
- 1 cup packed brown sugar
- ¾ cup butter, cubed
- 1 pkg. (3 oz.) cook-and-serve vanilla pudding mix
- 2 Tbsp. 2% milk
- 2 tsp. ground cinnamon

1. Cut dough into 1-in. pieces; place in a greased 13x9-in. baking dish. In a large saucepan, combine remaining ingredients; bring to a boil. Cook and stir for 1 minute; remove from heat. Pour sauce over the dough pieces.

2. Cover loosely with parchment paper or nonstick foil; let rise in a warm place until almost doubled, about 45 minutes. Preheat oven to 350°. Bake, uncovered, until golden brown, for 20-25 minutes. Immediately invert onto a serving plate.

1 serving: 247 cal., 9g fat (4g sat. fat), 18mg chol., 339mg sod., 36g carb. (16g sugars, 2g fiber), 5g pro.

NOTES

_____
_____
_____
_____
_____
_____
_____
_____
_____
_____

VANILLA FRENCH TOAST

When in Mexico, we couldn't figure out what made the French toast so delicious until we learned the secret—vanilla. Now we add vanilla to our waffle and pancake recipes, too!
—Joe and Bobbi Schott, Castroville, TX

TAKES: 15 min. • **MAKES:** 6 servings

- 4 large eggs, lightly beaten
- 1 cup 2% milk
- 2 Tbsp. sugar
- 2 tsp. vanilla extract
- ⅛ tsp. salt
- 12 slices day-old sandwich bread
  Optional toppings: butter, maple syrup, fresh berries and confectioners' sugar

1. In a shallow dish, whisk together the first five ingredients. Preheat a greased griddle over medium heat.

2. Dip bread in egg mixture, allowing to soak 30 seconds on each side. Cook until golden brown on both sides. Serve with toppings as desired.

2 slices: 218 cal., 6g fat (3g sat. fat), 127mg chol., 376mg sod., 30g carb. (9g sugars, 1g fiber), 10g pro. **Diabetic exchanges:** 2 starch, 1 medium-fat meat.

Whole Wheat Cinnamon French Toast:
Omit vanilla. Substitute 1½ tsp. honey for sugar and whole wheat bread for the day-old bread. Add ¼ tsp. ground cinnamon to the milk mixture.

BONUS: BAKED FRENCH TOAST WITH HOME STYLE SYRUP

This cruchy-coated variation of typical French toast is both simple to prepare and delicious. And the homemade syrup has more flavor than bottled syrup ever could!
—Deloris Asmus, Waseca, MN

TAKES: 25 min. • **MAKES:** 8 servings

- 4 large eggs, lightly beaten
- 1 cup whole milk
- 2 tsp. vanilla extract
- 1 tsp. salt
- 12 slices day-old French bread (½ in. thick)
- 1¼ cups crushed cornflakes
- 1 to 2 Tbsp. butter

SYRUP
- 1½ cups sugar
- ⅔ cup light corn syrup
- ½ cup water
- 1 tsp. ground cinnamon
- 1 can (5 oz.) evaporated milk
- ½ tsp. butter flavoring
- ½ tsp. almond extract

1. In a shallow dish, combine eggs, milk, vanilla and salt. Add bread; soak for 5 minutes, turning once to coat. Coat each slice with cornflake crumbs; place on a greased baking sheet. Dot with butter. Bake at 450° for 10-12 minutes or until golden brown.

2. For syrup, combine sugar, corn syrup, water and cinnamon in a saucepan. Bring to a boil. Boil, stirring constantly, for 2 minutes. Remove from the heat; stir in evaporated milk and flavorings. Serve over warm French toast.

2 slices: 416 cal., 7g fat (3g sat. fat), 120mg chol., 610mg sod., 82g carb. (55g sugars, 1g fiber), 8g pro.

SAUSAGE EGG BAKE

This hearty egg dish is wonderful for any meal of the day. I fix it frequently for special occasions because it's easy to prepare and really versatile. For a change, use spicier sausage or substitute a flavored cheese blend.
—Molly Swallow, Pocatello, ID

PREP: 10 min. • **BAKE:** 40 min.
MAKES: 12 servings

- 1 **lb. bulk Italian sausage**
- 2 **cans (10¾ oz. each) condensed cream of potato soup, undiluted**
- 9 **large eggs, lightly beaten**
- ¾ **cup 2% milk**
- ¼ **tsp. pepper**
- 1 **cup shredded cheddar cheese**

1. In a large skillet, cook sausage over medium heat until no longer pink; drain. Stir in soup. In a large bowl, whisk eggs, milk and pepper; stir in sausage mixture.
2. Transfer to a lightly greased 2-qt. baking dish. Sprinkle with cheese. Bake, uncovered, at 375° for 40-45 minutes or until a knife inserted in the center comes out clean.
1 serving: 181 cal., 13g fat (6g sat. fat), 189mg chol., 484mg sod., 5g carb. (2g sugars, 0 fiber), 11g pro.

Monterey Mushroom Breakfast Bake:
Cook sausage with 2 cups sliced fresh mushrooms. Substitute condensed cream of mushroom soup for the potato soup and shredded Monterey Jack cheese for the cheddar.

SAUSAGE CRESCENT ROLLS

I love the appetizer pigs in a blanket and thought I could turn it into an amazing breakfast dish. Boy, was I right! These are now on the menu for every family gathering.
—Jimmie Harvey, Bedias, TX

PREP: 25 min. + rising • **BAKE:** 15 min.
MAKES: 3 dozen

- 36 **frozen fully cooked breakfast sausage links**
- 1 **pkg. (¼ oz.) active dry yeast**
- 1 **cup warm water (110° to 115°)**
- ½ **cup sugar**
- ½ **cup butter, melted**
- 3 **large eggs**
- 1 **tsp. salt**
- 5½ **to 6 cups all-purpose flour**
TOPPING
- 1 **large egg white**
- 1 **Tbsp. water**
- 3 **Tbsp. sesame seeds, toasted**

1. In a large skillet, cook sausage over medium heat just until browned, turning frequently. Cool slightly; refrigerate.
2. Dissolve yeast in warm water. Add sugar, butter, eggs, salt and 2 cups flour. Beat on medium speed until smooth. Stir in enough remaining flour to form a soft dough. Refrigerate, covered, overnight.
3. Turn dough onto a lightly floured surface; divide into six portions. Roll each into a 10-in. circle; cut each circle into six wedges. Place a sausage at the wide end of each wedge and roll up from the wide end. Place rolls point sides down, 2 in. apart, on greased baking sheets. Cover with a kitchen towel; let rise in a warm place until doubled, about 1 hour.
4. Preheat oven to 350°. Beat egg white and water; brush over rolls. Sprinkle with sesame seeds. Bake until lightly browned, 12-14 minutes. Serve warm.
1 roll: 165 cal., 9g fat (4g sat. fat), 30mg chol., 218mg sod., 18g carb. (3g sugars, 1g fiber), 5g pro.

OVERNIGHT BAKED OATMEAL

After making a few tweaks to an oatmeal recipe from a nearby bed-and-breakfast, I now bake this breakfast treat whenever I want to relive those cozy mornings.
—Jennifer Cramer, Lebanon, PA

PREP: 10 min. + chilling • **BAKE:** 45 min.
MAKES: 8 servings

- 2 large eggs, lightly beaten
- 3 cups 2% milk
- ¾ cup packed brown sugar
- ¼ cup canola oil
- 1½ tsp. ground cinnamon
- 1 tsp. salt
- 2 cups old-fashioned oats
- ¼ cup dried blueberries
- ¼ cup dried cherries
- ¼ cup sliced almonds

1. In a large bowl, whisk together first six ingredients. Stir in oats, blueberries and cherries. Transfer mixture to a greased 8-in. square baking dish. Refrigerate, covered, 8 hours or overnight.

2. Preheat oven to 350°. Remove oatmeal from refrigerator while oven heats. Stir oatmeal; sprinkle with almonds. Bake, uncovered, until golden brown and a thermometer reads 160°, 40-50 minutes. Serve warm.

1 serving: 331 cal., 13g fat (2g sat. fat), 54mg chol., 364mg sod., 46g carb. (30g sugars, 4g fiber), 8g pro.

BONUS: MAPLE APPLE BAKED OATMEAL

I've tried different fruit for this recipe, but apple is my family's favorite. I mix the dry and wet ingredients in separate bowls the night before, and I combine them the next morning when it's time to make breakfast.
—Megan Brooks, Saint Lazare, Quebec

PREP: 20 min. • **COOK:** 25 min. • **MAKES:** 8 servings

- 3 cups old-fashioned oats
- 2 tsp. baking powder
- 1¼ tsp. ground cinnamon
- ½ tsp. salt
- ¼ tsp. ground nutmeg
- 2 large eggs
- 2 cups fat-free milk
- ½ cup maple syrup
- ¼ cup canola oil
- 1 tsp. vanilla extract
- 1 large apple, chopped
- ¼ cup sunflower kernels or pepitas

Preheat oven to 350°. In a large bowl, mix the first five ingredients. In a small bowl, whisk eggs, milk, syrup, oil and vanilla until blended; stir into dry ingredients. Let stand 5 minutes. Stir in apple. Transfer to an 11x7-in. baking dish coated with cooking spray. Sprinkle with sunflower kernels. Bake, uncovered, 25-30 minutes or until set and edges are lightly browned.

1 serving: 305 cal., 13g fat (2g sat.fat), 48mg chol., 325mg sod., 41g carb. (20g sugars, 4g fiber), 8g pro.

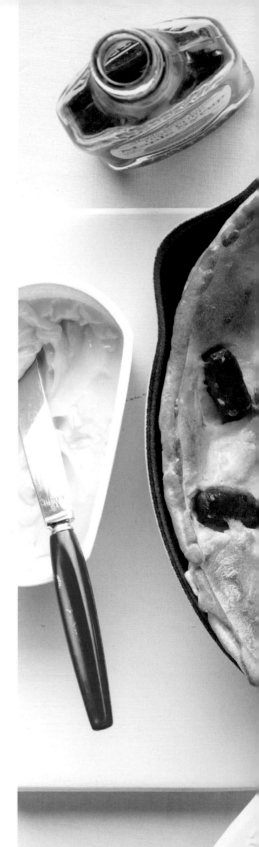

GRANDMOTHER'S TOAD IN A HOLE

I have fond memories of my grandmother's Yorkshire pudding wrapped around sausages, a puffy dish my kids called "The Boat." Slather it with butter and maple syrup.
—Susan Kieboam, Streetsboro, OH

PREP: 10 min. + standing • **BAKE:** 25 min.
MAKES: 6 servings

- 3   **large eggs**
- 1   **cup 2% milk**
- ½   **tsp. salt**
- 1   **cup all-purpose flour**
- 1   **pkg. (12 oz.) uncooked maple breakfast sausage links**
- 3   **Tbsp. olive oil**
    Butter and maple syrup, optional

1. Preheat oven to 400°. In a small bowl, whisk eggs, milk and salt. Whisk flour into the egg mixture until blended. Let stand for 30 minutes. Meanwhile, cook sausage according to the package directions; cut each sausage into three pieces.

2. Place oil in a 12-in. nonstick ovenproof skillet. Place in oven for 3-4 minutes or until hot. Stir the batter and pour into the prepared skillet; top with sausages. Bake for 20-25 minutes or until golden brown and puffed. Remove from the skillet; cut into wedges. If desired, serve with butter and syrup.

1 wedge: 336 cal., 22g fat (6g sat. fat), 126mg chol., 783mg sod., 20g carb. (2g sugars, 1g fiber), 14g pro.

NOTES

_____
_____
_____
_____
_____
_____
_____
_____
_____
_____

TOP TIP

Instead of small breakfast sausage links, you can use full-size links of any flavor in this dish. To use, brown three or four sausages in the ovenproof skillet, then pour the batter over top and bake as directed.

5 INGREDIENTS

LOADED BREAKFAST POTATOES

My kids really love loaded potatoes in restaurants, so I modified them to make at home. Using the microwave for the potatoes will save you about 10 minutes. Instead of russets, I use thin-skinned red potatoes and leave the skins on to save on peeling time.
—Tena Kropp, Aurora, IL

TAKES: 30 min. • **MAKES:** 6 servings

- 1½ **lbs. red potatoes, cubed**
- ¼ **lb. bacon strips, chopped**
- ¾ **cup cubed fully cooked ham**
- 1 **cup shredded cheddar cheese**
- ½ **tsp. salt**
- ¼ **tsp. pepper**
  Sour cream

1. Place potatoes in a microwave-safe dish and cover with water. Cover and microwave on high for 4-5 minutes or until tender.

2. Meanwhile, in a large skillet, cook bacon over medium heat until crisp. Remove to paper towels with a slotted spoon. Drain potatoes; saute in bacon drippings until lightly browned. Add the ham, cheese, salt, pepper and bacon. Cook and stir over medium heat until cheese is melted. Serve with sour cream.

¾ cup: 273 cal., 16g fat (8g sat. fat), 45mg chol., 776mg sod., 19g carb. (1g sugars, 2g fiber), 13g pro.

5 INGREDIENTS

RISE & SHINE PARFAIT

Start your day with a smile. This yogurt, fruit and granola parfait is so easy to make. You can use whatever favorite fresh fruit is in season and looking best at the supermarket.
—Diana Laskaris, Chicago, IL

TAKES: 15 min. • **MAKES:** 4 servings

- 4 **cups fat-free vanilla yogurt**
- 2 **medium peaches, chopped**
- 2 **cups fresh blackberries**
- ½ **cup granola without raisins or Kashi Go Lean Crunch cereal**

Layer half of the yogurt, peaches, blackberries and granola into 4 parfait glasses. Repeat the layers. Serve immediately or chill until serving. ¾ cup:

1 serving: 259 cal., 3g fat (0 sat. fat), 7mg chol., 6mg sod., 48g carb. (27g sugars, 7g fiber), 13g pro.

APPETIZERS & BEVERAGES

GET YOUR PARTY OFF THE GROUND WITH THESE CLASSIC STARTERS AND DELICIOUS DRINKS!

BACON CHEDDAR POTATO SKINS

Both crisp and hearty, this restaurant-quality snack is one my family requests all the time.

—Trish Perrin, Keizer, OR

TAKES: 30 min. • **MAKES:** 8 servings

- 4 large baking potatoes, baked
- 3 Tbsp. canola oil
- 1 Tbsp. grated Parmesan cheese
- ½ tsp. salt
- ¼ tsp. garlic powder
- ¼ tsp. paprika
- ⅛ tsp. pepper
- 8 bacon strips, cooked and crumbled
- 1½ cups shredded cheddar cheese
- ½ cup sour cream
- 4 green onions, sliced

1. Preheat oven to 475°. Cut potatoes in half lengthwise; scoop out the pulp, leaving a ¼-in. shell (save the pulp for another use). Place potato skins on a greased baking sheet.

2. Combine oil with next five ingredients; brush mixture over both sides of skins.

3. Bake until crisp, about 7 minutes on each side. Sprinkle bacon and cheddar cheese inside the skins. Bake until the cheese is melted, about 2 minutes longer. Top with sour cream and onions, or serve toppings on the side. Serve immediately.

1 potato skin: 350 cal., 19g fat (7g sat. fat), 33mg chol., 460mg sod., 34g carb. (2g sugars, 4g fiber), 12g pro.

TOP TIP

Cut down your kitchen time: Instead of prebaking the potatoes in an oven for 50-60 minutes, microwave them for 4 minutes. Scoop out the pulp and then make the potato skins as directed.

AUNT FRANCES' LEMONADE

When my sister and I visited our Aunt Frances each summer, she always had this refreshing lemonade in a stoneware crock in the refrigerator.

—Debbie Reinhart, New Cumberland, PA

TAKES: 15 min.
MAKES: 16 servings (1 gallon)

- 5 lemons
- 5 limes
- 5 oranges
- 3 qt. water
- 1½ to 2 cups sugar

1. Squeeze the juice from four each of the lemons, limes and oranges; pour into a gallon container.

2. Thinly slice the remaining fruit and set aside for garnish. Add water and sugar to the juices; mix well. Store in refrigerator. Serve over ice with fruit slices.

1 cup: 122 cal., 0 fat (0 sat. fat), 0 chol., 2mg sod., 33g carb. (25g sugars, 3g fiber), 1g pro.

CLASSIC HUMMUS

We love hummus, and this version is really amazing. If you have a pressure cooker, this is an easy, tasty reason to pull it out! We pair hummus with fresh veggies for a meal or snack.
—Monica and David Eichler, Lawrence, KS

PREP: 20 min. + soaking
COOK: 25 min. + chilling • **MAKES:** 2½ cups

- 1 cup dried chickpeas
- 1 medium onion, quartered
- 1 bay leaf
- 4 cups water
- ¼ cup minced fresh parsley
- ¼ cup lemon juice
- ¼ cup tahini
- 4 to 6 garlic cloves, minced
- 1 tsp. ground cumin
- ¾ tsp. salt
- ⅛ tsp. cayenne pepper
- ¼ cup olive oil
  Assorted fresh vegetables

TOP TIP

To keep fresh parsley in the refrigerator for several weeks, wash the entire bunch in warm water, then shake off the excess moisture, wrap the parsley in a paper towel and seal the bundle in a plastic bag. You can store parsley in the freezer for even longer periods (just remove the paper towel and freeze the sealed bag), but use this only for cooked dishes like soups and stews.

1. Sort beans and rinse in cold water. Place beans in a large bowl; add water to cover by 2 in. Cover and let stand overnight.
2. Drain and rinse beans, discarding liquid. Transfer beans to a pressure cooker; add the onion, bay leaf and 4 cups water.
3. Close cover securely according to manufacturer's directions. Bring cooker to full pressure over high heat. Reduce heat to medium-high and cook beans for 12 minutes. (Pressure regulator should maintain a slow, steady rocking motion or release of steam; adjust heat if needed.)
4. Remove from the heat; allow pressure to drop on its own. Immediately cool according to manufacturer's directions until pressure is completely reduced. Drain bean mixture, reserving ½ cup cooking liquid. Discard onion and bay leaf.
5. Place the beans, parsley, lemon juice, tahini, garlic, cumin, salt and cayenne in a food processor; cover and process until smooth. While processing, gradually add the oil in a steady stream. Add enough of the reserved cooking liquid to achieve desired consistency.
6. Cover and refrigerate for at least 1 hour. Serve with vegetables.
¼ cup: 139 cal., 10g fat (1g sat. fat), 0 chol., 190mg sod., 14g carb. (1g sugars, 6g fiber), 5g pro. **Diabetic exchanges:** 1½ fat, 1 starch.

JALAPENO POPPERS WITH LIME CILANTRO DIP

Crispy and crunchy with a creamy filling, these little pepper bites always earn rave reviews. They're fit for any event, from a cocktail soiree to a neighborhood picnic.
—Tana Rogers, New York, NY

PREP: 30 min. • **BAKE:** 20 min.
MAKES: 2 dozen (2 cups dip)

- 12 **jalapeno peppers**
- 1 **pkg. (8 oz.) cream cheese, softened**
- 1¼ **cups shredded sharp cheddar cheese**
- 4 **green onions, finely chopped**
- ⅓ **cup all-purpose flour**
- 6 **large egg whites, lightly beaten**
- 1½ **cups panko (Japanese) bread crumbs**
- ½ **tsp. salt**
- ½ **tsp. pepper**

LIME CILANTRO DIP
- 2 **cups sour cream**
- 4 **green onions, finely chopped**
- ¼ **cup lime juice**
- 2 **Tbsp. minced fresh cilantro**
- ½ **tsp. garlic salt**

1. Cut jalapenos in half lengthwise and remove the seeds. Place jalapenos on an ungreased baking sheet. Broil 4-in. from the heat for 4-6 minutes on each side or until lightly blistered. Cool slightly.

2. In a small bowl, beat cream cheese and cheddar cheese until blended. Stir in the onions. Spoon into pepper halves.

3. Place the flour, egg whites and bread crumbs in separate shallow bowls. Coat jalapenos with flour, then dip in egg whites and coat with crumbs. Place on a greased baking sheet; sprinkle with the salt and pepper. Bake at 350° for 18-20 minutes or until lightly browned.

4. For the lime dip, combine all ingredients in a small bowl. Serve with poppers.

Note: Wear disposable gloves when cutting hot peppers; the oils can burn skin. Avoid touching your face.

1 popper with 4 tsp. dip: 119 cal., 8g fat (6g sat. fat), 30mg chol., 179mg sod., 6g carb. (1g sugars, 0 fiber), 4g pro.

NOTES

TOP TIP

When cutting a large number of jalapeno peppers, first cut off the tops, then slice them in half lengthwise. Use the small end of a melon baller to scrape out the seeds and membranes. It speeds the job and keeps you from slicing your gloves—which you should be wearing!

—Julaine Svacina, Richland Center, WI

SWISS CHEESE BREAD

This bread will receive rave reviews, whether you serve it as an appetizer or with a meal. For real convenience, you can make it ahead of time and freeze it!
—Karla Boice, Mahtomedi, MN

TAKES: 30 min. • **MAKES:** 24 servings

- 1 loaf (18-20 in.) French bread
- 8 oz. (2 sticks) butter, softened
- 2 cups shredded Swiss cheese
- ¾ tsp. celery seed
- ¾ tsp. garlic powder
- 3 Tbsp. dehydrated parsley flakes

1. Cut the bread in half. Make diagonal cuts, 1 in. thick, through bread but not through bottom. Combine all remaining ingredients. Spread half of the butter mixture between bread slices. Spread remaining cheese mixture over top and sides of bread.

2. Place bread on double thickness of foil; cover loosely with more foil. Bake at 425° for 20-30 minutes. For the last 5 minutes, remove foil covering the bread to allow it to brown.

1 piece: 154 cal., 11g fat (6g sat. fat), 29mg chol., 217mg sod., 10g carb. (1g sugars, 1g fiber), 4g pro.

5 INGREDIENTS
SANGRIA WINE

Citrus-spiked wine is always the life of the party, whether I serve it on a hot summer evening or a chilly winter day. The soda bubbles give it some extra pop.
—Colleen Sturma, Milwaukee, WI

TAKES: 10 min. • **MAKES:** 10 servings

- 1 bottle (750 milliliters) dry red wine
- 1 cup lemon-flavored rum
- 2 cans (12 oz. each) lemon-lime soda, chilled
- 2 medium lemons, sliced
- 2 medium limes, sliced
  Ice cubes

In a pitcher, combine the wine, rum and soda; add lemon and lime slices. Serve sangria over ice.

¾ cup: 151 cal., 0 fat (0 sat. fat), 0 chol., 12mg sod., 12g carb. (8g sugars, 1g fiber), 0 pro.

HOMEMADE GUACAMOLE

Nothing is better than fresh guacamole when you're eating something spicy. It's easy to whip together in a matter of minutes, and it quickly tames anything that's too hot.
—Joan Hallford, North Richland Hills, TX

TAKES: 10 min. • **MAKES:** 2 cups

- 3 medium ripe avocados, peeled and cubed
- 1 garlic clove, minced
- ¼ to ½ tsp. salt
- 2 medium tomatoes, seeded and chopped, optional
- 1 small onion, finely chopped
- 1 to 2 Tbsp. lime juice
- 1 Tbsp. minced fresh cilantro
  Tortilla chips

Mash avocados with garlic and salt. Stir in the remaining ingredients. Serve with tortilla chips.

Note: Wear disposable gloves when cutting hot peppers; the oils can burn exposed skin. Avoid touching your face.

¼ cup: 90 cal., 8g fat (1g sat. fat), 0 chol., 78mg sod., 6g carb. (1g sugars, 4g fiber), 1g pro. **Diabetic exchanges:** 1½ fat.

BONUS: MANGO GUACAMOLE

As a change from standard guacamole, I added mango for a touch of sweetness. It really complements the heat from the chili pepper, and it looks beautiful, too!
—Adam Landau, Englewood Cliffs, NJ

TAKES: 20 min. • **MAKES:** 3 cups

- 2 medium ripe avocados, peeled and quartered
- 1 medium mango, peeled and chopped
- ½ cup finely chopped red onion
- ¼ cup minced fresh cilantro
- 1 jalapeno pepper, seeded and finely chopped
- 2 Tbsp. lime juice
- 1½ tsp. grated lime zest
- ½ tsp. salt
- ⅛ tsp. coarsely ground pepper
  Tortilla or pita chips

In a small bowl, mash avocados. Stir in the mango, onion, cilantro, jalapeno, lime juice, lime zest, salt and pepper. Serve with chips.

Note: Wear disposable gloves when cutting hot peppers; the oils can burn exposed skin. Avoid touching your face.

¼ cup: 63 cal., 5g fat (1g sat. fat), 0 chol., 101mg sod., 6g carb. (3g sugars, 2g fiber), 1g pro. **Diabetic exchanges:** ½ starch, ½ fat.

CHICKEN POTSTICKERS

Chicken and mushrooms make up the filling in these potstickers, a traditional Chinese dumpling. Greasing the steamer rack makes it easy to remove them once they're steamed.

—Jacquelynne Stine, Las Vegas, NV

PREP: 50 min. • **COOK:** 10 min.
MAKES: 4 dozen

- 1 lb. boneless skinless chicken thighs, cut into chunks
- 1½ cups sliced fresh mushrooms
- 1 small onion, cut into wedges
- 2 Tbsp. hoisin sauce
- 2 Tbsp. prepared mustard
- 2 Tbsp. Sriracha Asian hot chili sauce or 1 Tbsp. hot pepper sauce
- 1 pkg. (10 oz.) pot sticker or gyoza wrappers
- 1 large egg, lightly beaten

SAUCE
- 1 cup reduced-sodium soy sauce
- 1 green onion, chopped
- 1 tsp. ground ginger

1. In a food processor, combine the uncooked chicken, mushrooms, onion, hoisin sauce, mustard and chili sauce; cover and process until blended.

2. Place 1 Tbsp. of chicken mixture in the center of one wrapper. (Always keep the remaining wrappers covered with a damp towel until ready to use to prevent them from drying out.) Moisten entire edge with egg. Fold the wrapper over the filling to form a semicircle. Press edges firmly to seal, pleating the front side to form several folds.

3. Holding the sealed edges, stand each dumpling on an even surface; press to flatten the bottom. Curve the ends to form a crescent shape. Repeat with the remaining wrappers and filling.

4. Working in batches, arrange potstickers in a single layer on a large greased steamer basket rack; place in a Dutch oven over 1 in. of water. Bring to a boil; cover and steam for 5-7 minutes or until the filling juices run clear. Repeat with the remaining potstickers.

5. Meanwhile, in a small bowl, combine the sauce ingredients. Serve with potstickers. Refrigerate leftovers.

Freeze option: Cover and freeze uncooked potstickers in a single layer on waxed paper-lined sheets until firm. Transfer them to resealable plastic freezer bags; return to freezer. To use, steam as directed until heated through and juices run clear.

1 potsticker: 43 cal., 1g fat (0 sat. fat), 11mg chol., 374mg sod., 5g carb. (0 sugars, 0 fiber), 3g pro.

"These were delicious! I used fresh ginger in the dipping sauce as well as 1 teaspoon of honey. I definitely will be making these for our next party."
— KATEJUDY311,
TASTEOFHOME.COM

SPICY SHRIMP & CRAB COCKTAIL

I don't usually like radishes, but I love them in this shrimp cocktail. Serve it straight up, with tortilla chips or on a bed of butter lettuce. A zippy Bloody Mary mix works just as well as spicy V8.
—Heidi Knaak, Liberty, MO

PREP: 25 min. + chilling
MAKES: 12 servings (¾ cup each)

- 2   medium cucumbers, peeled, seeded and chopped
- 8   radishes, halved and thinly sliced (about 2 cups)
- 2   cups Spicy Hot V8 juice (about 16 oz.)
- 1   cup Clamato juice
- ½   cup finely chopped red onion
- ½   cup ketchup
- 5   jalapeno peppers, seeded and finely chopped
- ¼   cup coarsely chopped fresh cilantro
- 2   garlic cloves, minced
- ½   tsp. salt
- 1   lb. peeled and deveined cooked small shrimp
- 1   lb. lump crabmeat, drained
- 2   medium ripe avocados, peeled and cubed

Combine the first 10 ingredients. Gently fold in the shrimp, crab and avocados. Refrigerate, covered, for at least 2 hours or until cold. Serve in martini glasses.
¾ cup: 162 cal., 6g fat (1g sat. fat), 91mg chol., 604mg sod., 11g carb. (6g sugars, 3g fiber), 17g pro.

5 INGREDIENTS
MIMOSA

A standard offering at brunch, mimosas are as pretty as they are tasty. Make sure the wine you use is extra dry or dry (not brut), so it doesn't overpower the orange juice.
—*Taste of Home* Test Kitchen

TAKES: 5 min. • **MAKES:** 1 serving

- 2   oz. champagne or other sparkling wine, chilled
- ½   oz. Triple Sec
- 2   oz. orange juice
      Orange slice (for garnish), optional

Pour champagne into a champagne flute or wine glass. Add Triple Sec and orange juice. Garnish with an orange slice or as desired.
Note: For a batch of mimosas (12 servings), slowly pour one bottle (750 ml) of chilled champagne into a pitcher. Stir in 3 cups of orange juice and ¾ cup of Triple Sec.
1 serving: 119 cal., 0 fat (0 sat. fat), 0 chol., 0 sod., 13g carb. (11g sugars, 0 fiber), 0 pro.

FREEZE IT
TOMATO-HERB FOCACCIA

With its medley of herbs and tomatoes, this rustic bread is sure to liven up any occasion, whether it's a family dinner or a game-day get-together. It will vanish in no time at all!

—Janet Miller, Indianapolis, IN

PREP: 30 min. + rising • **BAKE:** 20 min.
MAKES: 12 servings

- 1 pkg. (¼ oz.) active dry yeast
- 1 cup warm water (110° to 115°)
- 2 Tbsp. olive oil, divided
- 1½ tsp. salt
- 1 tsp. sugar
- 1 tsp. garlic powder
- 1 tsp. each dried oregano, thyme and rosemary, crushed
- ½ tsp. dried basil
  Dash pepper
- 2 to 2½ cups all-purpose flour, divided
- 2 plum tomatoes, thinly sliced
- ¼ cup shredded part-skim mozzarella cheese
- 1 Tbsp. grated Parmesan cheese

1. In a large bowl, dissolve yeast in warm water. Add 1 Tbsp. oil, salt, sugar, garlic powder, herbs, pepper and 1½ cups flour. Beat until smooth. Stir in enough remaining flour to form a soft dough (dough will be sticky).

2. Turn onto a floured surface; knead until smooth and elastic, about 6-8 minutes. Place in a greased bowl, turning once to grease the top. Cover and let rise in a warm place until doubled, about 1 hour.

3. Punch dough down. Cover and let rest for 10 minutes. Shape into a 13x9-in. rectangle; place on a greased baking sheet. Cover and let rise until doubled, about 30 minutes. With fingertips, make several dimples over the top of the dough.

4. Preheat oven to 400°. Brush dough with the remaining oil; arrange tomatoes over the top. Sprinkle with cheeses. Bake for 20-25 minutes or until golden brown. Remove to a wire rack.

Freeze option: Freeze the cooled focaccia squares in freezer containers, separating layers with waxed paper. To use, reheat squares on a baking sheet in a preheated 400° oven until heated through.

1 slice: 112 cal., 3g fat (1g sat. fat), 2mg chol., 320mg sod., 18g carb. (1g sugars, 1g fiber), 3g pro. **Diabetic exchanges:** 1 starch, ½ fat.

BAKED CHICKEN NACHOS

This party appetizer is delicious and so simple. Rotisserie (or leftover) chicken keeps it quick, and the seasonings and splash of lime juice give it fantastic flavor. My husband likes this snack so much that he often requests it for dinner.
—Gail Cawsey, Geneseo, IL

PREP: 20 min. • **BAKE:** 15 min.
MAKES: 16 servings

- 2 medium sweet red peppers, diced
- 1 medium green pepper, diced
- 3 tsp. canola oil, divided
- 1 can (15 oz.) black beans, rinsed and drained
- 1 tsp. minced garlic
- 1 tsp. dried oregano
- ¼ tsp. ground cumin
- 2¼ cups shredded rotisserie chicken
- 4½ tsp. lime juice
- ⅛ tsp. salt
- ⅛ tsp. pepper
- 7½ cups tortilla chips
- 8 oz. pepper jack cheese, shredded
- ¼ cup thinly sliced green onions
- ½ cup minced fresh cilantro
- 1 cup sour cream
- 2 to 3 tsp. diced pickled jalapeno peppers, optional

1. Preheat oven to 350°. In a large skillet, saute peppers in 1½ tsp. oil for 3 minutes or until crisp-tender; transfer to a small bowl. In the same skillet, saute the beans, garlic, oregano and cumin in remaining oil for 3 minutes or until heated through.

2. Meanwhile, combine the chicken, lime juice, salt and pepper. In a greased 13x9-in. baking dish, layer half of each of the tortilla chips, pepper mixture, bean mixture, shredded chicken, cheese, onions and cilantro. Repeat the layers.

3. Bake, uncovered, for 15-20 minutes or until heated through. Serve with sour cream and pickled jalapenos if desired.

1 serving: 221 cal., 13g fat (5g sat. fat), 41mg chol., 314mg sod., 14g carb. (2g sugars, 2g fiber), 12g pro.

"This is fantastic! I've made it three times and it's a keeper. It's such an easy and flexible recipe...we used carne asada for one of our batches."

—MMSKULSKI, TASTEOFHOME.COM

SLOW COOKER
FIVE-CHEESE SPINACH & ARTICHOKE DIP

This is the dish everyone asks me to bring to weddings, Christmas parties and more! You can also bake it at 400° for 30 minutes or until hot and bubbly.
—Noelle Myers, Grand Forks, ND

PREP: 20 min. • **COOK:** 2½ hours
MAKES: 16 servings (¼ cup each)

- 1 jar (12 oz.) roasted sweet red peppers
- 1 jar (6½ oz.) marinated quartered artichoke hearts
- 1 pkg. (10 oz.) frozen chopped spinach, thawed and squeezed dry
- 8 oz. fresh mozzarella cheese, cubed
- 1½ cups shredded Asiago cheese
- 6 oz. cream cheese, softened and cubed
- 1 cup crumbled feta cheese
- ⅓ cup shredded provolone cheese
- ⅓ cup minced fresh basil
- ¼ cup finely chopped red onion
- 2 Tbsp. mayonnaise
- 2 garlic cloves, minced
  Assorted crackers

1. Drain peppers, reserving 1 Tbsp. liquid; chop peppers. Drain artichokes, reserving 2 Tbsp. liquid; coarsely chop artichokes.
2. In a 3-qt. slow cooker coated with cooking spray, combine spinach, cheeses, basil, onion, mayonnaise, garlic, artichoke hearts and peppers. Stir in the reserved pepper and artichoke liquids. Cook dip, covered, on high 2 hours. Stir mixture; cook, covered, 30-60 minutes longer or until cheese is melted. Stir before serving; serve with crackers.
¼ cup: 197 cal., 16g fat (8g sat. fat), 38mg chol., 357mg sod., 4g carb. (2g sugars, 1g fiber), 9g pro.

SLOW COOKER
SLOW-COOKER CIDER

There's no last-minute rush when you slowly simmer this punch.
—Alpha Wilson, Roswell, NM

PREP: 5 min. • **COOK:** 2 hours • **MAKES:** 2 qt.

- 2 cinnamon sticks (3 in.)
- 1 tsp. whole cloves
- 1 tsp. whole allspice
- 2 qt. apple cider
- ½ cup packed brown sugar
- 1 orange, sliced

1. Place cinnamon, cloves and allspice on a double thickness of cheesecloth; bring up corners of the cloth and tie with a string to form a bag.
2. Place cider and brown sugar in a 3-qt. slow cooker; stir until sugar dissolves. Add the spice bag. Place orange slices on top. Cover and cook on low for 2-3 hours or until heated through. Discard spice bag.
1 cup: 177 cal., 0 fat (0 sat. fat), 0 chol., 30mg sod., 44g carb. (40g sugars, 0 fiber), 0 pro.

5 INGREDIENTS

GARLIC TOMATO BRUSCHETTA

Bruschetta makes a great introduction to any Italian entree. For this version, I started with my grandmother's recipe and added fresh tomatoes.
—Jean Franzoni, Rutland, VT

PREP: 30 min. + chilling • **MAKES:** 12 servings

- ¼ cup olive oil
- 3 Tbsp. chopped fresh basil
- 3 to 4 garlic cloves, minced
- ½ tsp. salt
- ¼ tsp. pepper
- 4 medium tomatoes, diced
- 2 Tbsp. grated Parmesan cheese
- 1 loaf (1 lb.) unsliced French bread

1. In a large bowl, combine oil, basil, garlic, salt and pepper. Add tomatoes and toss gently. Sprinkle with cheese. Refrigerate for at least 1 hour.

2. Bring the tomato mixture to room temperature before serving. Cut bread into 24 slices; toast under broiler until lightly browned. Top with tomato mixture. Serve immediately.

2 bruschetta : 156 cal., 6g fat (1g sat. fat.), 1mg chol., 347mg sod., 22g carb. (0 sugars, 1g fiber), 4g pro.

BONUS: CREAMY MUSHROOM BRUSCHETTA

Mushrooms—button, portobello and shiitake—plus a lovely blend of herbs makes a hearty, flavorful topping for bruschetta.
—Amy Chase, Vanderhoof, BC

PREP: 15 min. • **COOK:** 30 min. • **MAKES:** 28 appetizers

- 1½ cups sliced fresh mushrooms
- 1½ cups sliced baby portobello mushrooms
- 1 cup sliced fresh shiitake mushrooms
- ¾ cup chopped onion
- 2 Tbsp. olive oil
- 1 cup heavy whipping cream
- 2 Tbsp. Worcestershire sauce
- ¼ tsp. kosher salt
- ¼ tsp. coarsely ground pepper
- 28 slices French bread baguette (½ in. thick)
- 1 garlic clove, peeled and halved
- 1 Tbsp. each minced fresh basil, parsley and thyme

1. In a large skillet, saute the mushrooms and onion in oil for 6-7 minutes or until mushrooms are browned. Stir in cream, Worcestershire sauce, salt and pepper. Bring to a boil. Reduce heat; simmer, uncovered, for 20-25 minutes or until thickened, stirring occasionally.

2. Meanwhile, place baguette slices on ungreased baking sheets. Broil 4-6 in. from the heat for 1 to 1½ minutes on each side or until toasted. Rub garlic clove over toasts; discard the garlic.

3. Stir basil, parsley and thyme into the mushroom mixture; heat through. Spoon about 1 tablespoonful on each toast. Serve immediately.

1 bruschetta: 94 cal., 5g fat (2g sat. fat), 12mg chol., 104mg sod., 10g carb. (0 sugars, 1g fiber), 2g pro. **Diabetic exchanges:** 1 fat, ½ starch.

COZY HOT CHOCOLATE

A steaming mug of this smooth beverage is a nice anytime treat to share with my husband, Ken.
—Marie Hattrup, Sonoma, CA

TAKES: 10 min. • **MAKES:** 2 servings

- 2 **Tbsp. baking cocoa**
- 2 **Tbsp. sugar**
- ¼ **cup water**
- 2 **cups 2% milk**
- ½ **tsp. vanilla extract**
- ¼ **cup whipped cream**
  Ground cinnamon, optional

1. In a small saucepan, mix the cocoa and sugar. Add water; stir until smooth. Bring to a boil, stirring constantly. Boil mixture for 1 minute. Reduce heat; stir in milk and heat through.

2. Remove from heat and stir in the vanilla. Serve hot chocolate with whipped cream; if desired, sprinkle with cinnamon.

1 cup: 241 cal., 11g fat (7g sat. fat), 40mg chol., 121mg sod., 28g carb. (25g sugars, 1g fiber), 9g pro.

Cozy Hot Mocha: Reduce milk to 1 cup. Add 1 cup strong brewed coffee. Proceed as directed.

Maple Hot Chocolate: Omit whipped cream and cinnamon. Add 1 Tbsp. butter to cocoa mixture before bringing it to a boil. Add 3 large marshmallows with the milk and heat until marshmallows are melted. Add ½ tsp. maple flavoring with the vanilla. Pour into mugs and top with additional marshmallows.

BONUS: KAHLUA HOT CHOCOLATE

When we want a cup of hot chocolate, we prefer homemade over store mixes. A splash of Kahlua adds a touch of fabulous.
—Chung-Ah Rhee, Hollywood, CA

TAKES: 20 min. • **MAKES:** 2 servings

- 2 **Tbsp. sugar**
- 2 **Tbsp. Dutch-processed cocoa**
- ¼ **tsp. ground cinnamon**
  Dash ground nutmeg
- 2 **cups 2% milk**
- 2 **to 4 Tbsp. Kahlua (coffee liqueur)**
  Optional toppings: whipped cream, marshmallows and miniature marshmallows, salted caramel sauce and chocolate syrup

In a small saucepan, whisk the sugar, cocoa, cinnamon and nutmeg. Gradually whisk in milk; cook and stir until heated through. Remove from heat; stir in Kahlua. Ladle into mugs; serve with toppings as desired.

1 cup: 280 cal., 8g fat (5g sat. fat), 20mg chol., 116mg sod., 40g carb. (31g sugars, 6g fiber), 11g pro.

HOW TO MAKE WHIPPED CREAM

1. In a chilled small glass bowl and using chilled beaters, beat 1 cup heavy whipping cream until it begins to thicken.

2. Add 3 Tbsp. confectioners' sugar and ½ tsp. vanilla extract. Beat until soft peaks form.

To make ahead of time, slightly underwhip the cream, then cover and refrigerate for several hours. Beat briefly just before using.

To quickly chill the bowl and beaters, put them in the freezer for 10-15 minutes.

Instead of confectioners' sugar, use an equal amount of granulated sugar, maple syrup or honey. Other flavors—¼ tsp. of almond or maple extract—can take the place of the vanilla. Or use 1 Tbsp. of a liquor, like bourbon, rum or Irish Cream.

1.

2.

SWEET SAUSAGE ROLLS

Refrigerated crescent dough makes these appetizers a snap to prepare. Sausage gives them a little smoky heat, while honey and brown sugar lend an appealing sweetness. It all adds up to finger food that's downright addicting!
—Lori Cabuno, Canfield, OH

PREP: 25 min. • **BAKE:** 15 min.
MAKES: 2 dozen

- 1   tube (8 oz.) refrigerated crescent rolls
- 24 miniature smoked sausage links
- ½   cup butter, melted
- ½   cup chopped nuts
- 3   Tbsp. honey
- 3   Tbsp. brown sugar

1. Preheat oven to 400°. Unroll crescent dough and separate into triangles; cut each lengthwise into three triangles. Place a sausage on the wide end of each triangle; roll up tightly.
2. Combine the remaining ingredients in an 11x7-in. baking dish. Arrange sausage rolls, seam side down, in butter mixture. Bake, uncovered, for 15-20 minutes or until golden brown.
1 roll: 128 cal., 10g fat (4g sat. fat), 16mg chol., 194mg sod., 8g carb. (5g sugars, 0 fiber), 2g pro.

HERB-HAPPY GARLIC BREAD

You'll love the fresh garlic and herbs in this recipe. The mild cheesy duo sprinkled on top makes it extra rich and wonderful.
—*Taste of Home* Test Kitchen

TAKES: 15 min. • **MAKES:** 12 servings

- ½   cup butter, softened
- ¼   cup grated Romano cheese
- 2   Tbsp. minced fresh basil or 2 tsp. dried basil
- 1   Tbsp. minced fresh parsley
- 3   garlic cloves, minced
- 1   French bread baguette
- 4   oz. crumbled goat cheese

1. Preheat oven to 425°. In a small bowl, mix the first five ingredients until blended. Cut baguette crosswise in half; cut each piece lengthwise in half. Spread cut sides with butter mixture. Place bread on an ungreased baking sheet.
2. Bake, uncovered, for 7-9 minutes or until lightly toasted. Sprinkle with goat cheese; bake 1-2 minutes longer or until goat cheese is softened. Cut into slices.
1 slice: 169 cal., 11g fat (7g sat. fat), 35mg chol., 307mg sod., 14g carb. (0 sugars, 1g fiber), 5g pro.

SALSA ROJA

With the help of my food processor, I can have fresh, homemade salsa ready in just 15 minutes. The lime juice works wonders bringing out all the flavors.
—Amber Massey, Argyle, TX

TAKES: 15 min. • **MAKES:** 7 cups

- 1 can (28 oz.) whole tomatoes, drained
- 1 can (14½ oz.) diced tomatoes with garlic and onion, drained
- 1 can (14½ oz.) Mexican stewed tomatoes, drained
- 1 can (10 oz.) diced tomatoes and green chilies, drained
- 1 medium onion, quartered
- 2 banana peppers, seeded and coarsely chopped
- 2 jalapeno peppers, seeded and coarsely chopped
- 3 garlic cloves, minced
- 2 tsp. salt
- ¼ tsp. ground cumin
- ½ cup minced fresh cilantro
- ¼ cup lime juice
- 2 medium ripe avocados, peeled and cubed
  Tortilla chips

1. Place the first 10 ingredients in a food processor; cover and process until chopped. Add cilantro and lime juice; cover and pulse until combined.
2. Transfer to a bowl; stir in avocados. Serve with tortilla chips.
Note: Wear disposable gloves when cutting hot peppers; the oils can burn skin. Avoid touching your face.
¼ cup: 42 cal., 2g fat (0 sat. fat), 0 chol., 381mg sod., 6g carb. (3g sugars, 2g fiber), 1g pro.

BONUS: TOMATILLO SALSA

Dare to deviate from tomato salsa and try this tomatillo-based version for a deliciously addictive change of pace. It's fantastic on its own with tortilla chips or served as a condiment alongside a variety of meats.
—Lori Kostecki, Wausau, WI

TAKES: 20 min. • **MAKES:** 2¼ cups

- 8 tomatillos, husks removed
- 1 medium tomato, quartered
- 1 small onion, cut into chunks
- 1 jalapeno pepper, seeded
- 3 Tbsp. fresh cilantro leaves
- 3 garlic cloves, peeled
- 1 Tbsp. lime juice
- ½ tsp. salt
- ¼ tsp. ground cumin
- ⅛ tsp. pepper
  Tortilla chips

1. In a large saucepan, bring 4 cups water to a boil. Add tomatillos. Reduce heat; simmer, uncovered, for 5 minutes. Drain.
2. Place the tomatillos, tomato, onion, jalapeno, cilantro, garlic, lime juice and seasonings in a food processor. Cover and process until blended. Serve with chips.
Note: Wear disposable gloves when cutting hot peppers; the oils can burn skin. Avoid touching your face.
¼ cup: 19 cal., 0 fat (0 sat. fat), 0 chol., 133mg sod., 4g carb. (2g sugars, 1g fiber), 1g pro. **Diabetic exchanges:** 1 Free food.

SAUSAGE MUSHROOM APPETIZERS

These hors d'oeuvres are oh-so-good! For interesting variations, I sometimes replace the pork sausage in the stuffing with ground venison or crabmeat.
—Sheryl Siemonsma, Sioux Falls, SD

PREP: 15 min. • **BAKE:** 20 min.
MAKES: 4 dozen

- 48 large fresh mushrooms
- 2 large eggs, lightly beaten
- 1 lb. bulk pork sausage, cooked and crumbled
- 1 cup shredded Swiss cheese
- ¼ cup mayonnaise
- 3 Tbsp. butter, melted
- 2 Tbsp. finely chopped onion
- 2 tsp. spicy brown or horseradish mustard
- 1 tsp. garlic salt
- 1 tsp. Cajun seasoning
- 1 tsp. Worcestershire sauce

1. Preheat oven to 350°. Remove mushroom stems (discard or save for another use); set caps aside. In a large bowl, combine remaining ingredients. Stuff mixture into the mushroom caps.
2. Place the mushrooms in two greased 13x9-in. baking dishes. Bake, uncovered, for 16-20 minutes or until heated through.
2 mushrooms: 103 cal., 9g fat (3g sat. fat), 33mg chol., 234mg sod., 2g carb. (1g sugars, 1g fiber), 4g pro.

BONUS: GOAT CHEESE MUSHROOMS

Stuffed mushrooms are superstars in the hot appetizer category. I use baby portobello mushrooms and load them with creamy goat cheese and sweet red peppers.
—Mike Bass, Alvin, TX

TAKES: 30 min. • **MAKES:** 2 dozen

- 24 baby portobello mushrooms (about 1 lb.), stems removed
- ½ cup crumbled goat cheese
- ½ cup chopped drained roasted sweet red peppers
  Pepper to taste
- 4 tsp. olive oil
  Chopped fresh parsley

1. Preheat oven to 375°. Place mushroom caps in a greased 15x10x1-in. baking pan. Fill each with 1 tsp. cheese; top each with 1 tsp. red pepper. Sprinkle with pepper; drizzle with oil.
2. Bake for 15-18 minutes or until the mushrooms are tender. Sprinkle with parsley.
1 stuffed mushroom: 19 cal., 1g fat (0 sat. fat), 3mg chol., 31mg sod., 1g carb. (1g sugars, 0 fiber), 1g pro.

"Rave reviews for this one. I've used different kinds of sausage to change the taste...and all are good. I make these for all our family parties and birthday celebrations, by request!"

—GRAMMA AMY,
TASTEOFHOME.COM

BRIE PUFF PASTRY

My husband was in the Air Force, so we've entertained guests in many parts of the world. I acquired this recipe while in California. It's one of my favorite special appetizers.

—Sandra Twait, Tampa, FL

PREP: 15 min. • **BAKE:** 20 min. + standing
MAKES: 10 servings

- 1 round (13.2 oz.) Brie cheese
- ½ cup crumbled blue cheese
- 1 sheet frozen puff pastry, thawed
- ¼ cup apricot jam
- ½ cup slivered almonds, toasted
- 1 large egg, lightly beaten
  Assorted crackers

1. Preheat oven to 400°. Cut Brie round horizontally in half. Sprinkle the bottom half with blue cheese; replace top half.
2. On a lightly floured surface, roll pastry into a 14-in. square. Trim the corners to make a circle. Spoon jam onto the center of the pastry; sprinkle with almonds. Top with Brie.
3. Lightly brush the edges of the pastry with beaten egg. Fold the pastry over the cheese, pinching edges to seal; trim excess pastry as desired.
4. Transfer to an ungreased baking sheet, seam side down. Brush pastry with the beaten egg. Bake for 20-25 minutes or until golden brown.
5. Immediately remove from pan to a serving plate; let stand for 45 minutes before serving. Serve with crackers.
Note: To toast nuts, bake in a shallow pan in a 350° oven for 5-10 minutes or cook in a skillet over low heat until lightly browned, stirring occasionally.
1 serving: 328 cal., 22g fat (10g sat. fat), 64mg chol., 424mg sod., 20g carb. (3g sugars, 2g fiber), 13g pro.

BEST DEVILED EGGS

Thanks to the herbs lending an amazing flavor, these are the best deviled eggs you can make!

—Jesse and Anne Foust, Bluefield, WV

TAKES: 15 min. • **MAKES:** 2 dozen

- ½ cup mayonnaise
- 2 Tbsp. 2% milk
- 1 tsp. dried parsley flakes
- ½ tsp. dill weed
- ½ tsp. minced chives
- ½ tsp. ground mustard
- ¼ tsp. salt
- ¼ tsp. paprika
- ⅛ tsp. garlic powder
- ⅛ tsp. pepper
- 12 hard-boiled large eggs
  Minced fresh parsley and additional paprika

Combine the first 10 ingredients. Slice eggs in half lengthwise; remove yolks and set whites aside. In another bowl, mash the yolks; add to the mayonnaise mixture, mixing well. Stuff or pipe the filling into the egg whites. Sprinkle tops with parsley and additional paprika. Refrigerate until serving.
1 stuffed egg half: 73 cal., 6g fat (1g sat. fat), 108mg chol., 81mg sod., 0 carb. (0 sugars, 0 fiber), 3g pro.

SANDWICHES

LUNCH OR DINNER, COOKING OUT OR EATING IN, THESE SANDWICHES NEVER GO OUT OF STYLE!

CHILI CONEY DOGS

Everyone in our family, from the smallest kids to the oldest adults, loves these hot dogs. Throw it together in the slow cooker in the morning or the night before, then pop in a bun and top to serve.
—Michele Harris, Vicksburg, MI

PREP: 20 min. • **COOK:** 4 hours
MAKES: 8 servings

- 1 lb. lean ground beef (90% lean)
- 1 can (15 oz.) tomato sauce
- ½ cup water
- 2 Tbsp. Worcestershire sauce
- 1 Tbsp. dried minced onion
- ½ tsp. garlic powder
- ½ tsp. ground mustard
- ½ tsp. chili powder
- ½ tsp. pepper
  Dash cayenne pepper
- 8 hot dogs
- 8 hot dog buns, split
  Optional toppings: shredded cheddar cheese, relish and chopped onion

1. In a large skillet, cook beef over medium heat for 6-8 minutes or until no longer pink, breaking into crumbles; drain. Stir in tomato sauce, water, Worcestershire sauce, onion and seasonings.
2. Place hot dogs in a 3-qt. slow cooker; top with beef mixture. Cook, covered, on low for 4-5 hours or until heated through. Serve on buns with toppings as desired.
1 chili dog: 371 cal., 20g fat (8g sat. fat), 53mg chol., 992mg sod., 26g carb. (5g sugars, 2g fiber), 21g pro.

AVOCADO QUESADILLAS

Avocado slices give these quesadillas a nutritional boost, and fortunately my son likes them, too. Add chicken or beef if you want some extra protein.
—Debbie Limas, North Andover, MA

TAKES: 20 min.
MAKES: 4 servings

- 1 Tbsp. canola oil
- 16 corn tortillas (6 in.)
- 2 cups shredded Mexican cheese blend
- 1 cup pico de gallo
- 1 large ripe avocado, peeled and thinly sliced
- 3 Tbsp. minced fresh cilantro
  Additional pico de gallo

1. Grease a griddle with oil; heat over medium heat. Lightly sprinkle tortillas with water to moisten.
2. Place eight tortillas on the griddle; sprinkle with cheese. After the cheese has melted slightly, top with pico de gallo, avocado and cilantro. Top with the remaining tortillas.
3. Cook for 3-4 minutes on each side or until the tortillas are lightly browned and cheese is melted. Serve with additional pico de gallo.
2 quesadillas: 611 cal., 37g fat (15g sat. fat), 50mg chol., 455mg sod., 54g carb. (2g sugars, 12g fiber), 20g pro.

BLT WITH PEPPERED BALSAMIC MAYO

Here's my twist on a classic. Creamy avocado, balsamic mayo and crisp salad greens make this BLT legendary in my book. For a lighter take, I often use turkey bacon.
—Ami Boyer, San Francisco, CA

TAKES: 25 min. • **MAKES:** 4 servings

- 8 bacon strips, halved
- ½ cup mayonnaise
- 1 Tbsp. balsamic vinegar
- ½ tsp. pepper
- ⅛ tsp. salt
- 8 slices bread, toasted
- 2 cups spring mix salad greens
- 8 cherry tomatoes, sliced
- 1 medium ripe avocado, peeled and sliced

1. In a large skillet, cook the bacon over medium heat until crisp. Remove to paper towels to drain.

2. In a small bowl, the mix mayonnaise, vinegar, pepper and salt. Spread half of the mixture over four toast slices. Layer with bacon, salad greens, tomatoes and avocado. Spread remaining mayonnaise over remaining toast; place over top.

1 sandwich: 501 cal., 37g fat (6g sat. fat), 27mg chol., 870mg sod., 32g carb. (4g sugars, 5g fiber), 11g pro.

BONUS: HOMEMADE MAYONNAISE

America's go-to dressing can be prepared right in your own kitchen with only a handful of everyday pantry items. This handy recipe makes it a cinch!
—*Taste of Home* Test Kitchen

PREP: 15 min. • **COOK:** 10 min. • **MAKES:** 1½ cups

- 2 large egg yolks
- 2 Tbsp. water
- 2 Tbsp. lemon juice
- ½ tsp. salt
  Dash white pepper
- 1 cup olive oil

1. In a double boiler or metal bowl over simmering water, constantly whisk the egg yolks, water and lemon juice until mixture reaches 160° or is thick enough to coat the back of a spoon. While stirring, quickly place the bottom of the pan in a bowl of ice water; continue stirring for 2 minutes or until cooled.

2. Transfer to a blender. Add salt and pepper. While processing, gradually add oil in a steady stream. Transfer to a small bowl. Cover and refrigerate for up to 7 days.

1 tablespoon: 84 cal., 9g fat (1g sat. fat), 17mg chol., 50mg sod., 0 carb. (0 sugars, 0 fiber), 0 pro. **Diabetic exchanges:** 2 fat.

5 INGREDIENTS

PAT'S KING OF STEAKS PHILLY CHEESESTEAK

This ultimate cheesesteak, an iconic sandwich in Philly, is a best-seller at Pat's King of Steaks Restaurant. Patrons praise its thinly cut beef and crusty Italian rolls.
—Frank Olivieri, Philadelphia, PA

TAKES: 20 min. • **MAKES:** 4 servings

- 1 large onion, sliced
- ½ lb. sliced fresh mushrooms, optional
- 1 small green pepper, sliced, optional
- 1 small sweet red pepper, sliced, optional
- 6 Tbsp. canola oil, divided
- 1½ lbs. beef ribeye steaks, thinly sliced
- 4 crusty Italian rolls, split
  Process cheese sauce

1. In a large skillet, saute the onion and, if desired, mushrooms and peppers in 3 Tbsp. oil until tender. Remove and keep warm. In the same pan, saute the beef in remaining oil in batches for 45-60 seconds or until meat reaches desired doneness.

2. On each roll bottom, layer the beef and onion mixture. Drizzle with cheese sauce, then replace tops.

1 sandwich: 714 cal., 49g fat (12g sat. fat), 101mg chol., 299mg sod., 31g carb. (3g sugars, 2g fiber), 36g pro.

TOP TIP

Philadelphia residents hold strong opinions about what makes the perfect cheesesteak and aren't shy about expressing them. Some will even tell you that a cheesesteak isn't really a cheesesteak unless the roll comes from a particular Philly bakery.

The cheese sauce is a hot topic for debate. Instead of sauce, you can melt a cheese of your choice—provolone is the leading contender—over the steak before putting it in the roll.

Peppers, mushrooms and onions are all common toppings, but depending on who you ask, one or all of them are must-haves—but the others should never touch a cheesesteak.

Most agree that the steak should be very thinly sliced (although some go for shredded). Freezing the steak slightly before cutting it will help you get the thinnest slices possible.

Other than the cheese, the steak and the toppings, is there anything Philadelphians can agree on? Yes—all will tell you the best Philly cheesesteak is the one from the place on the corner in their old neighborhood.

"This recipe was easy and delicious. The only change I made was to add a little salt and pepper. I will make these again!"

—BILLIEPOCK, TASTEOFHOME.COM

SNAPPY TUNA MELTS

Traditional tuna melts use mayo, but I lighten things up by using a creamy balsamic vinaigrette instead. Kids and adults both go for this quick meal.
—Christine Schenher, Exeter, CA

TAKES: 15 min. • **MAKES:** 4 servings

- 1 pouch (11 oz.) light tuna in water
- 1 hard-boiled large egg, coarsely chopped
- 2 Tbsp. reduced-fat creamy balsamic vinaigrette
- 1 Tbsp. stone-ground mustard, optional
- 4 whole wheat hamburger buns, split
- 8 slices tomato
- 8 slices reduced-fat Swiss cheese

1. In a small bowl, mix the tuna, egg, vinaigrette and, if desired, mustard. Place the buns on an ungreased baking sheet, cut side up. Broil 4-6 in. from heat for 1-2 minutes or until golden brown.
2. Spread tuna mixture over buns; top with tomato and cheese. Broil 2-3 minutes longer or until the cheese is melted.
2 open-faced sandwiches: 341 cal., 13g fat (5g sat. fat), 105mg chol., 557mg sod., 27g carb. (6g sugars, 4g fiber), 35g pro. **Diabetic exchanges:** 4 lean meat, 2 starch, 1 fat.

THE BEST EVER GRILLED CHEESE SANDWICH

Spreading a mixture of mayo and butter on the bread creates a delightfully crispy crust plus the well-loved, wonderful flavor of butter one expects of a grilled cheese sandwich.
—Josh Rink, Milwaukee, WI

TAKES: 30 min. • **MAKES:** 4 servings

- 6 Tbsp. butter, softened, divided
- 8 slices sourdough bread
- 3 Tbsp. mayonnaise
- 3 Tbsp. finely shredded Manchego or Parmesan cheese
- ⅛ tsp. onion powder
- ½ cup shredded sharp white cheddar cheese
- ½ cup shredded Monterey Jack cheese
- ½ cup shredded Gruyere cheese
- 4 oz. Brie cheese, rind removed and sliced

1. Spread 3 Tbsp. butter on one side of each bread slice. Toast bread, butter side down, in a large skillet or electric griddle over medium-low heat until golden brown, 2-3 minutes; remove. In a small bowl, mix together the mayonnaise, Manchego cheese, onion powder and remaining 3 Tbsp. butter. In another bowl, combine cheddar, Monterey Jack and Gruyere cheeses.
2. To assemble sandwiches, top the toasted side of four of the bread slices with sliced Brie. Sprinkle the cheddar cheese mixture evenly over the Brie. Top with remaining the bread slices, toasted side facing inward. Spread the mayonnaise mixture on the outside of each sandwich. Place in same skillet and cook until the bread is golden brown and the cheese is melted, 5-6 minutes on each side. Serve sandwiches immediately.
1 sandwich: 659 cal., 49g fat (27g sat. fat), 122mg chol., 1017mg sod., 30g carb. (3g sugars, 1g fiber), 24g pro.

ALL-AMERICAN BACON CHEESEBURGERS

With this delicious recipe, you can get a juicy bacon cheeseburger right in your own backyard that is superior to any drive-thru fare.
—Jackie Burns, Kettle Falls, WA

TAKES: 30 min. • **MAKES:** 4 servings

- 2 Tbsp. finely chopped onion
- 2 Tbsp. ketchup
- 1 garlic clove, minced
- 1 tsp. sugar
- 1 tsp. Worcestershire sauce
- 1 tsp. steak sauce
- ¼ tsp. cider vinegar
- 1 lb. ground beef
- 4 slices sharp cheddar cheese
- 4 hamburger buns, split and toasted
- 8 cooked bacon strips
  Optional toppings: lettuce and tomato, onion and pickle slices

1. In a large bowl, combine the first seven ingredients. Crumble beef over mixture and mix well. Shape into four patties.
2. Grill burgers, covered, over medium heat or broil the patties 3 in. from the heat for 4-7 minutes on each side or until a thermometer reads 160° and the juices run clear. Top with cheese. Grill 1 minute longer or until the cheese is melted. Serve on buns with bacon and the toppings of your choice.

1 burger: 472 cal., 25g fat (10g sat. fat), 98mg chol., 947mg sod., 27g carb. (7g sugars, 1g fiber), 33g pro.

BONUS: BUFFALO TURKEY BURGERS

Celery and blue cheese dressing help tame the hot sauce on these juicy burgers. For a lighter version, skip the buns and serve with lettuce leaves, onion and tomato.
—Mary Pax-Shipley, Bend, OR

TAKES: 25 min. • **MAKES:** 4 servings

- 2 Tbsp. Louisiana-style hot sauce, divided
- 2 tsp. ground cumin
- 2 tsp. chili powder
- 2 garlic cloves, minced
- ½ tsp. salt
- ⅛ tsp. pepper
- 1 lb. lean ground turkey
- 4 whole wheat hamburger buns, split
- 1 cup shredded lettuce
- 2 celery ribs, chopped
- 2 Tbsp. fat-free blue cheese salad dressing

1. Combine 1 Tbsp. hot sauce, cumin, chili powder, garlic, salt and pepper. Add turkey; mix lightly but thoroughly. Shape into four ½-in.-thick patties.
2. In a large nonstick skillet coated with cooking spray, cook burgers over medium heat for 4-6 minutes on each side or until a thermometer reads 165°.
3. Serve burgers on buns with lettuce, celery, salad dressing and the remaining hot sauce.

1 burger: 312 cal., 12g fat (3g sat. fat), 90mg chol., 734mg sod., 28g carb. (5g sugars, 5g fiber), 24g pro. **Diabetic exchanges:** 3 lean meat, 2 starch, ½ fat.

CHICKEN GYROS

These yummy Greek specialties are a snap to prepare. Tender chicken and a creamy sauce are tucked into pitas.
—*Taste of Home* Test Kitchen

PREP: 20 min. + marinating • **COOK:** 10 min.
MAKES: 2 servings

- ¼ cup lemon juice
- 2 Tbsp. olive oil
- ¾ tsp. minced garlic, divided
- ½ tsp. ground mustard
- ½ tsp. dried oregano
- ½ lb. boneless skinless chicken breasts, cut into ½-in. strips
- ½ cup chopped peeled cucumber
- ⅓ cup plain yogurt
- ¼ tsp. dill weed
- 2 whole pita breads
- ½ small red onion, thinly sliced

1. In a large resealable plastic bag, combine the lemon juice, oil, ½ tsp. garlic, mustard and oregano; add chicken. Seal bag and turn to coat; refrigerate for at least 1 hour. In a small bowl, combine cucumber, yogurt, dill and the remaining garlic; cover and refrigerate until serving.
2. Drain and discard the marinade. In a large nonstick skillet, cook and stir the chicken for 7-8 minutes or until no longer pink. Spoon onto pita breads. Top with yogurt mixture and onion; fold in half.
1 gyro: 367 cal., 9g fat (2g sat. fat), 68mg chol., 397mg sod., 39g carb. (4g sugars, 2g fiber), 30g pro. **Diabetic exchanges:** 3 lean meat, 2½ starch, 1 fat.

BONUS: BEEF GYROS

Going out for gyros can be expensive, so I came up with this homemade version. Usually I set out the fixings so everyone can assemble their own.
—Sheri Scheerhorn, Hills, MN

TAKES: 30 min. • **MAKES:** 5 servings

- 1 cup ranch salad dressing
- ½ cup chopped seeded peeled cucumber
- 1 pound beef top sirloin steak, cut into thin strips
- 2 Tbsp. olive oil
- 5 whole pita breads
- 1 medium tomato, chopped
- 1 can (2¼ oz.) sliced ripe olives, drained
- ½ small onion, thinly sliced
- 1 cup (4 oz.) cumbled feta cheese
- 2½ cups shredded lettuce

1. In a small bowl, combine salad dressing and cucumber; set aside. In a large skillet, cook beef in oil over medium heat until no longer pink. Layer half of each pita with steak, tomato, olives, onion, cheese, lettuce and dressing mixture. Fold each pita over filling.
1 gyro: 654 cal., 41g fat (9g sat. fat), 57mg chol., 1086mg sod., 41g carb. (4g sugars, 3g fiber), 30g pro.

BLUE PLATE OPEN-FACED TURKEY SANDWICH

Turkey with gravy makes divine comfort food that reminds me of old-time diners on the East Coast. Happily, my gravy is not from a can!
—Christine Schwester, Divide, CO

TAKES: 25 min. • **MAKES:** 6 servings

- ⅓ cup butter, cubed
- 1 small onion, chopped
- ⅓ cup all-purpose flour
- 2 tsp. minced fresh parsley
- ¼ tsp. pepper
- ⅛ tsp. garlic powder
- ⅛ tsp. dried thyme
- 3 cups reduced-sodium chicken broth
- 1¼ lbs. sliced deli turkey
- 12 slices white bread

1. In a large saucepan, heat butter over medium heat. Add onion; cook and stir for 4-5 minutes or until tender. Stir in flour, parsley and seasonings until blended; gradually whisk in broth. Bring to a boil, stirring constantly; cook and stir for 1-2 minutes or until slightly thickened.
2. Add turkey, one slice at a time; heat through. Serve over bread.

2 open-faced sandwiches: 361 cal., 14g fat (7g sat. fat), 60mg chol., 1462mg sod., 33g carb. (4g sugars, 2g fiber), 25g pro.

FRENCH DIP

The seasonings in this perfected version of a traditional French Dip give the broth a wonderful flavor, and the meat cooks up tender and juicy. This recipe could soon be a favorite at your house, too.
—Margaret McNeil, Germantown, TN

PREP: 15 min. • **COOK:** 5 hours
MAKES: 8 servings

- 1 beef chuck roast (3 lbs.), trimmed
- 2 cups water
- ½ cup reduced-sodium soy sauce
- 1 tsp. dried rosemary, crushed
- 1 tsp. dried thyme
- 1 tsp. garlic powder
- 1 bay leaf
- 3 to 4 whole peppercorns
- 8 French rolls, split

1. Place roast in a 5-qt. slow cooker. Add the water, soy sauce and seasonings. Cover and cook on high for 5-6 hours or until the beef is tender.
2. Remove the meat from broth; shred with two forks and keep warm. Strain broth; skim the fat. Pour the broth into small cups to use for dipping. Serve beef on rolls.

1 sandwich: 467 cal., 19g fat (7g sat. fat), 111mg chol., 1300mg sod., 31g carb. (3g sugars, 2g fiber), 41g pro.

SLOW COOKER

BLACKBERRY SRIRACHA CHICKEN SLIDERS

Dump everything in a slow cooker and watch these spicy-sweet sliders become an instant party time classic.
—Julie Peterson, Crofton, MD

PREP: 20 min. • **COOK:** 5 hours
MAKES: 1 dozen

- 1 jar (10 oz.) seedless blackberry spreadable fruit
- ¼ cup ketchup
- ¼ cup balsamic vinegar
- ¼ cup Sriracha Asian hot chili sauce
- 2 Tbsp. molasses
- 1 Tbsp. Dijon mustard
- ¼ tsp. salt
- 3½ lbs. bone-in chicken thighs
- 1 large onion, thinly sliced
- 4 garlic cloves, minced
- 12 pretzel mini buns, split
  Additional Sriracha Asian hot chili sauce
  Leaf lettuce and tomato slices

1. In a 4- or 5-qt. slow cooker, stir together the first seven ingredients. Add chicken, onion and garlic. Toss to combine.
2. Cook, covered, on low until chicken is tender, 5-6 hours. Remove chicken. When cool enough to handle, remove bones and skin; discard. Shred meat with two forks. Reserve 3 cups cooking juices; discard remaining juices. Skim fat from reserved juices. Return chicken and reserved juices to slow cooker; heat through. Using slotted spoon, serve on pretzel buns. Drizzle with additional Sriracha; top with lettuce and tomato.

1 slider: 352 cal., 14g fat (3g sat. fat), 63mg chol., 413mg sod., 35g carb. (12g sugars, 1g fiber), 21g pro.

BONUS:

SLOW COOKER

TANGY PULLED PORK SANDWICHES

The slow cooker makes this an easy meal, and it keeps the pork tender, moist and loaded with flavor. The sandwiches are so satisfying without being heavy.
—Beki Kosydar-Krantz, Mayfield, PA

PREP: 10 min. • **COOK:** 4 hours • **MAKES:** 4 servings

- 1 pork tenderloin (1 lb.)
- 1 cup ketchup
- 2 Tbsp. plus 1½ tsp. brown sugar
- 2 Tbsp. plus 1½ tsp. cider vinegar
- 1 Tbsp. plus 1½ tsp. Worcestershire sauce
- 1 Tbsp. spicy brown mustard
- ¼ tsp. pepper
- 4 rolls or buns, split and toasted
  Coleslaw, optional

1. Cut tenderloin in half; place in a 3-qt. slow cooker. Combine ketchup, brown sugar, vinegar, Worcestershire sauce, mustard and pepper; pour over pork.
2. Cover and cook on low for 4-5 hours or until meat is tender. Remove meat; shred with two forks. Return to slow cooker; heat through. Serve on toasted rolls or buns, and, if desired, with coleslaw.

1 sandwich: 402 cal., 7g fat (2g sat. fat), 63mg chol., 1181mg sod., 56g carb. (18g sugars, 2g fiber), 29g pro. **Diabetic exchanges:** 3½ starch, 3 lean meat, 1 fat.

TURKEY FOCACCIA CLUB

My family thinks this sandwich is pure heaven, thanks to the cranberry-pecan mayo. I make it with leftover turkey at Thanksgiving, but it's so good, they ask me to make it all year long!
—Judy Wilson, Sun City West, AZ

TAKES: 20 min. • **MAKES:** 4 servings

- ½ **cup mayonnaise**
- ½ **cup whole-berry cranberry sauce**
- 2 **Tbsp. chopped pecans, toasted**
- 2 **Tbsp. Dijon mustard**
- 1 **Tbsp. honey**
- 1 **loaf (8 oz.) focaccia bread**
- 3 **lettuce leaves**
- ½ **lb. thinly sliced cooked turkey**
- ¼ **lb. sliced Gouda cheese**
- 8 **slices tomato**
- 6 **bacon strips, cooked**

In a small bowl, mix first five ingredients until blended. Using a long serrated knife, cut the focaccia horizontally in half. Spread cut sides with mayonnaise mixture. Layer bottom half with lettuce, turkey, cheese, tomato and bacon; replace bread top. Cut the loaf into wedges to serve.

Note: To toast nuts, bake in a shallow pan in a 350° oven for 5-10 minutes or cook in a skillet over low heat until lightly browned, stirring occasionally.

1 wedge: 707 cal., 41g fat (10g sat. fat),96mg chol., 1153mg sod., 53g carb. (17g sugars, 2g fiber), 32g pro.

NOTES

TOASTED REUBENS

Reubens were made famous by the delis of New York, and New Yorkers tell me my Reubens taste like home. If you like a milder flavor, omit the horseradish.
—Patricia Kile, Elizabethtown, PA

TAKES: 20 min. • **MAKES:** 4 servings

- 4 tsp. prepared mustard
- 8 slices rye bread
- 4 slices Swiss cheese
- 1 lb. thinly sliced deli corned beef
- 1 can (8 oz.) sauerkraut, rinsed and well drained
- ½ cup mayonnaise
- 3 Tbsp. ketchup
- 2 Tbsp. sweet pickle relish
- 1 Tbsp. prepared horseradish
- 2 Tbsp. butter

1. Spread mustard over four slices of bread. Layer with cheese, corned beef and sauerkraut. In a small bowl, mix the mayonnaise, ketchup, relish and horseradish; spread over the remaining bread. Place over sauerkraut. Spread the outsides of the sandwiches with butter.
2. In a large skillet over medium heat, toast sandwiches for 3-4 minutes on each side or until the bread is golden brown and the cheese is melted.
1 sandwich: 705 cal., 45g fat (15g sat. fat), 124mg chol., 2830mg sod., 41g carb. (9g sugars, 6g fiber), 34g pro.

FREEZE IT
SUPER SLOPPY JOES

Mother made these fresh-tasting sloppy joes many times when I was growing up. She gave the recipe to me when I got married. My brother-in-law says they're the best sandwiches he's ever tasted. He ought to know, his name is Joe!
—Ellen Stringer, Bourbonnais, IL

PREP: 15 min. • **COOK:** 35 min.
MAKES: 10 servings

- 2 lbs. ground beef
- ½ cup chopped onion
- 2 celery ribs with leaves, chopped
- ¼ cup chopped green pepper
- 1 can (15 oz.) crushed tomatoes
- ¼ cup ketchup
- 2 Tbsp. brown sugar
- 1 Tbsp. white vinegar
- 1 Tbsp. Worcestershire sauce
- 1 Tbsp. steak sauce
- ½ tsp. garlic salt
- ¼ tsp. ground mustard
- ¼ tsp. paprika
- 10 hamburger or hoagie buns, split

1. In a Dutch oven over medium heat, cook the beef, onion, celery and green pepper until the meat is no longer pink and the vegetables are tender; drain.
2. Stir in the next nine ingredients. Simmer, uncovered, for 35-40 minutes or until heated through, stirring occasionally. Spoon about ½ cup of the meat mixture onto each bun.
Freeze option: Freeze individual portions of the cooled meat mixture in freezer containers. To use, partially thaw in refrigerator overnight. Microwave, covered, on high in a microwave-safe dish until heated through, gently stirring and adding a little broth or water if necessary.
1 sandwich: 306 cal., 13g fat (5g sat. fat), 60mg chol., 473mg sod., 25g carb. (7g sugars, 2g fiber), 22g pro.

BARBECUE BRATS & PEPPERS

We live in brat country, and this saucy, barbecue-style recipe feeds a crowd.
—Maria Zrucky, Kronenwetter, WI

PREP: 15 min. • **COOK:** 6 hours
MAKES: 10 servings

- 2 bottles (12 oz. each) beer or nonalcoholic beer
- 1 bottle (18 oz.) barbecue sauce
- ½ cup ketchup
- 1 large sweet onion, halved and sliced
- 1 large sweet yellow pepper, cut into strips
- 1 large sweet orange pepper, cut into strips
- 1 jalapeno pepper, thinly sliced
- 1 serrano pepper, thinly sliced
- 10 uncooked bratwurst links
- 10 brat or hot dog buns, split

1. Place the first eight ingredients in a 5-qt. slow cooker; stir to mixture combine. In a large skillet, brown bratwurst on all sides over medium-high heat; transfer to slow cooker.

2. Cook, covered, on low 6-8 hours or until sausages are cooked through and vegetables are tender. Using tongs, serve bratwurst and pepper mixture on buns.

Note: Wear disposable gloves when cutting hot peppers; the oils can burn your skin. Avoid touching your face.

1 bratwurst: 614 cal., 30g fat (10g sat. fat), 63mg chol., 1789mg sod., 66g carb. (27g sugars, 2g fiber), 21g pro.

BONUS: GRILLED BRATS WITH SRIRACHA MAYO

I'm a Sriracha fanatic, so that's what inspired this dish. You can boil the brats in your favorite beer to reduce the fat and give them flavor before grilling, or really ramp up the flavor by spreading garlic butter on lightly toasted buns.
—Quincie Bell, Olympia, WA

PREP: 10 min. • **COOK:** 10 min. • **MAKES:** 4 servings

- ½ cup mayonnaise
- ⅓ cup minced roasted sweet red peppers
- 3 Tbsp. Sriracha Asian hot chili sauce
- 4 fully cooked bratwurst links
- 4 brat buns or hot dog buns, split
- ½ cup dill pickle relish
- ½ cup finely chopped red onion
  Ketchup, optional

Mix the first four ingredients. Grill bratwursts, covered, over medium-low heat until browned and heated through, 7-10 minutes, turning occasionally. Serve in buns with mayonnaise mixture, relish, onion and, if desired, ketchup.

1 bratwurst: 742 cal., 49g fat (13g sat. fat), 65mg chol., 2020mg sod., 54g carb. (10g sugars, 2g fiber), 20g pro.

SAUSAGE & SPINACH CALZONES

These comforting calzones are perfect for quick meals—or even a midnight snack. My nurse coworkers always ask me to make them when it's my turn to bring in lunch.
—Kourtney Williams, Mechanicsville, VA

TAKES: 30 min. • **MAKES:** 4 servings

- ½ **lb. bulk Italian sausage**
- 3 **cups fresh baby spinach**
- 1 **tube (13.8 oz.) refrigerated pizza crust**
- ¾ **cup shredded part-skim mozzarella cheese**
- ½ **cup part-skim ricotta cheese**
- ¼ **tsp. pepper**
  Pizza sauce, optional

1. Preheat oven to 400°. In a large skillet, cook and crumble sausage over medium heat until no longer pink, 4-6 minutes; drain. Add spinach; cook and stir until wilted. Remove from heat.

2. On a lightly floured surface, unroll and pat dough into a 15x11-in. rectangle. Cut into four smaller rectangles. Sprinkle mozzarella cheese on one half of each rectangle to within 1 in. of edges.

3. Stir ricotta cheese and pepper into the sausage mixture; spoon over mozzarella cheese. Fold dough over the filling; press edges with a fork to seal. Place calzones on a greased baking sheet.

4. Bake until crust is light golden brown, 10-15 minutes. If desired, serve with pizza sauce on the side.

Freeze option: Freeze cooled calzones in a resealable plastic freezer bag. To use, microwave on high until heated through.

BONUS: PERFECT PIZZA CRUST

I spent years trying different techniques to achieve the perfect pizza crust recipe. I'm proud to say this is it. My family prefers my crust to the pizza parlor's!
—Lesli Dustin, Nibley, UT

TAKES: 20 min. + rising • **MAKES:** a 14-in. pizza crust (8 slices)

- 1 **Tbsp. active dry yeast**
- 1½ **cups warm water (110° to 115°)**
- 2 **Tbsp. sugar**
- ½ **tsp. salt**
- 2 **cups bread flour**
- 1½ **cups whole wheat flour**

In a large bowl, dissolve yeast in warm water. Add sugar, salt, 1 cup of the bread flour and the whole wheat flour. Beat until smooth. Stir in enough of the remaining bread flour to form a soft dough (dough will be sticky). Turn onto a floured surface; knead until smooth and elastic, 6-8 minutes. Place in a greased bowl, turning once to grease the top. Cover and let rise in a warm place until doubled, about 1 hour. Punch dough down; roll out and use how desired.

1 slice: 193 cal., 0 fat (0 sat. fat), 0 chol., 149mg sod., 42g carb. (3g sugars, 4g fiber), 8g pro.

TOP TIP
If you're using fresh or homemade pizza dough for this calzone, you may need to give it 5-10 minutes more cooking time. Sprinkle some cornmeal on the baking sheet to prevent sticking, and keep an eye on the color of the crust.

GIANT MEATBALL SUB

Whether you fix it for a party or on a weeknight for your family, this big sub will rise to the top of your list of favorites. Just don't count on having any leftovers!
—Deana Paul, San Dimas, CA

PREP: 15 min. • **COOK:** 30 min.
MAKES: 8 servings

- 2 large eggs, lightly beaten
- ⅓ cup milk
- 1 medium onion, chopped
- 2 garlic cloves, minced
- 1 cup soft bread crumbs
- ½ tsp. salt
- ½ tsp. Italian seasoning
- 1¼ lbs. bulk Italian sausage
- ¾ lb. ground beef
- 2 jars (26 oz. each) spaghetti sauce
- 1 loaf (1 lb.) unsliced French bread, halved lengthwise
- 8 slices part-skim mozzarella cheese
   Shredded Parmesan cheese, optional

1. Preheat oven to 425°. Combine eggs, milk, onion, garlic, bread crumbs, salt and Italian seasoning. Crumble sausage and beef over the egg mixture; mix well.
2. Shape into 1-in. balls. Place on a greased rack in a shallow baking pan. Bake for 15 minutes or until browned; drain.
3. In a Dutch oven, heat the spaghetti sauce over medium heat. Add meatballs; simmer for 15 minutes. Meanwhile, bake the bread at 325° for 10 minutes or until heated through.
4. Place mozzarella cheese on bottom half of bread; spoon meatballs onto cheese. Replace the top. Slice sandwich into eight portions; serve with extra spaghetti sauce and, if desired, Parmesan cheese.
1 serving: 686 cal., 40g fat (16g sat. fat), 161mg chol., 1649mg sod., 45g carb. (9g sugars, 4g fiber), 34g pro.

CAESAR CHICKEN WRAPS

When we have chicken for dinner, I cook extra for these full-flavored roll-ups. They're perfect paired with chips—or corn on the cob and a green vegetable.
—Christi Martin, Elko, NV

TAKES: 30 min. • **MAKES:** 5 servings

- ½ cup creamy Caesar salad dressing
- ½ cup grated Parmesan cheese, divided
- 1 tsp. lemon juice
- 1 garlic clove, minced
- ¼ tsp. pepper
- 1 pkg. (8 oz.) cream cheese, softened
- 3 cups shredded romaine
- ½ cup diced sweet red pepper
- 1 can (2¼ oz.) sliced ripe olives, drained
- 5 flour tortillas (10 in.)
- 1¾ cups cubed cooked chicken

1. In a small bowl, combine the salad dressing, ¼ cup of the Parmesan cheese, lemon juice, garlic and pepper. In a small bowl, beat cream cheese until smooth. Add half of the salad dressing mixture to the cream cheese and mix well; set aside.
2. In a large bowl, combine the romaine, red pepper and olives. Add the remaining salad dressing mixture; toss to coat.
3. Spread about ¼ cup of the cream cheese mixture over each tortilla. Top with the romaine mixture and chicken; sprinkle with the remaining Parmesan cheese. Roll up; cut in half.
1 wrap: 614 cal., 36g fat (15g sat. fat), 108mg chol., 1065mg sod., 36g carb. (2g sugars, 7g fiber), 29g pro.

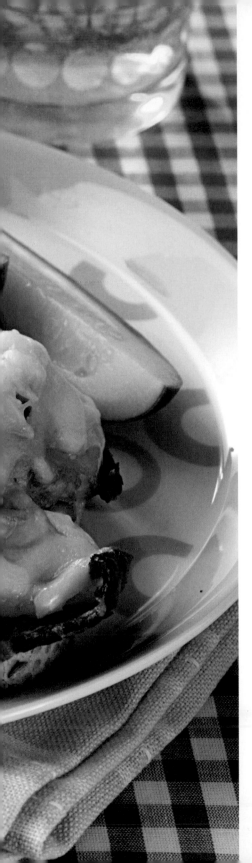

CORNED BEEF & COLESLAW SANDWICHES

These open-faced sandwiches with layers of savory corned beef, creamy slaw and melty Swiss are not only tasty but take just 15 minutes to create.
—Marilou Robinson, Portland, OR

TAKES: 15 min. • **MAKES:** 4 servings

- 2 **cups coleslaw mix**
- 3 **Tbsp. sour cream**
- 4 **tsp. mayonnaise**
- 1 **Tbsp. horseradish sauce**
- 1 **tsp. prepared mustard**
- ⅛ **tsp. salt**
- 4 **slices rye bread**
- ½ **lb. thinly sliced corned beef**
- 8 **slices Swiss cheese**

1. Place coleslaw mix in a small bowl. Combine the sour cream, mayonnaise, horseradish sauce, mustard and salt. Pour over coleslaw mix and toss to coat.

2. Place bread slices on an ungreased baking sheet. Broil 4 in. from the heat for 2-3 minutes on each side or until toasted golden brown. Layer with corned beef, coleslaw mixture and cheese. Broil for 2-3 minutes or until cheese is melted.

1 sandwich: 423 cal., 26g fat (14g sat. fat), 100mg chol., 1203mg sod., 19g carb. (3g sugars, 3g fiber), 26g pro.

NOTES

HEARTY BREADED FISH SANDWICHES

Fishing for a burger alternative? Consider it caught. A hint of cayenne is cooled by a creamy yogurt and mayo sauce in this pleasing fish sandwich.
—*Taste of Home* Test Kitchen

TAKES: 30 min. • **MAKES:** 4 servings

- ½ cup dry bread crumbs
- ½ tsp. garlic powder
- ½ tsp. cayenne pepper
- ½ tsp. dried parsley flakes
- 4 cod fillets (6 oz. each)
- 4 whole wheat hamburger buns, split
- ¼ cup plain yogurt
- ¼ cup fat-free mayonnaise
- 2 tsp. lemon juice
- 2 tsp. sweet pickle relish
- ¼ tsp. dried minced onion
- 4 lettuce leaves
- 4 slices tomato
- 4 slices sweet onion

1. In a shallow bowl, combine the bread crumbs, garlic powder, cayenne and parsley. Coat cod fillets with the bread crumb mixture.

2. On a lightly oiled grill rack, grill the cod, covered, over medium heat or broil 4 in. from the heat for 4-5 minutes on each side or until the fish flakes easily with a fork. Grill the hamburger buns over medium heat for 30-60 seconds or until toasted.

3. Meanwhile, in a small bowl, combine yogurt, mayonnaise, lemon juice, relish and minced onion; spread over the bun bottoms. Top with cod, lettuce, tomato and onion; replace bun tops.

1 sandwich: 292 cal., 4g fat (1g sat. fat), 68mg chol., 483mg sod., 32g carb. (7g sugars, 4g fiber), 32g pro. **Diabetic exchanges:** 5 lean meat, 2 starch.

Salsa Fish Sandwiches: Follow method as directed above but replace the plain yogurt with salsa and omit the lemon juice, relish and dried minced onion. Top sandwiches with sliced tomato and fresh cilantro.

Slaw-Topped Fish Sandwiches: Follow method as directed above but omit the relish, substitute red wine vinegar for the lemon juice and stir 1½ cups coleslaw mix into the mayonnaise mixture. Omit the lettuce, tomato and onion and top cod with the slaw mixture.

TOP TIP

These sandwiches are made with cod fillets, but any white fish—tilapia, catfish, halibut or haddock—would do nicely. You can bake the fillets instead of grilling them if you prefer.

CRISPY BUFFALO CHICKEN WRAPS

I'm big on wraps, even when I go out to eat. As a busy stay-at-home mom, I turn to this family favorite a lot. It's so good with chips and salsa on the side.
—Christina Addison, Blanchester, OH

TAKES: 30 min. • **MAKES:** 4 servings

- 1 **pkg. (12 oz.) frozen popcorn chicken**
- 1 **pkg. (8 oz.) shredded lettuce**
- 2 **medium tomatoes, finely chopped**
- 1 **cup shredded cheddar cheese**
- ⅓ **cup Buffalo wing sauce**
- 4 **flour tortillas (10 in.), warmed Ranch or chipotle ranch salad dressing, optional**

1. Cook chicken according to package directions; coarsely chop chicken. In a large bowl, mix chicken, lettuce, tomatoes and cheese. Drizzle with the wing sauce; toss to coat.

2. Spoon 1½ cups chicken mixture down center of each tortilla. Fold bottom of tortilla over filling; fold both sides to close. Serve the wraps immediately, with salad dressing if desired.

1 wrap: 570 cal., 26g fat (9g sat. fat), 55mg chol., 1895mg sod., 62g carb. (7g sugars, 4g fiber), 23g pro.

SLOW COOKER | FREEZE IT
ITALIAN SAUSAGE HOAGIES

In southeastern Wisconsin, our cuisine is influenced by both Germans and Italians who immigrated to this area. Sometimes we'll swap German bratwurst for Italian sausage in this recipe. Blending the two influences has delicious results.
—Craig Wachs, Racine, WI

PREP: 15 min. • **COOK:** 4 hours
MAKES: 10 servings

- 10 **Italian sausage links**
- 2 **Tbsp. olive oil**
- 1 **jar (24 oz.) meatless spaghetti sauce**
- ½ **medium green pepper, julienned**
- ½ **medium sweet red pepper, julienned**
- ½ **cup water**
- ¼ **cup grated Romano cheese**
- 2 **Tbsp. dried oregano**
- 2 **Tbsp. dried basil**
- 2 **loaves French bread (20 in.)**

1. In a large skillet over medium-high heat, brown the sausage in oil; drain. Transfer to a 5-qt. slow cooker. Add the spaghetti sauce, peppers, water, cheese, oregano and basil. Cover and cook on low for 4 hours or until the sausage is no longer pink.

2. Slice each French bread loaf lengthwise but not all of the way through; cut each loaf widthwise into five pieces. Fill each with sausage, peppers and sauce.

1 serving: 509 cal., 21g fat (7g sat. fat), 48mg chol., 1451mg sod., 56g carb. (7g sugars, 5g fiber), 22g pro.

SOUPS & STEWS

NOTHING SAYS HOME COOKING LIKE WARM, HEARTY SOUPS, STEWS AND CHILI!

HEARTY PASTA FAJIOLI

Here's a classic Italian favorite, made easier by using spaghetti sauce and canned broth for the flavorful base.
—Cindy Garland, Limestone, TN

PREP: 40 min. • **COOK:** 40 min.
MAKES: 24 servings (7½ qt.)

- 2 lbs. ground beef
- 6 cans (14½ oz. each) beef broth
- 2 cans (28 oz. each) diced tomatoes, undrained
- 2 jars (26 oz. each) spaghetti sauce
- 3 large onions, chopped
- 8 celery ribs, diced
- 3 medium carrots, sliced
- 1 can (16 oz.) canned kidney beans, rinsed and drained
- 1 can (15 oz.) cannellini beans, rinsed and drained
- 3 tsp. minced fresh oregano or 1 tsp. dried oregano
- 2½ tsp. pepper
- 1½ tsp. hot pepper sauce
- 8 oz. uncooked medium pasta shells
- 5 tsp. minced fresh parsley

1. In a large stockpot, cook the beef over medium heat until no longer pink; drain. Add broth, tomatoes, spaghetti sauce, onions, celery, carrots, beans, oregano, pepper and pepper sauce.
2. Bring to a boil. Reduce heat; simmer, covered, for 30 minutes. Add pasta and parsley; simmer, covered, 10-14 minutes or until pasta is tender.
1¼ cups: 212 cal., 6g fat (2g sat. fat), 20mg chol., 958mg sod., 25g carb. (8g sugars, 5g fiber), 14g pro.

SLOW COOKER
POTATO & LEEK SOUP

Full of veggies and bacon with just a little tanginess from sour cream, bowls of this comforting soup taste just as terrific with a sandwich as they do with crackers or breadsticks.
—Melanie Wooden, Reno, NV

PREP: 20 min. • **COOK:** 8 hours
MAKES: 8 servings (2 qt.)

- 4 cups chicken broth
- 3 medium potatoes, peeled and cubed
- 1½ cups chopped cabbage
- 2 medium carrots, chopped
- 1 medium leek (white portion only), chopped
- 1 medium onion, chopped
- ¼ cup minced fresh parsley
- ½ tsp. salt
- ½ tsp. caraway seeds
- ½ tsp. pepper
- 1 bay leaf
- ½ cup sour cream
- 1 lb. bacon strips, cooked and crumbled

1. Combine the first 11 ingredients in a 4- or 5-qt. slow cooker. Cover and cook on low for 8-10 hours or until the vegetables are tender.
2. Before serving, combine sour cream with 1 cup soup; return all to the slow cooker. Stir in bacon and discard bay leaf.
1 cup: 209 cal., 11g fat (4g sat. fat), 27mg chol., 1023mg sod., 18g carb. (4g sugars, 2g fiber), 10g pro.

QUICK CREAM OF MUSHROOM SOUP

My daughter-in-law, a gourmet cook, received this recipe from her mom and graciously shared it with me. Now I'm happy to share it with my own friends and family.
—Anne Kulick, Phillipsburg, NJ

TAKES: 30 min. • **MAKES:** 6 servings

- 2 Tbsp. butter
- ½ lb. sliced fresh mushrooms
- ¼ cup chopped onion
- 6 Tbsp. all-purpose flour
- ½ tsp. salt
- ⅛ tsp. pepper
- 2 cans (14½ oz. each) chicken broth
- 1 cup half-and-half cream

1. In a large saucepan, heat the butter over medium-high heat; saute mushrooms and onion until tender.

2. Mix the flour, salt, pepper and one can broth until smooth; stir into mushroom mixture. Stir in remaining broth. Bring to a boil; cook and stir mixture until thickened, about 2 minutes. Reduce heat; stir in the cream. Simmer the soup, uncovered, until flavors are blended, for about 15 minutes, stirring occasionally.

1 cup: 136 cal., 8g fat (5g sat. fat), 33mg chol., 842mg sod., 10g carb. (3g sugars, 1g fiber), 4g pro.

BONUS: CREAM OF ASPARAGUS SOUP

I developed this recipe myself by experimenting with and adapting an old recipe for cream of broccoli soup. It's a big favorite at our house!
—Westelle Griswa, Monroe, CT

PREP: 10 min. • **COOK:** 20 min. • **MAKES:** 6 servings

- 4 cups cut fresh asparagus (½-in. pieces)
- 2 cups water, divided
- ¼ cup finely chopped green onions or 1 tsp. onion powder
- 5 Tbsp. butter
- 5 Tbsp. all-purpose flour
- ½ to 1 tsp. salt
- 4 cups whole milk
- 1 Tbsp. chicken bouillon granules

1. Place asparagus in a large saucepan and cover with 1 cup water. Bring to a boil, cover and cook for 3-5 minutes or until crisp-tender. Drain, reserving liquid.

2. In a another saucepan, saute onions in butter until tender. Stir in the flour, salt and pepper until blended. Gradually stir in the milk, bouillon, reserved cooking liquid and remaining water. Bring to a boil. Cook and stir for 2 minutes or until thickened and bubbly. Stir in asparagus; heat through..

1 cup: 232 cal., 15g fat (9g sat. fat), 48mg chol., 795mg sod., 17g carb. (10g sugars, 2g fiber), 8g pro.

SPECIAL OCCASION BEEF BOURGUIGNON

I've found many rich and satisfying variations for boeuf bourguignon, and this is one of my favorites. White rice flour instead of all-purpose flour will make this stew gluten-free.
—Leo Cotnoir, Johnson City, NY

PREP: 50 min. • **BAKE:** 2 hours
MAKES: 8 servings

- 4 bacon strips, chopped
- 1 beef sirloin tip roast (2 lbs.), cut into 1½-in. cubes and patted dry
- ¼ cup all-purpose flour
- ½ tsp. salt
- ½ tsp. pepper
- 1 Tbsp. canola oil
- 2 medium onions, chopped
- 2 medium carrots, coarsely chopped
- ½ lb. medium fresh mushrooms, quartered
- 4 garlic cloves, minced
- 1 Tbsp. tomato paste
- 2 cups dry red wine
- 1 cup beef stock
- 2 bay leaves
- ½ tsp. dried thyme
- 8 oz. uncooked egg noodles
  Minced fresh parsley

1. Preheat oven to 325°. In a Dutch oven, cook bacon over medium-low heat until crisp, stirring occasionally. Remove with a slotted spoon, reserving drippings; drain on paper towels.

2. In batches, brown beef in drippings over medium-high heat; remove from the pan. Toss with flour, salt and pepper.

3. In the same pan, heat 1 Tbsp. oil over medium heat; saute onions, carrots and mushrooms until the onions are tender, 4-5 minutes. Add garlic and tomato paste; cook and stir for 1 minute. Add wine and stock, stirring to loosen the browned bits from the pan. Add herbs, bacon and beef; bring to a boil.

4. Transfer to oven; bake, covered, until the meat is tender, 2 to 2¼ hours. Remove bay leaves.

5. To serve, cook noodles according to package directions; drain. Serve stew with noodles; sprinkle with parsley.

Freeze option: Freeze cooled stew in freezer containers. To use, partially thaw the stew in refrigerator overnight. Heat through in a saucepan, stirring occasionally and adding a little stock or broth if necessary.

⅔ cup stew with ⅔ cup noodles: 422 cal., 14g fat (4g sat. fat), 105mg chol., 357mg sod., 31g carb. (4g sugars, 2g fiber), 31g pro. **Diabetic exchanges:** 4 lean meat, 2 fat, 1½ starch, 1 vegetable.

You can use stew meat for this recipe, but be aware that many stores package different cuts mixed together as stew meat, and they may cook at different rates. Look for a package with pieces that look similar and have the same amount of marbling.

BEER-CHEESE VELVET SOUP

This soup was a hit with a group of German exchange teachers who visited our high school. When I don't use bread bowls, I usually serve it with soft pretzels or crusty bread. And it's also a treat with slices of cooked bratwurst or kielbasa stirred into it.
—Paula Zsiray, Logan, UT

TAKES: 25 min. • **MAKES:** 8 servings

- ¾ cup butter, cubed
- ¾ cup all-purpose flour
- 1 bottle (12 oz.) light beer
- 4 cups chicken or vegetable stock, divided
- 2 tsp. Worcestershire sauce
- 1 tsp. ground mustard
- ½ tsp. salt
- ¼ tsp. pepper
- ¼ tsp. cayenne pepper
- 4 cups shredded cheddar cheese
  Bread bowls, crumbled bacon, shredded cheddar cheese, optional

1. In a large saucepan, melt butter over medium heat. Stir in flour until blended; gradually whisk in beer until smooth. Whisk in stock, Worcestershire sauce, mustard, salt, pepper and cayenne.
2. Bring to a boil, stirring soup constantly; cook and stir until thickened, 1-2 minutes. Reduce heat. Gradually stir in cheese until melted. If desired, serve the soup in bread bowls and top with crumbled bacon and shredded cheese.

¾ cup: 450 cal., 36g fat (22g sat. fat), 102mg chol., 925mg sod., 12g carb. (1g sugars, 0 fiber), 17g pro.

SPLIT PEA SOUP WITH HAM

To liven up pea soup, I load mine with potatoes and veggies. It's peppery rather than smoky, and I like to pass it around with warm rye bread.
—Barbara Link, Alta Loma, CA

PREP: 15 min. • **COOK:** 1¼ hours
MAKES: 12 servings (3 qt.)

- 1 pkg. (16 oz.) dried green split peas
- 8 cups water
- ¾ lb. potatoes (about 2 medium), cubed
- 2 large onions, chopped
- 2 medium carrots, chopped
- 2 cups cubed fully cooked ham (about 10 oz.)
- 1 celery rib, chopped
- 5 tsp. reduced-sodium chicken bouillon granules
- 1 tsp. dried marjoram
- 1 tsp. poultry seasoning
- 1 tsp. rubbed sage
- ½ to 1 tsp. pepper
- ½ tsp. dried basil

Place all ingredients in a Dutch oven; bring to a boil. Reduce heat; simmer, covered, 1¼ to 1½ hours or until peas and vegetables are tender, stirring the soup occasionally.

1 cup: 202 cal., 2g fat (0 sat. fat), 14mg chol., 396mg sod., 33g carb. (5g sugars, 11g fiber), 15g pro. **Diabetic exchanges:** 2 starch, 1 lean meat.

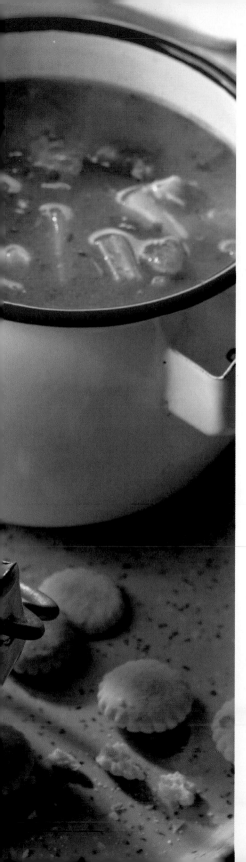

MANHATTAN CLAM CHOWDER

I typically serve this chowder with a tossed salad and hot rolls. It's easy to make and tastes wonderful; my family has enjoyed it for over 30 years.
—Joan Hopewell, Columbus, NJ

PREP: 10 min. • **COOK:** 40 min.
MAKES: 8 servings (about 2 qt.)

- 2   Tbsp. butter
- 1   cup chopped onion
- ⅔   cup chopped celery
- 2   tsp. minced green pepper
- 1   garlic clove, minced
- 2   cups hot water
- 1   cup cubed peeled potatoes
- 1   can (28 oz.) diced tomatoes, undrained
- 2   cans (6½ oz. each) minced clams, undrained
- 1   tsp. salt
- ½   tsp. dried thyme
- ¼   tsp. pepper
     Dash cayenne pepper
- 2   tsp. minced fresh parsley

1. In a large saucepan, heat butter over low heat. Add onion, celery, green pepper and garlic; cook, stirring frequently, for 20 minutes. Add water and potatoes; bring to a boil. Reduce heat; simmer, covered, until potatoes are tender, about 15 minutes.

2. Add the tomatoes, clams, salt, thyme, pepper and cayenne; heat through. Stir in parsley. Serve immediately.

1 cup: 91 cal., 3g fat (2g sat. fat), 15mg chol., 652mg sod., 13g carb. (5g sugars, 3g fiber), 5g pro.

NOTES

_____
_____
_____
_____
_____
_____
_____
_____
_____
_____
_____

SOUPY CHICKEN NOODLE SUPPER

At least once a week my 6-year-old son, also known as Doctor John, hands me a prescription for chicken noodle soup. I'm always happy to fill it.
—Heidi Hall, North Saint Paul, MN

TAKES: 30 min. • **MAKES:** 4 servings

- 1   **Tbsp. butter**
- 1   **medium carrot, sliced**
- 1   **celery rib, sliced**
- 1   **small onion, chopped**
- 4   **cups water**
- 4   **tsp. chicken bouillon granules**
- 1½   **tsp. dried parsley flakes**
- ¼   **tsp. Italian seasoning**
- ⅛   **tsp. celery seed**
- ⅛   **tsp. pepper**
- 3   **cups uncooked wide egg noodles**
- 1½   **cups cubed rotisserie chicken**
- 1   **can (10¾ oz.) condensed cream of chicken soup, undiluted**
- ½   **cup sour cream**

1. In a large saucepan, heat butter over medium-high heat. Add carrot, celery and onion; cook and stir about 6-8 minutes or until tender.

2. Stir in water, bouillon and seasonings; bring to a boil. Add the noodles; cook, uncovered, 5-7 minutes or until tender. Stir in chicken, soup and sour cream; heat through.

1⅔ cups: 392 cal., 19g fat (8g sat. fat), 92mg chol., 1497mg sod., 32g carb. (4g sugars, 3g fiber), 22g pro.

BONUS: THE ULTIMATE CHICKEN NOODLE SOUP

My first Wisconsin winter was so cold, all I wanted to eat was soup. This recipe is in heavy rotation from November to April at our house.
—Gina Nistico, Denver, CO

PREP: 15 min. • **COOK:** 45 min. + standing
MAKES: 10 servings (3½ qt.)

- 2½ lbs. bone-in chicken thighs
- 1¼ tsp. pepper, divided
- ½ tsp. salt
- 1 Tbsp. canola oil
- 1 large onion, chopped
- 1 garlic clove, minced
- 10 cups chicken broth
- 4 celery ribs, chopped
- 4 medium carrots, chopped
- 2 bay leaves
- 1 tsp. minced fresh thyme or ¼ tsp. dried thyme
- 3 cups uncooked kluski or other egg noodles (about 8 oz.)
- 1 Tbsp. chopped fresh parsley
- 1 Tbsp. lemon juice

1. Pat chicken dry with paper towels; sprinkle with ½ tsp. pepper and salt. In a 6-qt. stockpot, heat oil over medium-high heat. Add chicken in batches, skin side down; cook until dark golden brown, 3-4 minutes. Remove the chicken from pan; remove and discard skin. Discard drippings, reserving 2 Tbsp.

2. Add onion to the drippings; cook and stir over medium-high heat until tender, 4-5 minutes. Add garlic; cook 1 minute longer. Add broth, stirring to loosen the browned bits from pan. Bring to a boil. Return the chicken to pan. Add celery, carrots, bay leaves and thyme. Reduce heat; simmer, covered, until the chicken is tender, 25-30 minutes.

3. Transfer chicken to a plate. Remove soup from heat. Add noodles; let stand, covered, until the noodles are tender, 20-22 minutes.

4. Meanwhile, when the chicken is cool enough to handle, remove meat from bones; discard bones. Shred meat into bite-size pieces. Return meat to stockpot. Stir in parsley and lemon juice. Adjust seasoning with salt and the remaining ¾ tsp. pepper. Remove bay leaves.

1⅓ cups: 239 cal., 12g fat (3g sat. fat), 68mg chol., 1176mg sod., 14g carb. (3g sugars, 2g fiber), 18g pro.

COMFORTING BEEF BARLEY SOUP

When the weather outside is cool, this soup full of beef, barley and veggies is the most delicious way to warm up.
—Sue Jurack, Mequon, WI

PREP: 10 min. • **COOK:** 35 min.
MAKES: 8 servings (3 qt.)

- 1   **Tbsp. butter**
- 1   **medium carrot, chopped**
- 1   **celery rib, chopped**
- ½   **cup chopped onion**
- 4   **cups beef broth**
- 4   **cups water**
- 2   **cups chopped cooked roast beef**
- 1   **can (14½ oz.) diced tomatoes, undrained**
- 1   **cup quick-cooking barley**
- ½   **tsp. dried basil**
- ½   **tsp. dried oregano**
- ½   **tsp. pepper**
- ¼   **tsp. salt**
- ½   **cup frozen peas**

1. In a 6-qt. stockpot, heat butter over medium-high heat; saute carrot, celery and onion until tender, 4-5 minutes.
2. Add broth, water, beef, tomatoes, barley and seasonings; bring to a boil. Reduce heat; simmer, covered, for 20 minutes, stirring occasionally. Add peas; heat through, about 5 minutes.
1½ cups: 198 cal., 4g fat (2g sat. fat), 36mg chol., 652mg sod., 23g carb. (3g sugars, 6g fiber), 18g pro. **Diabetic exchanges:** 2 lean meat, 1½ starch, ½ fat.

FREEZE IT
PICO DE GALLO BLACK BEAN SOUP

Everyone who sits at my table goes for this velvety, feel-good soup. It's quick and delicious when you're pressed for time.
—Darlis Wilfer, West Bend, WI

TAKES: 20 min. • **MAKES:** 6 servings

- 4   **cans (15 oz. each) black beans, rinsed and drained**
- 2   **cups vegetable broth**
- 2   **cups pico de gallo**
- ½   **cup water**
- 2   **tsp. ground cumin**
      Optional toppings: chopped fresh cilantro, additional pico de gallo

1. In a Dutch oven, combine the first five ingredients; bring to a boil over medium heat, stirring occasionally. Reduce heat; simmer, uncovered, 5-7 minutes or until the vegetables in the pico de gallo are softened, stirring occasionally.
2. Puree soup using an immersion blender. Or cool slightly and puree in batches in a blender; return to the pan and heat through. Serve with toppings as desired.
Freeze option: Freeze the cooled soup in freezer containers. To use, partially thaw in refrigerator overnight. Heat through in a saucepan, stirring occasionally and adding a little broth or water if necessary. Top as desired.
1¼ cups: 241 cal., 0 fat (0 sat. fat), 0 chol., 856mg sod., 44g carb. (4g sugars, 12g fiber), 14g pro.

CLASSIC FRENCH ONION SOUP

When I make this traditional soup for my granddaughter Becky, I always serve it in a French onion soup bowl complete with garlic croutons and gobs of melted Swiss cheese on top.

—Lou Sansevero, Ferron, UT

PREP: 20 min. • **COOK:** 2 hours + broiling
MAKES: 12 servings

- 5 Tbsp. olive oil, divided
- 1 Tbsp. butter
- 8 cups thinly sliced onions (about 3 lbs.)
- 3 garlic cloves, minced
- ½ cup port wine
- 2 cartons (32 oz. each) beef broth
- ½ tsp. pepper
- ¼ tsp. salt
- 24 slices French bread baguette (½ in. thick)
- 2 large garlic cloves, peeled and halved
- ¾ cup shredded Gruyere or Swiss cheese (about 3 oz.)

1. In a Dutch oven, heat 2 Tbsp. of oil and the butter over medium heat. Add onions; cook and stir until softened, 10-13 minutes. Reduce heat to medium-low; cook, stirring occasionally, until the onions are deep golden brown, about 30-40 minutes. Add minced garlic; cook for 2 minutes longer.

2. Stir in wine. Bring to a boil; cook until liquid is reduced by half. Add the broth, pepper and salt; return to a boil. Reduce heat. Simmer the soup, covered, stirring occasionally, for 1 hour.

3. Meanwhile, preheat oven to 400°. Place baguette slices on a baking sheet; brush both sides with the remaining oil. Bake until toasted, 3-5 minutes on each side. Rub toasts with halved garlic.

4. To serve, place twelve 8-oz. broiler-safe bowls or ramekins on baking sheets. Place two toasts in each. Ladle with soup; top with cheese. Broil 4 in. from heat until the cheese is melted.

¾ cup soup with 2 slices bread and 1 Tbsp. cheese: 195 cal., 10g fat (3g sat. fat), 9mg chol., 805mg sod., 20g carb. (4g sugars, 2g fiber), 6g pro.

"I followed the recipe exactly and it is delicious! My family said it tastes like Grandma's soup that we used to have on Christmas Eve. Cooking the onions thoroughly and slowly is truly part of making the great flavor."

—LINDA, TASTEOFHOME.COM

CHEESY HAM CHOWDER

My five children all say this soothing recipe is wonderful. The best part is that it takes just a half-hour of hands-on time.
—Jennifer Trenhaile, Emerson, NE

PREP: 30 min. • **COOK:** 30 min.
MAKES: 10 servings

- 10 bacon strips, diced
- 1 large onion, chopped
- 1 cup diced carrots
- 3 Tbsp. all-purpose flour
- 3 cups whole milk
- 1½ cups water
- 2½ cups cubed potatoes
- 1 can (15¼ oz.) whole kernel corn, drained
- 2 tsp. chicken bouillon granules
- Pepper to taste
- 3 cups shredded cheddar cheese
- 2 cups cubed fully cooked ham

1. In a Dutch oven, cook the bacon over medium heat until crisp. Remove to paper towels to drain. Saute onion and carrots in the drippings until tender. Stir in flour until blended. Gradually add milk and water. Bring to a boil; cook and stir for 2 minutes or until thickened.

2. Add the potatoes, corn, bouillon and pepper. Reduce heat; simmer, uncovered, for 20 minutes or until the potatoes are tender. Add cheese and ham; heat until cheese is melted. Stir in bacon.

1 cup: 418 cal., 28g fat (14g sat. fat), 76mg chol., 1056mg sod., 21g carb. (8g sugars, 2g fiber), 19g pro.

BONUS: QUICK HAM & BEAN SOUP

If you like ham and bean soup but are short on time, this version is the one for you. It's delicious and takes just 30 minutes from start to finish.
—*Taste of Home* Test Kitchen

PREP: 10 min. • **COOK:** 20 min. • **MAKES:** 7 servings

- 2 medium carrots, sliced
- 2 celery ribs, chopped
- ½ cup chopped onion
- 2 Tbsp. butter
- 4 cans (15½ oz. each) great northern beans, rinsed and drained
- 4 cups chicken broth
- 2 cups cubed fully cooked ham
- 1 tsp. chili powder
- ½ tsp. minced garlic
- ¼ tsp. pepper
- 1 bay leaf

In a large saucepan, saute the carrots, celery and onion in butter until tender. Stir in the remaining ingredients. Bring to a boil. Reduce heat; cook for 15 minutes or until heated through. Discard bay leaf.

1 cup: 168 cal., 7g fat (3g sat. fat), 30mg chol., 1242mg sod., 14g carb. (3g sugars, 4g fiber), 12g pro.

TOP TIP

Chowder in the winter is even better if you freeze fresh corn in the summer. Cut the raw corn kernels off the cob, then microwave for 2 minutes. Stir and cook for 2 more minutes. Then package and freeze until ready to use.

ROASTED TOMATO SOUP WITH FRESH BASIL

Roasting really brings out the flavor of the tomatoes in this wonderful soup. It has a slightly chunky texture that indicates it's fresh and homemade.
—Marie Forte, Raritan, NJ

PREP: 20 min. • **BAKE:** 25 min.
MAKES: 6 servings

3½ lbs. tomatoes (about 11 medium), halved
1 small onion, quartered
2 garlic cloves, peeled and halved
2 Tbsp. olive oil
2 Tbsp. fresh thyme leaves
1 tsp. salt
¼ tsp. pepper
12 fresh basil leaves
  Optional toppings: croutons, thinly sliced fresh basil

1. Preheat oven to 400°. Place tomatoes, onion and garlic in a greased 15x10x1-in. baking pan; drizzle with oil. Sprinkle with thyme, salt and pepper; toss to coat. Roast for 25-30 minutes or until tender, stirring once. Cool slightly.
2. Process the tomato mixture with the basil leaves in batches in a blender until smooth. Transfer to a large saucepan; heat through. If desired, top soup with croutons and sliced basil.
1 cup: 107 cal., 5g fat (1g sat. fat), 0 chol., 411mg sod., 15g carb. (9g sugars, 4g fiber), 3g pro. **Diabetic exchanges:** 1 starch, 1 fat.

CREAMY WHITE CHILI

I got this wonderful recipe from my sister-in-law, who made a big batch to serve a crowd one night. It's easy and quick, which was a big help when I started cooking in college. In all my years of 4-H cooking, I'd never had a dish get so many compliments.
—Laura Brewer, Lafayette, IN

PREP: 10 min. • **COOK:** 40 min.
MAKES: 7 servings

1 lb. boneless skinless chicken breasts, cut into ½-in. cubes
1 medium onion, chopped
1½ tsp. garlic powder
1 Tbsp. canola oil
2 cans (15½ oz. each) great northern beans, rinsed and drained
1 can (14½ oz.) chicken broth
2 cans (4 oz. each) chopped green chilies
1 tsp. salt
1 tsp. ground cumin
1 tsp. dried oregano
½ tsp. pepper
¼ tsp. cayenne pepper
1 cup sour cream
½ cup heavy whipping cream
  Optional toppings: tortilla chips, shredded cheddar cheese, sliced seeded jalapeno pepper

1. In a large saucepan, saute the chicken, onion and garlic powder in oil until the chicken is no longer pink. Add the beans, broth, chilies and seasonings. Bring to a boil. Reduce heat; simmer, uncovered, for 30 minutes.
2. Remove from the heat; stir in sour cream and cream. If desired, top with tortilla chips, cheese and jalapenos.
1 cup: 334 cal., 16g fat (8g sat. fat), 81mg chol., 1045mg sod., 24g carb. (3g sugars, 7g fiber), 22g pro.

SLOW-COOKED CHUNKY CHILI

Pork sausage, ground beef and plenty of beans make this chili marvelous. I keep serving-size containers in my freezer so I can quickly warm up bowls on busy days.
—Margie Shaw, Greenbrier, AR

PREP: 15 min. • **COOK:** 4 hours • **MAKES:** 3 qt.

- 1 **lb. ground beef**
- 1 **lb. bulk pork sausage**
- 4 **cans (16 oz. each) kidney beans, rinsed and drained**
- 2 **cans (14½ oz. each) diced tomatoes, undrained**
- 2 **cans (10 oz. each) diced tomatoes and green chilies, undrained**
- 1 **large onion, chopped**
- 1 **medium green pepper, chopped**
- 1 **envelope taco seasoning**
- ½ **tsp. salt**
- ¼ **tsp. pepper**

Optional toppings: shredded cheddar cheese, chopped red onion, sour cream

1. In a large skillet, cook beef and sausage over medium heat until the meat is no longer pink; drain. Transfer to a 5-qt. slow cooker. Stir in the remaining ingredients.

2. Cover and cook on high for 4-5 hours or until the vegetables are tender. If desired, serve with shredded cheese, chopped onion and sour cream.

Freeze option: Before adding toppings, cool chili. Freeze chili and toppings separately in freezer containers. To use, partially thaw in refrigerator overnight. Heat through in a saucepan, stirring occasionally and adding a little water if necessary. Sprinkle with any desired toppings.

1 cup: 329 cal., 13g fat (4g sat. fat), 44mg chol., 1158mg sod., 33g carb. (5g sugars, 9g fiber), 21g pro.

NOTES

_____
_____
_____
_____
_____
_____
_____
_____
_____

EASY CHICKEN & DUMPLINGS

Perfect for fall nights, my simple version of chicken and dumplings is speedy, low in fat and a delicious one-dish meal.
—Nancy Tuck, Elk Falls, KS

TAKES: 30 min. • **MAKES:** 6 servings

- 3 celery ribs, chopped
- 2 medium carrots, sliced
- 3 cans (14½ oz. each) reduced-sodium chicken broth
- 3 cups cubed cooked chicken breast
- ½ tsp. poultry seasoning
- ⅛ tsp. pepper
- 1⅔ cups reduced-fat biscuit mix
- ⅔ cup fat-free milk

1. In a Dutch oven coated with cooking spray, cook and stir celery and carrots over medium heat until tender, about 5 minutes. Stir in broth, chicken and seasonings. Bring to a boil; reduce heat to a gentle simmer.

2. For dumplings, mix biscuit mix and milk until a soft dough forms. Drop by tablespoonfuls on top of the simmering liquid. Reduce heat to low; cover and cook 10-15 minutes or until a toothpick inserted in dumplings comes out clean (do not lift cover during the first 10 minutes).

1 cup: 260 cal., 4g fat (1g sat. fat), 54mg chol., 1039mg sod., 28g carb. (6g sugars, 2g fiber), 27g pro.

BONUS: TURKEY BISCUIT STEW

This chunky stew makes a hearty supper, especially in the fall and winter. It's also a great way to use extra turkey during the holidays.
—Lori Schlecht, Wimbledon, ND

PREP: 15 min. • **BAKE:** 20 min. • **MAKES:** 8 servings

- ⅓ cup chopped onion
- ¼ cup butter, cubed
- ⅓ cup all-purpose flour
- ½ tsp. salt
- ⅛ tsp. pepper
- 1 can (10½ oz.) condensed chicken broth, undiluted
- ¾ cup whole milk
- 2 cups cubed cooked turkey
- 1 cup cooked peas
- 1 cup cooked whole baby carrots
- 1 tube (10 oz.) refrigerated buttermilk biscuits

In an ovenproof skillet, saute onion in butter until tender. Stir in flour, salt and pepper until blended. Gradually add broth and milk. Bring to a boil. Cook and stir until thickened and bubbly, about 2 minutes. Add turkey, peas and carrots; heat through. Arrange biscuits over the stew. Bake at 375° until golden brown, 20-25 minutes.

1 serving: 263 cal., 10g fat (5g sat. fat), 45mg chol., 792mg sod., 27g carb. (4g sugars, 2g fiber), 17g pro.

TOP TIP

Broth and stock are made differently but can be used interchangeably. Stock is made by simmering bones (which may have meat); broth is made by simmering meat (which may have bones). Both are cooked with a mix of vegetables, and both are good for use in soups, stews and other cooked recipes.

CHICKEN WILD RICE SOUP

This savory soup has a lot of substance, and we enjoy brimming bowls of it all winter long. The biggest fans are the men in my family, who love it.
—Virginia Montmarquet, Riverside, CA

PREP: 10 min. • **COOK:** 40 min.
MAKES: 14 servings (3½ qt.)

- 2 qt. chicken broth
- ½ lb. fresh mushrooms, chopped
- 1 cup finely chopped celery
- 1 cup shredded carrots
- ½ cup finely chopped onion
- 1 tsp. chicken bouillon granules
- 1 tsp. dried parsley flakes
- ¼ tsp. garlic powder
- ¼ tsp. dried thyme
- ¼ cup butter, cubed
- ¼ cup all-purpose flour
- 1 can (10¾ oz.) condensed cream of mushroom soup, undiluted
- ½ cup dry white wine or additional chicken broth
- 3 cups cooked wild rice
- 2 cups cubed cooked chicken

1. In a large saucepan, combine the first nine ingredients. Bring to a boil. Reduce heat; cover and simmer for 30 minutes.
2. In Dutch oven, melt butter; stir in flour until smooth. Gradually whisk in broth mixture. Bring to a boil; cook and stir for 2 minutes or until thickened. Whisk in the soup and wine. Add rice and chicken; heat through.
1 cup: 154 cal., 6g fat (3g sat. fat), 27mg chol., 807mg sod., 14g carb. (2g sugars, 2g fiber), 10g pro.

LENTIL-TOMATO SOUP

Double the recipe and share this fabulous soup with friends and neighbors on cold winter nights. I serve it with cornbread for dunking.
—Michelle Curtis, Baker City, OR

PREP: 15 min. • **COOK:** 30 min.
MAKES: 6 servings

- 4½ cups water
- 4 medium carrots, sliced
- 1 medium onion, chopped
- ⅔ cup dried brown lentils, rinsed
- 1 can (6 oz.) tomato paste
- 2 Tbsp. minced fresh parsley
- 1 Tbsp. brown sugar
- 1 Tbsp. white vinegar
- 1 tsp. garlic salt
- ½ tsp. dried thyme
- ¼ tsp. dill weed
- ¼ tsp. dried tarragon
- ¼ tsp. pepper

In a large saucepan, combine the water, carrots, onion and lentils; bring to a boil. Reduce heat; cover and simmer for 20-25 minutes or until vegetables and lentils are tender. Stir in the remaining ingredients; return to a boil. Reduce heat; simmer, uncovered, for 5 minutes to allow flavors to blend.
¾ cup: 138 cal., 0 fat (0 sat. fat), 0 chol., 351mg sod., 27g carb. (9g sugars, 9g fiber), 8g pro. **Diabetic exchanges:** 1 starch, 1 lean meat, 1 vegetable.

FREEZE IT

CASSOULET FOR TODAY

Traditional rustic French cassoulet is cooked for hours; this version offers the same homey taste in less time. It's easy on the wallet, too!
—Virginia Anthony, Jacksonville, FL

PREP: 45 min. • **BAKE:** 50 min.
MAKES: 6 servings

- 6 boneless skinless chicken thighs (about 1½ lbs.)
- ¼ tsp. salt
- ¼ tsp. coarsely ground pepper
- 3 tsp. olive oil, divided
- 1 large onion, chopped
- 1 garlic clove, minced
- ½ cup white wine or chicken broth
- 1 can (14½ oz.) diced tomatoes, drained
- 1 bay leaf
- 1 tsp. minced fresh rosemary or ¼ tsp. dried rosemary, crushed
- 1 tsp. minced fresh thyme or ¼ tsp. dried thyme
- 2 cans (15 oz. each) cannellini beans, rinsed and drained
- ¼ lb. smoked turkey kielbasa, chopped
- 3 bacon strips, cooked and crumbled

TOPPING
- ½ cup soft whole wheat bread crumbs
- ¼ cup minced fresh parsley
- 1 garlic clove, minced

1. Preheat oven to 325°. Sprinkle chicken with salt and pepper. In a broiler-safe Dutch oven, heat 2 tsp. oil over medium heat; brown chicken on both sides. Remove from pan.

2. In the same pan, saute onion in the remaining oil over medium heat until crisp-tender. Add garlic; cook 1 minute. Add wine; bring to a boil, stirring to loosen browned bits from pan. Add tomatoes, herbs and chicken; return to a boil.

3. Transfer to oven; bake, covered, for 30 minutes. Stir in beans and kielbasa; bake, covered, until chicken is tender, 20-25 minutes.

4. Remove from oven; preheat broiler. Discard bay leaf; stir in bacon. Toss bread crumbs with parsley and garlic; sprinkle over top. Place in oven so the surface of the cassoulet is 4-5 in. from heat; broil until the bread crumbs are golden brown, 2-3 minutes.

1 serving: 394 cal., 14g fat (4g sat. fat), 91mg chol., 736mg sod., 29g carb. (4g sugars, 8g fiber), 33g pro. **Diabetic exchanges:** 4 lean meat, 2 starch, ½ fat.

TOP TIP

To make soft bread crumbs, tear the bread into pieces and place in a food processor or blender. Cover and pulse until crumbs form. One slice of bread yields 1/2 to 3/4 cup crumbs.

HOMEMADE CHICKEN TORTILLA SOUP

This soup is as good as (if not better than) any I've had in a restaurant. I get so many compliments when I serve it: you will, too.
—Laura Black Johnson, Largo, FL

TAKES: 30 min. • **MAKES:** 8 servings

2 Tbsp. olive oil
1 large onion, chopped
1 can (4 oz.) chopped green chilies
2 garlic cloves, minced
1 jalapeno pepper, seeded
   and chopped
1 tsp. ground cumin
1 can (15 oz.) tomato sauce
1 can (14½ oz.) diced tomatoes
   with garlic and onion, undrained
5 cups reduced-sodium
   chicken broth
1 rotisserie chicken,
   shredded, skin removed
¼ cup minced fresh cilantro
2 tsp. lime juice
¼ tsp. salt
¼ tsp. pepper
   Optional toppings: crushed
   tortilla chips, shredded Monterey
   Jack or cheddar cheese

1. In a Dutch oven, heat oil over medium heat; saute onion until tender, about 5 minutes. Add chilies, garlic, jalapeno and cumin; cook 1 minute. Stir in tomato sauce, tomatoes and broth. Bring to a boil; reduce heat. Stir in chicken.

2. Simmer, uncovered, for 10 minutes. Add cilantro, lime juice, salt and pepper. Top individual servings with tortilla chips and cheese if desired.

Freeze option: Before adding chips and cheese, cool the soup; freeze in freezer containers. To use, partially thaw soup in refrigerator overnight. Heat through in a large saucepan over medium-low heat, stirring occasionally and adding a little broth or water if necessary. Add chips and cheese before serving.

Note: Wear disposable gloves when cutting hot peppers; the oils can burn skin. Avoid touching your face.

1¼ cups: 200 cal., 8g fat (2g sat. fat), 55mg chol., 941mg sod., 9g carb. (4g sugars, 2g fiber), 22g pro.

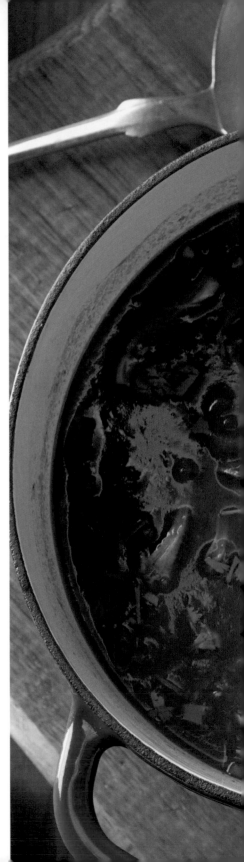

TOP TIP

To quickly chop an onion, peel and cut in half from the root to the top. Leaving the root attached, place flat side down on work surface. Cut vertically through the onion, leaving the root end uncut. Then cut across the onion, discarding the root end. The closer the cuts, the more finely chopped the onion pieces will be.

SLOW-COOKER BEEF STEW

When there's a chill in the air, I love to make my slow-cooked stew, full of tender chunks of beef, potatoes and carrots.
—Earnestine Wilson, Waco, TX

PREP: 25 min. • **COOK:** 85 hours
MAKES: 8 servings

1½ lbs. potatoes, peeled and cubed
6 medium carrots, cut into 1-in. slices
1 medium onion, coarsely chopped
3 celery ribs, coarsely chopped
3 Tbsp. all-purpose flour
1½ lbs. beef stew meat, cut into 1-in. cubes
3 Tbsp. canola oil
1 can (14½ oz.) diced tomatoes, undrained
½ to 1 cup beef broth
1 tsp. ground mustard
½ tsp. salt
½ tsp. pepper
½ tsp. dried thyme
½ tsp. browning sauce

1. Layer the potatoes, carrots, onion and celery in a 5-qt. slow cooker. Place flour in a large resealable plastic bag. Add stew meat; seal and toss to coat evenly. In a large skillet, brown meat in oil in batches. Place over vegetables.
2. In a large bowl, combine the tomatoes, broth, mustard, salt, pepper, thyme and browning sauce. Pour over the beef. Cover and cook on high for 1½ hours. Reduce heat to low; cook for 7-8 hours longer or until the meat and vegetables are tender.
1 cup: 272 cal., 11g fat (3g sat. fat), 53mg chol., 381mg sod., 23g carb. (7g sugars, 4g fiber), 19g pro.

PUMPKIN BISQUE WITH SMOKED GOUDA

I love the smell of this rich, cheesy soup as it bubbles on the stove. The Gouda cheese adds a delightful smokiness that just says autumn to me.
—Kerry Dingwall, Wilmington, NC

PREP: 20 min. • **COOK:** 35 min.
MAKES: 9 servings (2¼ qt.)

4 bacon strips, chopped
1 medium onion, chopped
3 garlic cloves, minced
6 cups chicken broth
1 can (29 oz.) solid-pack pumpkin
½ tsp. salt
¼ tsp. ground nutmeg
⅛ tsp. pepper
1 cup heavy whipping cream
1 cup shredded Gouda cheese
2 Tbsp. minced fresh parsley

Additional shredded Gouda cheese, optional

1. In a Dutch oven, cook the bacon over medium heat until crisp. Remove to paper towels with a slotted spoon; drain bacon, reserving 1 Tbsp. drippings. Saute onion in the drippings until tender. Add garlic; cook 1 minute longer.
2. Stir in the broth, pumpkin, salt, nutmeg and pepper. Bring to a boil. Reduce heat; simmer, uncovered, for 10 minutes. Cool mixture slightly.
3. In a blender, process the soup in batches until smooth. Return all to pan. Stir in cream; heat through. Add cheese; stir until melted. Sprinkle each serving with parsley, bacon and, if desired, with additional cheese.
1 cup: 214 cal., 17g fat (9g sat. fat), 58mg chol., 970mg sod., 11g carb. (5g sugars, 4g fiber), 7g pro.

MAIN COURSES

THESE HOMEY, SCRUMPTIOUS DINNERS ARE JUST LIKE MOM—AND GRANDMA—USED TO MAKE.

TENDERLOIN STEAK DIANE

My son loves mushrooms so I'll often toss a few extra into this recipe. They are fantastic with the steak.
—Carolyn Turner, Reno, NV

TAKES: 30 min. • **MAKES:** 4 servings

- 4 beef tenderloin steaks (6 oz. each)
- 1 tsp. steak seasoning
- 2 Tbsp. butter
- 1 cup sliced fresh mushrooms
- ½ cup reduced-sodium beef broth
- ¼ cup heavy whipping cream
- 1 Tbsp. steak sauce
- 1 tsp. garlic salt with parsley
- 1 tsp. minced chives

1. Sprinkle steaks with steak seasoning. In a large skillet, heat butter over medium heat. Add steaks; cook 4-5 minutes on each side or until meat reaches desired doneness. Remove steaks from pan.
2. Add mushrooms to skillet; cook and stir over medium-high heat until tender. Add broth, stirring to loosen browned bits from pan. Stir in the cream, steak sauce and garlic salt. Bring to a boil; cook and stir for 1-2 minutes or until the sauce is slightly thickened.
3. Return steaks to pan; turn to coat and heat through. Stir in chives.
1 steak with 2 Tbsp. sauce: 358 cal., 21g fat (11g sat. fat), 111mg chol., 567mg sod., 2g carb. (1g sugars, 0 fiber), 37g pro.

OVEN-FRIED CHICKEN DRUMSTICKS

This recipe uses Greek yogurt to create an amazing marinade that makes the chicken incredibly moist. No one will guess that it's been lightened up!
—Kimberly Wallace, Dennison, OH

PREP: 20 min. + marinating • **BAKE:** 40 min.
MAKES: 4 servings

- 1 cup fat-free plain Greek yogurt
- 1 Tbsp. Dijon mustard
- 2 garlic cloves, minced
- 8 chicken drumsticks (4 oz. each), skin removed
- ½ cup whole wheat flour
- 1½ tsp. paprika
- 1 tsp. baking powder
- 1 tsp. salt
- 1 tsp. pepper
  Olive oil-flavored cooking spray

1. In a large resealable plastic bag, combine the yogurt, mustard and garlic. Add the chicken; seal bag and turn to coat. Refrigerate 8 hours or overnight.
2. Preheat oven to 425°. In another plastic bag, mix flour, paprika, baking powder, salt and pepper. Remove chicken from the marinade and add, one piece at a time, to the flour mixture; close bag and shake each piece to coat. Place on a wire rack over a baking sheet; spritz with cooking spray. Bake for 40-45 minutes or until a thermometer reads 165°.
2 drumsticks: 227 cal., 7g fat (1g sat. fat), 81mg chol., 498mg sod., 9g carb. (2g sugars, 1g fiber), 31g pro. **Diabetic exchanges:** 4 lean meat, ½ starch.

HERB-GLAZED TURKEY

Honey and corn syrup blend with savoy herbs and seasonings to give this turkey a slightly sweet flavor. My tried-and-true recipe never fails to win compliments.
—Charlene Melenka, Vegreville, AB

PREP: 10 min. • **BAKE:** 4 hours + standing
MAKES: 18 servings

- 1 turkey (14 to 16 lbs.)
- ¼ cup olive oil
- 2 tsp. dried thyme
- 1½ tsp. salt, divided
- 1¼ tsp. pepper, divided
- 1 cup honey
- 1 cup corn syrup
- ¼ cup butter, melted
- 2 tsp. dried rosemary, crushed
- 1 tsp. rubbed sage
- 1 tsp. dried basil

1. Preheat oven to 325°. Brush turkey with oil; tie drumsticks together. Place turkey breast side up on a rack in a roasting pan. Combine thyme, 1 tsp. salt and 1 tsp. pepper; sprinkle evenly over turkey. Bake, uncovered, for 2 hours.

2. In a small bowl, combine the honey, corn syrup, butter, rosemary, sage, basil, and the remaining salt and pepper. Brush over turkey. Bake until a thermometer inserted in thickest part of thigh reads 170°-175°, basting frequently with pan drippings, about 90 minutes longer. Cover loosely with foil if turkey browns too quickly. Remove from oven. Cover and let stand for 15 minutes before carving.

7 oz. cooked turkey: 570 cal., 25g fat (8g sat. fat), 197mg chol., 380mg sod., 30g carb. (24g sugars, 0 fiber), 56g pro.

BONUS: CLASSIC TURKEY GRAVY

Making gravy is simple when you have the right proportions of ingredients. It starts with the drippings from your turkey, so it's always a perfect flavor match.
—Virginia Watson, Kirksville, MO

TAKES: 15 min. • **MAKES:** 2 cups

- Drippings from 1 roasted turkey
- 1 to 1½ cups turkey or chicken broth
- ¼ cup all-purpose flour
- Salt and white pepper to taste

Pour turkey drippings into a 2-cup measuring cup. Skim fat, reserving 2 Tbsp.; set aside. Add enough broth to the drippings to measure 2 cups. In a small saucepan, combine flour and the reserved fat until smooth. Gradually stir in the drippings mixture. Bring to a boil; cook and stir for 2 minutes or until thickened. Season with salt and white pepper to taste.

¼ cup: 45 cal., 3g fat (1g sat. fat), 4mg chol., 127mg sod., 3g carb. (0 sugars, 0 fiber), 1g pro.

CHICAGO-STYLE DEEP-DISH PIZZA

When my husband and I tried to duplicate the pizza from a popular Chicago restaurant, our recipe turned out even better. The secret is using a cast-iron skillet.
—Lynn Hamilton, Naperville, IL

PREP: 20 min. + rising • **BAKE:** 40 min.
MAKES: 2 pizzas (8 slices each)

- 3½ cups all-purpose flour
- ¼ cup cornmeal
- 1 pkg. (¼ oz.) quick-rise yeast
- 1½ tsp. sugar
- ½ tsp. salt
- 1 cup water
- ⅓ cup olive oil

TOPPINGS
- 6 cups shredded part-skim mozzarella cheese, divided
- 1 can (28 oz.) diced tomatoes, well drained
- 1 can (8 oz.) tomato sauce
- 1 can (6 oz.) tomato paste
- ½ tsp. salt
- ¼ tsp. each garlic powder, dried oregano, dried basil and pepper
- 1 lb. bulk Italian sausage, cooked and crumbled
- 48 slices pepperoni
- ½ lb. sliced fresh mushrooms
- ¼ cup grated Parmesan cheese

1. In a large bowl, combine 1½ cups flour, cornmeal, yeast, sugar and salt. In a saucepan, heat water and oil to 120°-130°. Add to the dry ingredients; beat just until moistened. Add the remaining flour to form a stiff dough.

2. Turn onto a floured surface; knead until smooth and elastic, 6-8 minutes. Place in a greased bowl, turning once to grease top. Cover and let the dough rise in warm place until doubled, about 30 minutes.

3. Punch dough down; divide in half. Roll each portion into an 11-in. circle. Press dough onto the bottom and up the sides of two greased 10-in. cast-iron or other ovenproof skillets. Sprinkle each with 2 cups mozzarella cheese.

4. In a large bowl, combine the tomatoes, tomato sauce, tomato paste and the seasonings. Spoon 1½ cups over each pizza. Layer each with half of the sausage, pepperoni and mushrooms; 1 cup of the mozzarella; and 2 Tbsp. Parmesan cheese.

5. Cover and bake at 450° for 35 minutes. Uncover; bake 5 minutes longer or until lightly browned.

1 slice: 407 cal., 23g fat (9g sat. fat), 49mg chol., 872mg sod., 32g carb. (4g sugars, 2g fiber), 20g pro.

TOP TIP
If you are using a
convection oven,
you may need to
adapt the cooking
time and temperature
of your recipe. As a
general rule, heat a
convection oven 25°
lower than the recipe
suggests and expect
foods to cook in
about 25 percent
less time, depending
on the food being
cooked. You may
need to experiment
to determine the best
oven temperature
and timing to use.

SOUTHERN SHRIMP & GRITS

A southern specialty sometimes called "breakfast shrimp," this dish tastes great for brunch, dinner and when company's coming. It's down-home comfort food at its finest.
—Mandy Rivers, Lexington, SC

PREP: 15 min. • **COOK:** 20 min.
MAKES: 4 servings

2 cups reduced-sodium chicken broth
2 cups 2% milk
⅓ cup butter, cubed
¾ tsp. salt
½ tsp. pepper
¾ cup uncooked old-fashioned grits
1 cup shredded cheddar cheese

SHRIMP

8 thick-sliced bacon strips, chopped
1 lb. uncooked medium shrimp, peeled and deveined
3 garlic cloves, minced
1 tsp. Cajun or blackened seasoning
4 green onions, chopped

1. In a large saucepan, bring the broth, milk, butter, salt and pepper to a boil. Slowly stir in grits. Reduce heat. Cover and cook for 12-14 minutes or until thickened, stirring occasionally. Stir in the cheese until melted. Set aside and keep warm.
2. In a large skillet, cook the bacon over medium heat until crisp. Remove bacon to paper towels with a slotted spoon; drain, reserving 4 tsp. of the drippings. Saute the shrimp, garlic and seasoning in reserved drippings until the shrimp turn pink. Serve with grits and sprinkle with onions.
1 cup grits with ½ cup shrimp mixture: 674 cal., 42g fat (22g sat. fat), 241mg chol., 1845mg sod., 33g carb. (7g sugars, 1g fiber), 41g pro.

PEPPERED RIBEYE STEAKS

A Southerner to the core, I love to cook—especially on the grill. This recipe is one of my favorites. The seasoning rub makes a wonderful marinade, and nothing beats the summertime taste of these flavorful grilled steaks.
—Sharon Bickett, Chester, SC

PREP: 10 min. + chilling • **GRILL:** 25 min.
MAKES: 8 servings

1 Tbsp. garlic powder
1 Tbsp. paprika
2 tsp. dried ground thyme
2 tsp. dried ground oregano
1½ tsp. kosher salt
1½ tsp. pepper
1 tsp. lemon-pepper seasoning
1 tsp. cayenne pepper
1 tsp. crushed red pepper flakes
4 beef ribeye steaks (1½ in. thick and 8 oz. each)

1. Combine all seasonings. Sprinkle over steaks, pressing mixture into both sides to help it adhere. Refrigerate, covered, for at least 1 hour or up to 24 hours.
2. Remove steaks; blot with paper towels to remove surface moisture, taking care to leave as much garlic mixture on steaks as possible. If desired, sprinkle with additional kosher salt. Grill the steaks, covered, turning occasionally, on a greased grill rack over medium indirect heat until a thermometer reads 110°. Move steaks to direct heat; continue grilling until meat reaches the desired level of doneness (for medium-rare, a thermometer should read 135°; medium, 140°; medium-well, 145°).
3. Let steaks stand 5 minutes before slicing. Place on a warm serving platter; cut across grain into thick slices.
3 oz. cooked beef: 257 cal., 18g fat (7g sat. fat), 67mg chol., 453mg sod., 2g carb. (0 sugars, 1g fiber), 21g pro.

BEEF BRISKET TACOS

Birthday parties back home were big gatherings of anyone we considered family. Hot pans of shredded brisket, or carne deshebrada, were served along with huge bowls of salads, frijoles, tostadas and salsas. The shredded brisket can be used in sandwiches too, or try spooning it over potatoes or egg noodles for a change.
—Yvette Marquez, Littleton, CO

PREP: 15 min. + marinating • **COOK:** 8 hours
MAKES: 10 servings

- 1   **bottle (12 oz.) beer or nonalcoholic beer**
- 1   **cup brisket marinade sauce or liquid smoke plus 1 Tbsp. salt**
- 2   **bay leaves**
- ½   **tsp. salt**
- ½   **tsp. pepper**
- 1   **fresh beef brisket (3 to 4 lbs.), fat trimmed**
- 20 **corn tortillas (6 in.), warmed**
      Optional toppings: Shredded cheddar cheese, lime wedges, media crema table cream, fresh cilantro leaves, thinly sliced green onions, avocado slices and salsa

1. In a large resealable plastic bag, combine the first five ingredients. Add brisket; seal the bag and turn to coat the meat in marinade. Refrigerate overnight.
2. Transfer brisket and marinade to a 6-qt. slow cooker. Cook, covered, on low until tender, 8-10 hours. Remove meat; discard bay leaves. Reserve juices in slow cooker. When cool enough to handle, shred meat with two forks. Return to slow cooker.
3. Using tongs, serve shredded brisket in tortillas. Add toppings as desired.
Freeze option: Freeze cooled meat mixture and juices in freezer containers. To use, partially thaw in refrigerator overnight. Heat through in a saucepan, stirring occasionally.
2 tacos: 278 cal., 7g fat (2g sat. fat), 58mg chol., 947mg sod., 21g carb. (0 sugars, 3g fiber), 31g pro.

BACON-TOPPED MEAT LOAF

I created this recipe for my meatloaf-loving family after trying and adjusting many other recipes over the years. Cheddar cheese tucked inside and a flavorful bacon topping dress it up just right for Sunday dinner.
—Sue Call, Beech Grove, IN

PREP: 10 min. • **BAKE:** 70 min. + standing
MAKES: 8 servings

- ½ cup chili sauce
- 2 large eggs, lightly beaten
- 1 Tbsp. Worcestershire sauce
- 1 medium onion, chopped
- 1 cup shredded cheddar cheese
- ⅔ cup dry bread crumbs
- ½ tsp. salt
- ¼ tsp. pepper
- 2 lbs. lean ground beef (90% lean)
- 2 bacon strips, halved

1. Preheat oven to 350°. In a large bowl, combine the first eight ingredients. Crumble the beef over the mixture and mix well. Shape into a loaf in an ungreased 13x9-in. baking dish. Top with bacon.

2. Bake, uncovered, for 70-80 minutes or until the meat is no longer pink and a thermometer reads 160°. Drain; let stand for 10 minutes before cutting.

1 slice: 329 cal., 17g fat (8g sat. fat), 127mg chol., 692mg sod., 13g carb. (5g sugars, 1g fiber), 28g pro.

BONUS: SWEET-AND-SOUR MEAT LOAF

The sweet-and-sour flavor combo adds a deliciously different twist to a longtime standby. I hardly ever make plain meat loaf anymore!
—Debbie Haneke, Stafford, KS

PREP: 15 min. • **BAKE:** 1 hour
MAKES: 6 servings

- 1 cup dry bread crumbs
- 1 tsp. salt
- ¼ tsp. pepper
- 2 large eggs, lightly beaten
- 1½ lbs. ground beef
- 1 tsp. dried minced onion
- 1 can (15 oz.) tomato sauce, divided
- ½ cup sugar
- 2 Tbsp. brown sugar
- 2 Tbsp. cider vinegar
- 2 tsp. prepared mustard

1. Preheat oven to 350°. In a large bowl, combine the bread crumbs, salt, pepper and eggs; crumble beef over top and mix well. Add onion and half of the tomato sauce. Press into a 9x5-in. loaf pan.

2. Bake for 50 minutes. In a saucepan, combine the sugars, vinegar, mustard and the remaining tomato sauce; bring to a boil. Pour over meat loaf; bake about 10 minutes longer or until no pink remains and a thermometer reads 160°.

1 slice: 419 cal., 17g fat (6g sat. fat), 146mg chol., 969mg sod., 38g carb. (23g sugars, 1g fiber), 28g pro.

COUNTRY RIBS DINNER

Ribs slow-cooked with carrots, celery, onions and red potatoes are pure comfort food for us. To add a little zip, we sometimes sprinkle in cayenne.
—Rose Ingall, Manistee, MI

PREP: 10 min. • **COOK:** 6¼ hours
MAKES: 4 servings

- 2 lbs. boneless country-style pork ribs
- ½ tsp. salt
- ¼ tsp. pepper
- 8 small red potatoes (about 1 lb.), halved
- 4 medium carrots, cut into 1-in. pieces
- 3 celery ribs, cut into ½-in. pieces
- 1 medium onion, coarsely chopped
- ¾ cup water
- 1 garlic clove, crushed
- 1 can (10¾ oz.) condensed cream of mushroom soup, undiluted

1. Sprinkle ribs with salt and pepper; transfer to a 4-qt. slow cooker. Add potatoes, carrots, celery, onion, water and garlic. Cook, covered, on low until the meat and vegetables are tender, for 6-8 hours.

2. Remove meat and vegetables; skim fat from cooking juices. Whisk soup into the cooking juices; return the meat and vegetables to slow cooker. Cook mixture, covered, until heated through, about 15-30 minutes longer.

5 oz. cooked meat with 1 cup vegetables and ¼ cup gravy: 528 cal., 25g fat (8g sat. fat), 134mg chol., 1016mg sod., 30g carb. (6g sugars, 6g fiber), 43g pro.

CHICKEN MARSALA WITH GORGONZOLA

This delicious chicken dish is quick enough for a weeknight but elegant enough for a dinner party. We live near caves used to age a lovely Gorgonzola cheese, so this is a favorite for us.
—Jill Anderson, Sleepy Eye, MN

PREP: 10 min. • **COOK:** 30 min.
MAKES: 4 servings

- 4 boneless skinless chicken breast halves (6 oz. each)
- ¼ tsp. plus ⅛ tsp. salt, divided
- ¼ tsp. pepper
- 3 Tbsp. olive oil, divided
- ½ lb. sliced baby portobello mushrooms
- 2 garlic cloves, minced
- 1 cup Marsala wine
- ⅔ cup heavy whipping cream
- ½ cup crumbled Gorgonzola cheese, divided
- 2 Tbsp. minced fresh parsley

1. Sprinkle chicken with ¼ tsp. salt and pepper. In a large skillet, cook chicken in 2 Tbsp. oil over medium heat 6-8 minutes on each side or until a thermometer reads 165°. Remove and keep warm.

2. In same skillet, saute mushrooms in the remaining oil until tender. Add garlic; cook for 1 minute.

3. Add wine, stirring to loosen browned bits from pan. Bring to a boil; cook until liquid is reduced by a third. Stir in cream and remaining salt. Return to a boil; cook until slightly thickened.

4. Return chicken to pan; add ⅓ cup of cheese. Cook until melted. Sprinkle with remaining cheese; garnish with parsley.

1 serving: 514 cal., 33g fat (15g sat. fat), 161mg chol., 514mg sod., 8g carb. (3g sugars, 1g fiber), 40g pro.

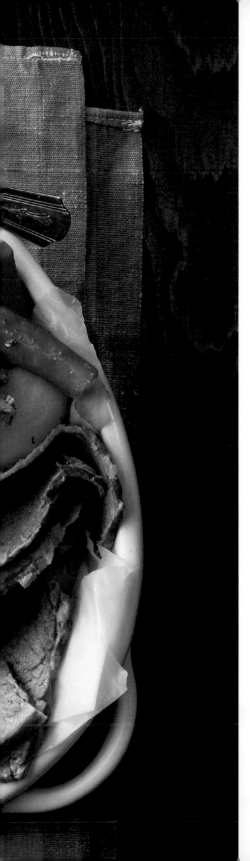

FAVORITE CORNED BEEF & CABBAGE

It may be the most famous dish to eat on St. Patrick's Day, but this Irish-American classic is a favorite at our table all year.
—Evelyn Kenney, Trenton, NJ

PREP: 10 min. • **COOK:** 2¾ hours
MAKES: 10 servings

- 1 **corned beef brisket (about 4 lbs.) with spice packet**
- 2 **Tbsp. brown sugar**
- 2 **bay leaves**
- 3½ **lbs. small potatoes (10-15), peeled**
- 8 **medium carrots, halved crosswise**
- 1 **medium head cabbage, cut into wedges**

HORSERADISH SAUCE
- 3 **Tbsp. butter**
- 2 **Tbsp. all-purpose flour**
- 1 **to 1½ cups reserved cooking juices from corned beef**
- 1 **Tbsp. sugar**
- 1 **Tbsp. cider vinegar**
- ¼ **cup horseradish**

1. Place brisket, contents of seasoning packet, brown sugar and bay leaves in a large Dutch oven or stockpot; cover with water. Bring to a boil. Reduce the heat; simmer, covered, 2 hours.

2. Add potatoes and carrots; return to a boil. Reduce heat; simmer, covered, just until the beef and vegetables are tender, 30-40 minutes.

3. Add cabbage to pot; return to a boil. (If the pot is too full, remove potatoes and carrots before adding cabbage; reheat before serving.) Reduce heat; simmer, covered, until cabbage is tender, about 15 minutes. Remove vegetables and corned beef; keep warm.

4. Strain and reserve 1½ cups cooking juices to make horseradish sauce; skim fat from the reserved juices. Discard any remaining juices.

5. Cut beef across the grain into slices. Serve with vegetables and horseradish sauce.

6. For the horseradish sauce: In a small saucepan, melt butter over medium heat; stir in flour until smooth. Gradually whisk in 1 cup reserved juices. Stir in sugar, vinegar and horseradish; bring to a boil, stirring constantly. Cook and stir until thickened. If desired, thin with additional juices. Season to taste with additional sugar, vinegar or horseradish.

1 serving (with horseradish sauce):
564 cal., 28g fat (10g sat. fat), 134mg chol., 1616mg sod., 50g carb. (11g sugars, 8g fiber), 29g pro.

TOP TIP
As an alternative to the horseradish sauce, you can make a simple mustard sauce by mixing 1 cup sour cream, 2 Tbsp. Dijon mustard, and ¼ tsp. sugar.

PORK CHOPS WITH SCALLOPED POTATOES

Mom always managed to put a delicious hearty meal on the table for us and our farmhands. This all-in-one comforting main dish reminds me of home.
—Bernice Morris, Marshfield, MO

PREP: 25 min. • **BAKE:** 1½ hours
MAKES: 6 servings

- 3 Tbsp. butter
- 3 Tbsp. all-purpose flour
- 1½ tsp. salt
- ¼ tsp. pepper
- 1 can (14½ oz.) chicken broth
- 6 pork rib or loin chops (¾ in. thick)
- 2 Tbsp. canola oil
  Additional salt and pepper, optional
- 6 cups thinly sliced peeled potatoes
- 1 medium onion, sliced
  Paprika and minced fresh parsley, optional

1. In a small saucepan, melt butter; stir in the flour, salt and pepper until smooth. Add broth. Bring to a boil; cook and stir for 1 minute or until thickened. Remove from the heat and set aside.

2. In a large skillet, brown pork chops on both sides in oil; sprinkle with additional salt and pepper if desired.

3. In a greased 13x9-in. baking dish, layer potatoes and onion. Pour broth mixture over layers. Place pork chops on top.

4. Cover and bake at 350° for 1 hour; uncover and bake 30 minutes longer or until meat and potatoes are tender. If desired, sprinkle with paprika and parsley.

1 serving: 574 cal., 29g fat (11g sat. fat), 128mg chol., 1015mg sod., 36g carb. (3g sugars, 3g fiber), 40g pro.

NOTES

TOP TIP

To remove the odor of raw onions from your hands, salt is the answer! When you've finished cutting or chopping onions, sprinkle some table salt on your hands, rub them together for a few moments, then wash them. Presto—no more smelly hands!

—*Connie S., Amherst, OH*

COMPANY POT ROAST

The aroma of this roast slowly cooking in the oven is absolutely mouthwatering. It gives the home such a cozy feeling, even on the chilliest winter days.
—Anita Osborne, Thomasburg, ON

PREP: 20 min. • **BAKE:** 2¾ hours
MAKES: 6 servings

- 1 boneless beef chuck roast (3 to 4 lbs.)
- 2 Tbsp. olive oil
- 1 cup sherry or beef broth
- ½ cup reduced-sodium soy sauce
- ¼ cup sugar
- 2 tsp. beef bouillon granules
- 1 cinnamon stick (3 in.)
- 8 medium carrots, cut into 2-in. pieces
- 6 medium potatoes, peeled and cut into 1½-in. pieces
- 1 medium onion, sliced
- 2 Tbsp. cornstarch
- 2 Tbsp. cold water

1. Brown roast in oil in a Dutch oven on all sides; drain. Combine the sherry, soy sauce, sugar, bouillon and cinnamon stick; pour over roast.
2. Cover and bake at 325° for 2¾ to 3¼ hours or until meat and vegetables are tender, adding the carrots, potatoes and onion during the last 30 minutes of cooking.
3. Remove roast and vegetables to a serving platter; keep warm. Combine cornstarch and water until smooth. Stir into pan. Bring to a boil; cook and stir for 2 minutes or until thickened. Serve with roast and vegetables.
6 oz. cooked meat with 2 cups vegetables and ¼ cup gravy: 713 cal., 26g fat (9g sat. fat), 148mg chol., 1437mg sod., 56g carb. (17g sugars, 5g fiber), 49g pro.

5 INGREDIENTS
ZIPPY BREADED PORK CHOPS

These chops with ranch dressing and a light breading will bring a delightful zing to your dinner table.
—Ann Ingalls, Gladstone, MO

TAKES: 25 min. • **MAKES:** 6 servings

- ⅓ cup prepared ranch salad dressing
- 1 cup seasoned bread crumbs
- 2 Tbsp. grated Parmesan cheese
- 6 bone-in pork loin chops (8 oz. each)

1. Preheat oven to 425°. Place the salad dressing in a shallow bowl. In a separate shallow bowl, mix bread crumbs and cheese. Dip pork chops in the dressing, then in the crumb mixture, patting to help coating adhere.
2. Place chops on a rack in an ungreased 15x10x1-in. baking pan. Bake 15-20 minutes or until a thermometer reads 145°. Let stand 5 minutes before serving.
1 pork chop: 201 cal., 12g fat (3g sat. fat), 22mg chol., 437mg sod., 14g carb. (1g sugars, 1g fiber), 9g pro.

CHICKEN PAPRIKASH

Some recipes for chicken paprikash include vegetables like bell peppers and celery, but not my Alta's. Hers was a simple combination of chicken, onions, garlic, paprika and sour cream.
—Lily Julow, Lawrenceville, GA

PREP: 20 min. • **COOK:** 45 min.
MAKES: 12 servings

2 broiler/fryer chickens (about 3½ to 4 lbs. each), cut into 8 pieces each
2 tsp. kosher salt
1 tsp. pepper
2 Tbsp. peanut oil or canola oil
2 medium onions, halved and sliced
2 large garlic cloves, chopped
3 Tbsp. all-purpose flour
1 Tbsp. sweet Hungarian paprika
2 cups hot chicken broth or water
1 cup sour cream
   Minced fresh parsley and additional sweet Hungarian paprika, optional
   Hot cooked noodles or mashed potatoes, optional

1. Season chicken with kosher salt and pepper. In a Dutch oven, heat peanut oil over medium-high heat. Brown chicken in batches. Remove with a slotted spoon; drain and keep warm.

2. Reduce heat to medium-low. Add onions; cook, stirring to loosen browned bits from pan, until the onions begin to soften, 6-8 minutes. Add garlic; cook 1 minute longer.

3. Stir in flour and paprika; reduce heat to low. Cook until the paprika is fragrant, 3-5 minutes. Add broth; cook, stirring constantly, until smooth, 6-8 minutes. Return the chicken to pan; simmer, covered, until a thermometer inserted into deepest part of thigh reads 170°, about 30 minutes. Transfer chicken to a serving platter.

4. Skim fat. Stir in sour cream; heat just until warmed through, 3-5 minutes (do not allow to boil). If desired, sprinkle with parsley and additional paprika. Serve with hot cooked noodles or mashed potatoes if desired.

1 serving: 422 cal., 26g fat (8g sat. fat), 127mg chol., 596mg sod., 5g carb. (2g sugars, 1g fiber), 40g pro.

CHEESY SPINACH-STUFFED SHELLS

I'm proud of this personal recipe because it was the first one I created. Adjust it to your own liking by adding more spinach or a meat to it.
—Laci Hooten, McKinney, TX

PREP: 45 min. • **BAKE:** 45 min.
MAKES: 12 servings

- 1 pkg. (12 oz.) jumbo pasta shells
- 1 Tbsp. butter
- 1 cup sliced mushrooms
- 1 small onion, finely chopped
- 4 garlic cloves, minced
- 2 large eggs, lightly beaten
- 1 carton (15 oz.) part-skim ricotta cheese
- 1 pkg. (10 oz.) frozen chopped spinach, thawed and squeezed dry
- 2 Tbsp. minced fresh basil or 2 tsp. dried basil
- ¼ tsp. pepper
- 1 can (4¼ oz.) chopped ripe olives
- 1½ cups shredded Italian cheese blend, divided
- 1½ cups shredded part-skim mozzarella cheese, divided
- 1 jar (24 oz.) marinara sauce Additional minced fresh basil, optional

1. Preheat oven to 375°. Cook pasta shells according to the package directions for al dente. Drain; rinse with cold water.

2. Meanwhile, in a small skillet, heat butter over medium-high heat. Add mushrooms and onion; cook and stir 4-6 minutes or until the vegetables are tender. Add garlic; cook 1 minute longer. Remove from heat; cool slightly.

3. In a large bowl, mix eggs, ricotta cheese, spinach, basil and pepper. Stir in olives, mushroom mixture and ¾ cup each of the cheese blend and mozzarella cheese.

4. Spread 1 cup sauce into a 13x9-in. baking dish coated with cooking spray. Fill pasta shells with the cheese mixture; place in baking dish, overlapping the ends slightly. Spoon remaining sauce over top.

5. Bake, covered, 40-45 minutes or until heated through. Uncover; sprinkle with remaining cheeses. Bake 5 minutes longer or until the cheese is melted. Let stand for 5 minutes before serving. If desired, sprinkle with additional basil.

3 stuffed shells: 313 cal., 13g fat (7g sat. fat), 65mg chol., 642mg sod., 32g carb. (5g sugars, 3g fiber), 18g pro. **Diabetic exchanges:** 2 starch, 2 medium-fat meat, ½ fat.

TOP TIP

Did you know you can make ricotta cheese at home? This simple method makes 2 cups of ricotta, enough for this recipe.

Line a large strainer with two layers of cheesecloth dampened with water; place over a large bowl.

In a Dutch oven, bring 2 quarts whole milk, 1 cup heavy whipping cream and ½ tsp. salt just to a boil over medium heat, stirring occasionally to prevent scorching.

Remove from heat. Stir in 3 Tbsp. white vinegar; let stand until curds form, about 5 minutes.

Pour into prepared strainer. Let stand until the ricotta reaches desired consistency, 30-60 minutes.

Discard liquid. Store ricotta in a covered container in the refrigerator for up to 5 days.

BAKED TILAPIA

I've decided to cook healthier food for my family, and that includes having more fish at home. This recipe is not only tasty but it's fast, too.
—Hope Stewart, Raleigh, NC

TAKES: 20 min. • **MAKES:** 4 servings

- 4 tilapia fillets (6 oz. each)
- 3 Tbsp. butter, melted
- 3 Tbsp. lemon juice
- 1½ tsp. garlic powder
- ⅛ tsp. salt
- 2 Tbsp. capers, drained
- ½ tsp. dried oregano
- ⅛ tsp. paprika

1. Preheat oven to 425°. Place tilapia in an ungreased 13x9-in. baking dish. In a small bowl, combine the butter, lemon juice, garlic powder and salt; pour over the fillets. Sprinkle with the capers, oregano and paprika.

2. Bake, uncovered, for 10-15 minutes or until fish flakes easily with a fork.

1 fillet: 224 cal., 10g fat (6g sat. fat), 106mg chol., 304mg sod., 2g carb. (0 sugars, 0 fiber), 32g pro.

PORK SHEPHERD'S PIE

Of all the shepherd's pie recipes I've tried, this one is the best. My family all agree: this meat pie is a keeper.
—Mary Arthurs, Etobicoke, ON

PREP: 30 min. • **BAKE:** 45 min.
MAKES: 6 servings

- 1 lb. ground pork
- 1 small onion, chopped
- 2 garlic cloves, minced
- 1 cup cooked rice
- ½ cup pork gravy or ¼ cup chicken broth
- ½ tsp. salt
- ½ tsp. dried thyme

CABBAGE LAYER
- 1 medium carrot, diced
- 1 small onion, chopped
- 2 Tbsp. butter or margarine
- 6 cups chopped cabbage
- 1 cup chicken broth
- ½ tsp. salt
- ¼ tsp. pepper

POTATO LAYER
- 2 cups mashed potatoes
- ¼ cup shredded cheddar cheese

1. In a skillet over medium heat, brown pork. Add onion and garlic. Cook until onions are tender; drain. Stir in the rice, gravy, salt and thyme. Spoon mixture into a greased 11x7-in. baking dish.

2. In the same skillet, saute carrot and onion in butter over medium heat for 5 minutes. Stir in the cabbage; cook for 1 minute. Add broth, salt and pepper; cover and cook for 10 minutes. Spoon over pork layer.

3. Spoon the mashed potatoes on top; sprinkle with cheese. Bake, uncovered, at 350° for 45 minutes or until browned.

1 cup: 365 cal., 19g fat (8g sat. fat), 66mg chol., 1045mg sod., 28g carb. (5g sugars, 4g fiber), 19g pro.

SPICY SAUSAGE MEATBALL SAUCE

I threw together three favorite veggies and spicy sausage for this incredible sauce that makes our mouths water the whole time it's cooking. Besides serving this with pasta, we've had it with brown basmati rice, on toasted rolls as sloppy subs, and with garlic bread as a stew.
—Ann Sheehy, Lawrence, MA

PREP: 40 min. • **COOK:** 5 hours
MAKES: 12 servings (3¾ qt.)

- 2   **cans (28 oz. each) crushed tomatoes**
- 2   **cans (14½ oz. each) diced tomatoes, undrained**
- ¾   **lb. sliced fresh mushrooms**
- 5   **garlic cloves, minced**
- 4   **tsp. Italian seasoning**
- 1   **tsp. pepper**
- ¼   **tsp. salt**
- ¼   **tsp. crushed red pepper flakes**
- 1   **large sweet onion**
- 1   **large green pepper**
- 1   **medium sweet red pepper**
- 1   **medium sweet orange pepper**
- 1   **medium sweet yellow pepper**
- 10 **hot Italian sausage links (4 oz. each), casings removed**
- ¼   **cup all-purpose flour**
- 2   **Tbsp. canola oil**
     Hot cooked pasta

1. Place the first eight ingredients in a 6-qt. slow cooker. Chop onion and peppers; stir into the tomato mixture.
2. Shape sausage into 1¾-in. balls; roll in flour to coat lightly. In a large skillet, heat oil over medium-high heat; cook the meatballs in batches for 5-8 minutes until lightly browned, turning occasionally. Drain on paper towels. Add to the slow cooker, stirring gently into the sauce.
3. Cook, covered, on low until meatballs are cooked through and the vegetables are tender, 5-6 hours. Serve with pasta.
Freeze option: Freeze the cooled meatball mixture in freezer containers. To use, partially thaw in refrigerator overnight. Place meatball mixture in a large skillet; heat through, stirring occasionally and adding water if necessary.
1¼ cups meatball sauce: 343 cal., 23g fat (7g sat. fat), 51mg chol., 984mg sod., 22g carb. (11g sugars, 5g fiber), 15g pro.

BONUS: PASTA ALLA PUTTANESCA

Want a zesty, spicy meal? Look no further than this puttanesca. Adjust the amount of red pepper flakes to get the level of spiciness you desire.
—Katie Theken, Durham, NC

PREP: 15 min. • **COOK:** 20 min.
MAKES: 3½ cups

- 3 anchovy fillets
- 3 Tbsp. olive oil
- 1 garlic clove, minced
- 1 can (14½ oz.) diced tomatoes, undrained
- 1¼ cups water
- 1 can (6 oz.) tomato paste
- 1 tsp. dried basil
- 1 tsp. dried parsley flakes
- ½ tsp. salt
- ¼ to ½ tsp. crushed red pepper flakes
- ¼ tsp. dried oregano
- ¼ tsp. pepper
- ¼ cup chopped pitted Greek olives
- 2 Tbsp. capers, drained and chopped
  Hot cooked pasta

1. In a large saucepan over medium heat, cook anchovy fillets in oil for 2 minutes. Add garlic; cook 1 minute longer. Stir in the tomatoes, water, tomato paste and seasonings.

2. Bring to a boil. Reduce heat; simmer, uncovered, for 10-15 minutes or until slightly thickened. Stir in olives and capers; heat through. Serve with pasta.

⅔ cup: 146 cal., 10g fat (1g sat. fat), 2mg chol., 668mg sod., 12g carb. (8g sugars, 4g fiber), 3g pro.

CRISPY BEER-BATTERED FISH

A local restaurant made a similar breading for their shrimp po' boys, but we think this version's better. I serve it with a ranch dressing and hot sauce mixture as a dip.
—Jenny Wenzel, Gulfport, MS

PREP: 25 min. • **COOK:** 5 min./batch
MAKES: 4 servings

- ½ cup cornstarch
- 1½ tsp. baking powder
- ¾ tsp. salt
- ½ tsp. Creole seasoning
- ¼ tsp. paprika
- ¼ tsp. cayenne pepper
- 1 cup all-purpose flour, divided
- ½ cup 2% milk
- ⅓ cup beer or nonalcoholic beer
- 2 cups crushed unsalted top saltines (about 40)
- 4 cod fillets (6 oz. each)
  Oil for deep-fat frying

1. In a shallow bowl, combine the cornstarch, baking powder, salt, Creole seasoning, paprika, cayenne and ½ cup of flour. Stir in milk and beer until smooth. Place crackers and the remaining flour in separate shallow bowls. Coat fillets with flour, then dip in the batter and coat with crackers.

2. In an electric skillet or deep-fat fryer, heat oil to 375°. Fry fish in batches for 2-3 minutes on each side or until golden brown. Drain on paper towels.

Note: The following spice mixture may be substituted for 1 tsp. Creole seasoning: ¼ tsp. each salt, garlic powder and paprika; and a pinch each of dried thyme, ground cumin and cayenne pepper.

1 fillet: 513 cal., 27g fat (3g sat. fat), 66mg chol., 775mg sod., 35g carb. (2g sugars, 1g fiber), 30g pro.

"This batter isn't just for fish! It works very well with chicken, too. Who would believe that beer and milk would work so well together? They do, and the amount of heat is just enough."

—APPY_GIRL, TASTEOFHOME.COM

ROASTED CHICKEN WITH ROSEMARY

Herbs, garlic and butter give this hearty meal-in-one a classic flavor.
—Isabel Zienkosky, Salt Lake City, UT

PREP: 20 min. • **BAKE:** 2 hours + standing
MAKES: 9 servings

- ½ cup butter, cubed
- 4 Tbsp. minced fresh rosemary or 2 Tbsp. dried rosemary, crushed
- 2 Tbsp. minced fresh parsley
- 1 tsp. salt
- ½ tsp. pepper
- 3 garlic cloves, minced
- 1 whole roasting chicken (5 to 6 lbs.)
- 6 small red potatoes, halved
- 6 medium carrots, halved lengthwise and cut into 2-in. pieces
- 2 medium onions, quartered

1. Preheat the oven to 350°. In a small saucepan, melt the butter; stir in the rosemary, parsley, salt, pepper and garlic. Place the chicken breast side up on a rack in a shallow roasting pan; tie drumsticks together with kitchen string. Spoon half the butter mixture over the chicken. Place potatoes, carrots and onions around the chicken. Drizzle remaining butter mixture over the vegetables.
2. Bake for 1½ hours. Baste with cooking juices; bake 30-60 minutes longer, basting occasionally, until a thermometer inserted in thickest part of thigh reads 170°-175°. (Cover loosely with foil if chicken browns too quickly.)
3. Tent with foil and let chicken stand for 10-15 minutes before carving. Serve with the vegetables.
1 serving: 449 cal., 28g fat (11g sat. fat), 126mg chol., 479mg sod., 16g carb. (5g sugars, 3g fiber), 33g pro.

BLUE CHEESE-CRUSTED SIRLOIN STEAKS

According to my wife, this smothered steak is my specialty. I often make it for her on Friday nights to say goodbye to a long week.
—Michael Rouse, Minot, ND

TAKES: 30 min. • **MAKES:** 4 servings

- 2 Tbsp. butter, divided
- 1 medium onion, chopped
- ⅓ cup crumbled blue cheese
- 2 Tbsp. soft bread crumbs
- 1 beef top sirloin steak (1 in. thick and 1½ lbs.)
- ¾ tsp. salt
- ½ tsp. pepper

1. Preheat broiler. In a large broil-safe skillet, heat 1 Tbsp. butter over medium heat; saute onion until tender. Transfer to a bowl; stir in cheese and bread crumbs.
2. Cut the steak into four pieces; sprinkle with salt and pepper. In the same pan, heat the remaining butter over medium heat; cook steaks until desired doneness (for medium-rare, a thermometer should read 135°; medium, 140°), 4-5 minutes per side.
3. Spread the onion mixture over the steaks. Broil 4-6 in. from heat until lightly browned, 2-3 minutes.
Note: To make soft bread crumbs, tear bread into pieces and place in a food processor or blender. Cover and pulse until crumbs form. One slice of bread yields ½ to ¾ cup crumbs.
1 serving: 326 cal., 16g fat (8g sat. fat), 92mg chol., 726mg sod., 5g carb. (2g sugars, 1g fiber), 39g pro.

CHEESY STUFFED PEPPERS

This is my favorite summertime dinner because I can use peppers and tomatoes fresh from my garden.
—Betty DeRaad, Sioux Falls, SD

PREP: 20 min. • **BAKE:** 20 min.
MAKES: 6 servings

6	medium green peppers
1½	lbs. ground beef
1	medium onion, chopped
½	tsp. salt
2	cups shredded cheddar cheese
2½	cups chopped tomatoes (3 medium)
1½	cups cooked rice

1. Cut the tops off the peppers and remove the seeds. In a Dutch oven, cook peppers in boiling water for 6-8 minutes or until crisp-tender.

2. Meanwhile, brown the beef, onion and salt in a skillet; drain. Cool slightly. Stir in the cheese, tomatoes and rice.

3. Drain the peppers and stuff with the meat mixture. Place in a baking dish. Bake, uncovered, at 350° for 20 minutes or until heated through.

1 serving: 419 cal., 21g fat (13g sat. fat), 96mg chol., 509mg sod., 26g carb. (7g sugars, 4g fiber), 31g pro.

NOTES

_____
_____
_____
_____
_____
_____
_____
_____
_____
_____
_____

CASSEROLES

WARM AND SATISFYING, CLASSIC CASSEROLES MAKE GREAT MAINS, SIDES AND BREAKFASTS

SOUTHWESTERN CASSEROLE

This family-pleasing casserole tastes wonderful, fits our budget and, best of all, makes a second one to freeze.
—Joan Hallford, North Richland Hills, TX

PREP: 15 min. • **BAKE:** 40 min.
MAKES: 2 casseroles (6 servings each)

- 2 cups (8 oz.) uncooked elbow macaroni
- 2 lbs. ground beef
- 1 large onion, chopped
- 2 garlic cloves, minced
- 2 cans (14½ oz. each) diced tomatoes, undrained
- 1 can (16 oz.) kidney beans, rinsed and drained
- 1 can (6 oz.) tomato paste
- 1 can (4 oz.) chopped green chilies, drained
- 1½ tsp. salt
- 1 tsp. chili powder
- ½ tsp. ground cumin
- ½ tsp. pepper
- 2 cups shredded Monterey Jack cheese
- 2 jalapeno peppers, seeded and chopped

1. Cook macaroni according to package directions. In a large saucepan, cook beef and onion over medium heat, crumbling beef, until no longer pink. Add garlic; cook 1 minute longer. Drain. Stir in next eight ingredients. Bring to a boil. Reduce heat; simmer, uncovered, for 10 minutes. Drain macaroni; stir into beef mixture.
2. Preheat oven to 375°. Transfer the macaroni mixture to two greased 2-qt. baking dishes. Top with the cheese and jalapenos. Cover and bake for 30 minutes. Uncover; bake until bubbly and heated through, about 10 minutes longer.

Freeze option: Cover baked casserole; freeze up to 3 months. To use, thaw in refrigerator 8 hours or overnight. Remove dish from refrigerator 30 minutes before baking. Cover; bake at 375° as directed, increasing time as necessary to heat through and for a thermometer inserted in the center to read 165° (20-25 minutes).
Note: Wear disposable gloves when cutting hot peppers; the oils can burn skin. Avoid touching your face.
1 cup: 321 cal., 15g fat (7g sat. fat), 64mg chol., 673mg sod., 23g carb. (5g sugars, 4g fiber), 24g pro.

CHICKEN ENCHILADA BAKE

Good thing the recipe makes a lot, because your family won't want to stop eating this simple, cheesy southwestern casserole. The green enchilada sauce brightens it right up.
—Melanie Burns, Pueblo West, CO

PREP: 20 min. • **BAKE:** 50 min. + standing
MAKES: 10 servings

- 4½ cups shredded rotisserie chicken
- 1 can (28 oz.) green enchilada sauce
- 1¼ cups sour cream
- 9 corn tortillas (6 in.), cut into 1½-in. pieces
- 4 cups shredded Monterey Jack cheese

1. Preheat oven to 375°. In a greased 13x9-in. baking dish, layer half of each of the following: chicken, enchilada sauce, sour cream, tortillas and cheese. Repeat the layers.
2. Bake, covered, for 40 minutes. Uncover dish; bake until bubbly, about 10 minutes longer. Let stand for 15 minutes before serving enchiladas.
Freeze option: Cover and freeze unbaked casserole. To use, partially thaw in refrigerator overnight. Remove from the refrigerator 30 minutes before baking. Preheat oven to 375°. Bake as directed, increasing time as necessary to heat through and for a thermometer inserted in center to read 165°.
1 cup: 469 cal., 29g fat (14g sat. fat), 113mg chol., 1077mg sod., 16g carb. (3g sugars, 1g fiber), 34g pro.

EASY SCALLOPED POTATOES

We all loved my mom's super rich scalloped potatoes. I tweaked her recipe to keep all the flavor but cut some of the fat. The cheese blend is the clincher.
—Diane Bramlett, Stockton, CA

PREP: 30 min. • **BAKE:** 20 min.
MAKES: 12 servings (½ cup each)

3	**lbs. Yukon Gold potatoes (about 11 medium), peeled and thinly sliced**
¼	**cup water**
¼	**cup butter, cubed**
1	**large sweet onion, chopped**
4	**garlic cloves, chopped**
¼	**cup all-purpose flour**
1	**tsp. salt**
1	**tsp. pepper**
⅛	**tsp. cayenne pepper**
2	**cups chicken broth**
⅓	**cup half-and-half cream**
1	**cup shredded Gruyere or Swiss cheese**
1	**cup shredded Monterey Jack or cheddar cheese**
	Minced fresh chives, optional

1. Preheat oven to 400°. Place potatoes and water in a large microwave-safe bowl; microwave, covered, on high until almost tender, 12-14 minutes.

2. In a 6-qt. stockpot, heat butter over medium-high heat; saute onion and garlic until tender, 5-7 minutes. Stir in flour and seasonings until blended; gradually stir in broth and cream. Bring to a boil, stirring occasionally; cook and stir until slightly thickened, 2-3 minutes. Stir in cheeses until melted.

3. Drain potatoes; add to sauce, stirring gently. Transfer to a greased 13x9-in. baking dish. Bake, uncovered, until lightly browned, about 20 minutes. If desired, sprinkle with chives.

½ cup: 245 cal., 11g fat (7g sat. fat), 33mg chol., 526mg sod., 29g carb. (4g sugars, 2g fiber), 8g pro.

CHICKEN PENNE CASSEROLE

I make this family-favorite casserole every week or two and we never tire of it. I like that I can put it together and then relax while it bakes.
—Carmen Vanosch, Vernon, BC

PREP: 35 min. • **BAKE:** 45 min.
MAKES: 4 servings

- 1½ cups uncooked penne pasta
- 1 Tbsp. canola oil
- 1 lb. boneless skinless chicken thighs, cut into 1-in. pieces
- ½ cup chopped onion
- ½ cup chopped green pepper
- ½ cup chopped sweet red pepper
- 1 tsp. dried basil
- 1 tsp. dried oregano
- 1 tsp. dried parsley flakes
- ½ tsp. salt
- ½ tsp. crushed red pepper flakes
- 3 garlic cloves, minced
- 1 can (14½ oz.) diced tomatoes, undrained
- 3 Tbsp. tomato paste
- ¾ cup chicken broth
- 2 cups shredded part-skim mozzarella cheese
- ½ cup grated Romano cheese

1. Preheat oven to 350°. Cook pasta according to the package directions. Meanwhile, in a large saucepan, heat oil over medium heat. Add chicken, onion, peppers and seasonings; saute until the chicken is no longer pink. Add the garlic; cook 1 minute longer.

2. In a blender, pulse the tomatoes and tomato paste, covered, until blended. Add to chicken mixture. Stir in broth; bring to a boil over medium-high heat. Reduce heat; cover and simmer until slightly thickened, 10-15 minutes.

3. Drain pasta; toss with chicken mixture. Spoon half of the mixture into a greased 2-qt. baking dish. Sprinkle with half of the cheeses. Repeat layers.

4. Cover and bake 30 minutes. Uncover the casserole; bake until heated through, 15-20 minutes longer.

1½ cups: 579 cal., 28g fat (12g sat. fat), 128mg chol., 1357mg sod., 36g carb. (9g sugars, 4g fiber), 47g pro.

TOP TIP
This simple dish is extremely adaptable and easy to change up. Substitute chicken breasts for the thighs, spiral pasta for the penne and provolone for the mozzarella, and you'll have a different take on the same basic casserole. Feel free to experiment!

CHILI MAC CASSEROLE

This nicely spiced dish uses some of my family's favorite ingredients—macaroni, kidney beans, tomatoes and cheese. Just add a green salad for a complete meal.
—Marlene Wilson, Rolla, ND

PREP: 15 min. • **BAKE:** 30 min.
MAKES: 10 servings

- 1 cup uncooked elbow macaroni
- 2 lbs. lean ground beef (90% lean)
- 1 medium onion, chopped
- 2 garlic cloves, minced
- 1 can (28 oz.) diced tomatoes, undrained
- 1 can (16 oz.) kidney beans, rinsed and drained
- 1 can (6 oz.) tomato paste
- 1 can (4 oz.) chopped green chilies
- 1¼ tsp. salt
- 1 tsp. chili powder
- ½ tsp. ground cumin
- ½ tsp. pepper
- 2 cups shredded reduced-fat Mexican cheese blend
  Thinly sliced green onions, optional

1. Cook macaroni according to package directions. Meanwhile, in a large nonstick skillet, cook the beef, onion and garlic over medium heat until meat is no longer pink; drain. Stir in the tomatoes, beans, tomato paste, chilies and seasonings. Drain the macaroni; add to the beef mixture.
2. Transfer to a 13x9-in. baking dish coated with cooking spray. Cover and bake at 375° for 25-30 minutes or until bubbly. Uncover; sprinkle with cheese. Bake 5-8 minutes longer or until cheese is melted. If desired, top with sliced green onions.
1 cup: 313 cal., 13g fat (6g sat. fat), 69mg chol., 758mg sod., 22g carb. (6g sugars, 5g fiber), 30g pro. **Diabetic exchanges:** 3 lean meat, 1½ starch, 1 fat.

SAUSAGE & EGG CASSEROLE

This casserole is the perfect combination of eggs, sausage, bread and cheese. My mom and I like it because it bakes up tender and golden, slices beautifully and goes over well whenever we serve it.
—Gayle Grigg, Phoenix, AZ

PREP: 15 min. + chilling • **BAKE:** 40 min.
MAKES: 10 servings

- 1 lb. bulk pork sausage
- 6 large eggs
- 2 cups milk
- 1 tsp. salt
- 1 tsp. ground mustard
- 6 slices white bread, cut into ½-in. cubes
- 1 cup shredded cheddar cheese

1. In a skillet, brown and crumble sausage; drain and set aside. In a large bowl, beat eggs; add milk, salt and mustard. Stir in the bread cubes, cheese and sausage.
2. Pour into a greased 11x7-in. baking dish. Cover and refrigerate for 8 hours or overnight. Preheat oven to 350°. Remove from the refrigerator 30 minutes before baking. Bake, uncovered, for 40 minutes or until a knife inserted in center comes out clean.
1 serving: 248 cal., 17g fat (7g sat. fat), 163mg chol., 633mg sod., 11g carb. (4g sugars, 0 fiber), 12g pro.

CHILIES RELLENOS

I find that chilies almost always improve a recipe that uses cheese. To make this a heartier main dish, I often add shredded cooked chicken after the chili layer.
—Irene Martin, Portales, NM

PREP: 10 min. • **BAKE:** 50 min.
MAKES: 8 servings

- 1 can (7 oz.) whole green chilies
- 2 cups shredded Monterey Jack cheese
- 2 cups shredded cheddar cheese
- 3 large eggs
- 3 cups whole milk
- 1 cup biscuit/baking mix
  Seasoned salt to taste
  Salsa

1. Split chilies; rinse and remove seeds. Dry on paper towels. Arrange chilies in an 11x7-in. baking dish. Top with cheeses.
2. In a large bowl, beat eggs; add milk and biscuit mix. Pour over cheese. Sprinkle with salt. Bake at 325° for 50-55 minutes or until golden brown. Serve with salsa.
1 cup: 352 cal., 24g fat (14g sat. fat), 144mg chol., 598mg sod., 15g carb. (5g sugars, 0 fiber), 19g pro.

NOTES

BEST LASAGNA

You can't go wrong with this deliciously rich and meaty lasagna. My grown sons and daughter-in-law request it for their birthdays, too.
—Pam Thompson, Girard, IL

PREP: 1 hour • **BAKE:** 50 min. + standing
MAKES: 12 servings

- 9 lasagna noodles
- 1¼ lbs. bulk Italian sausage
- ¾ lb. ground beef
- 1 medium onion, diced
- 3 garlic cloves, minced
- 2 cans (one 28 oz., one 15 oz.) crushed tomatoes
- 2 cans (6 oz. each) tomato paste
- ⅔ cup water
- 2 to 3 Tbsp. sugar
- 3 Tbsp. plus ¼ cup minced fresh parsley, divided
- 2 tsp. dried basil
- ¾ tsp. fennel seed
- ¾ tsp. salt, divided
- ¼ tsp. coarsely ground pepper
- 1 large egg, lightly beaten
- 1 carton (15 oz.) ricotta cheese
- 4 cups shredded part-skim mozzarella cheese
- ¾ cup grated Parmesan cheese

1. Cook noodles according to package directions; drain. Meanwhile, in a Dutch oven, cook the sausage, beef and onion over medium heat for 8-10 minutes or until the meat is no longer pink, breaking up meat into crumbles. Add garlic; cook 1 minute longer. Drain.

2. Stir in the tomatoes, tomato paste, water, sugar, 3 Tbsp. parsley, basil, fennel, ½ tsp. salt and the pepper; bring to a boil. Reduce heat; simmer sauce, uncovered, for 30 minutes, stirring occasionally.

3. In a small bowl, mix egg, ricotta cheese, and the remaining parsley and salt.

4. Preheat oven to 375°. Spread 2 cups meat sauce into an ungreased 13x9-in. baking dish. Layer with three noodles and a third of the ricotta mixture. Sprinkle with 1 cup mozzarella cheese and 2 Tbsp. Parmesan cheese. Repeat layers twice. Top with the remaining meat sauce and cheeses (the dish will be full).

5. Bake, covered, for 25 minutes. Bake, uncovered, 25 minutes longer or until bubbly. Let stand for 15 minutes before serving.

1 serving: 519 cal., 27g fat (13g sat. fat), 109mg chol., 1013mg sod., 35g carb. (10g sugars, 4g fiber), 35g pro.

BONUS: MEXICAN LASAGNA

I collect recipes (this one is from my son's mother-in-law). My husband teases me that I won't live long enough to try half of the recipes in my files!
—Rose Ann Buhle, Minooka, IL

PREP: 20 min. • **BAKE:** 65 min. + standing
MAKES: 12 servings

- 2 lbs. ground beef
- 1 can (16 oz.) refried beans
- 1 can (4 oz.) chopped green chilies
- 1 envelope taco seasoning
- 2 Tbsp. hot salsa
- 12 oz. uncooked lasagna noodles
- 4 cups shredded Colby-Monterey Jack cheese, divided
- 1 jar (16 oz.) mild salsa
- 2 cups water
- 2 cups sour cream
- 1 can (2¼ oz.) sliced ripe olives, drained
- 3 green onions, chopped
- 1 medium tomato, chopped, optional

1. Preheat oven to 350°. In a large skillet, cook beef over medium heat until no longer pink; drain. Stir in beans, chilies, taco seasoning and hot salsa.
2. In a greased 13x9-in. baking dish, layer a third of the noodles and meat mixture. Sprinkle with 1 cup of cheese. Repeat layers twice.
3. Combine mild salsa and water; pour over top. Cover and bake for 1 hour or until heated through.
4. Top with sour cream, olives, onions, tomatoes if desired, and the remaining cheese. Bake, uncovered, 5 minutes. Let stand 10-15 minutes before cutting.
1 serving: 521 cal., 28g fat (16g sat. fat), 110mg chol., 909mg sod., 36g carb. (4g sugars, 3g fiber), 29g pro.

SAUSAGE SPINACH BAKE

A friend gave me this delicious recipe years ago. A salad and bread of your choice is all you'll need for a filling lunch or dinner. It's so versatile, you can even serve it at brunch.
—Kathleen Grant, Swan Lake, MT

PREP: 20 min. • **BAKE:** 40 min.
MAKES: 12 servings

- 1 pkg. (6 oz.) savory herb-flavored stuffing mix
- ½ lb. bulk pork sausage
- ¼ cup chopped green onions
- ½ tsp. minced garlic
- 1 pkg. (10 oz.) frozen chopped spinach, thawed and squeezed dry
- 1½ cups shredded Monterey Jack cheese
- 1½ cups half-and-half cream
- 3 large eggs
- 2 Tbsp. grated Parmesan cheese

1. Preheat oven to 400°. Prepare the stuffing according to package directions. Meanwhile, crumble sausage into a large skillet. Add onions; cook over medium heat until meat is no longer pink. Add garlic; cook 1 minute longer. Drain.
2. In a large bowl, combine the stuffing, sausage mixture and spinach. Transfer to a greased 11x7-in. baking dish; sprinkle with Monterey Jack cheese. In a small bowl, combine cream and eggs; pour over the sausage mixture.
3. Bake for 35-40 minutes or until a thermometer reads 160°. Sprinkle with Parmesan cheese; bake 5 minutes longer or until bubbly.
1 serving: 258 cal., 17g fat (9g sat. fat), 95mg chol., 494mg sod., 14g carb. (2g sugars, 2g fiber), 11g pro.

CORN DOG CASSEROLE

Reminiscent of traditional corn dogs, this fun main dish really hits the spot. It tastes especially good right from the oven.
—Marcy Suzanne Olipane, Belleville, IL

PREP: 25 min. • **BAKE:** 30 min.
MAKES: 12 servings

- 2 cups thinly sliced celery
- 2 Tbsp. butter
- 1½ cups sliced green onions
- 1½ lbs. hot dogs
- 2 large eggs
- 1½ cups 2% milk
- 2 tsp. rubbed sage
- ¼ tsp. pepper
- 2 pkg. (8½ oz. each) cornbread/muffin mix
- 2 cups shredded sharp cheddar cheese, divided

1. In a small skillet, saute celery in butter 5 minutes. Add onions; saute 5 minutes longer or until the vegetables are tender. Place in a large bowl; set aside.
2. Preheat oven to 400°. Cut hot dogs into ½-in. slices. In the same skillet, saute the hot dogs for 5 minutes or until lightly browned; add to the vegetables. Set aside 1 cup.
3. In a large bowl, whisk eggs, milk, sage and pepper. Add the remaining hot dog mixture. Stir in cornbread mixes. Add 1½ cups of the cheese. Spread into a shallow 3-qt. baking dish. Top casserole with the reserved hot dog mixture and the remaining cheese.
4. Bake, uncovered, for 30 minutes or until golden brown.
1 serving: 389 cal., 28g fat (14g sat. fat), 101mg chol., 925mg sod., 20g carb. (7g sugars, 1g fiber), 14g pro.

TUNA MUSHROOM CASEROLE

The first time I made this dish, my uncle asked for seconds even though tuna casseroles are not usually his favorite. The green beans make it a whole meal.
—Jone Furlong, Santa Rosa, CA

PREP: 30 min. • **BAKE:** 25 min.
MAKES: 6 servings

½ cup water
1 tsp. chicken bouillon granules
1 pkg. (9 oz.) frozen cut green beans
1 cup chopped onion
1 cup sliced fresh mushrooms
¼ cup chopped celery
1 garlic clove, minced
½ tsp. dill weed
½ tsp. salt
⅛ tsp. pepper
4 tsp. cornstarch
1½ cups cold whole milk
½ cup shredded Swiss cheese
¼ cup mayonnaise
2½ cups egg noodles, cooked and drained

1 can (12 oz.) light tuna in water, drained and flaked
⅓ cup dry bread crumbs
1 Tbsp. butter

1. Preheat oven to 350°. In a large saucepan, bring the water and bouillon to a boil; stir until bouillon is dissolved. Add the next eight ingredients; bring to a boil. Reduce heat; cover and simmer the mixture for 5 minutes or until the vegetables are tender.
2. In a small bowl, combine cornstarch and milk until smooth; gradually add to the vegetable mixture. Bring to a boil; cook and stir for 2 minutes or until thickened. Remove from the heat; stir in cheese and mayonnaise until cheese is melted. Fold in noodles and tuna.
3. Pour into a greased 2½-qt. baking dish. In a small skillet, brown bread crumbs in butter; sprinkle over the casserole. Bake, uncovered, for 25-30 minutes or until heated through.

1 serving: 343 cal., 15g fat (5g sat. fat), 57mg chol., 770mg sod., 27g carb. (7g sugars, 2g fiber), 24g pro.

TOP TIP

In recipes that call for mayonnaise and are heated or baked, such as this one, reduced-fat and fat-free mayonnaise are not recommended, as they can break down when heated and leave an unpleasant texture.

CHICKEN & EGG NOODLE CASSEROLE

A friend and her family recently went through a really difficult time—bringing over this casserole was one thing I could think of to help in a tiny way and let them know I was thinking of them.

—Lin Krankel, Oxford, MI

PREP: 20 min. • **BAKE:** 30 min.
MAKES: 8 servings

- 6 **cups uncooked egg noodles (about 12 oz.)**
- 2 **cans (10¾ oz. each) condensed cream of chicken soup, undiluted**
- 1 **cup (8 oz.) sour cream**
- ¾ **cup 2% milk**
- ¼ **tsp. salt**
- ¼ **tsp. pepper**
- 3 **cups cubed cooked chicken breasts**
- 1 **cup crushed Ritz crackers (about 20 crackers)**
- ¼ **cup butter, melted**

1. Preheat oven to 350°. Cook noodles according to the package directions for al dente; drain.

2. In a large bowl, whisk soup, sour cream, milk, salt and pepper until blended. Stir in the chicken and noodles. Transfer to a greased 13x9-in. baking dish. In a small bowl, mix crushed crackers and butter; sprinkle over top. Bake 30-35 minutes or until bubbly.

1¼ cups: 446 cal., 22g fat (10g sat. fat), 107mg chol., 820mg sod., 37g carb. (4g sugars, 2g fiber), 23g pro.

NOTES

TOP TIP

Wide egg noodles are wonderful in casseroles because they rarely clump together, are quick to cook and have a solid bite. But you can also substitute traditional pasta for the noodles, if you like. Use a short pasta like penne or fusili. Cook the pasta al dente, according to package directions, and then proceed as directed in the recipe.

CONTEST-WINNING EGGPLANT PARMESAN

My recipe calls for baking the eggplant instead of frying, so it's healthier than most. It takes a little extra time, but the flavors and rustic elegance are worth it.
—Laci Hooten, McKinney, TX

PREP: 40 min. • **COOK:** 25 min.
MAKES: 8 servings

3 large eggs, beaten
2½ cups panko (Japanese) bread crumbs
3 medium eggplants, cut into ¼-in. slices
2 jars (4½ oz. each) sliced mushrooms, drained
½ tsp dried basil
⅛ tsp. dried oregano
2 cups shredded part-skim mozzarella cheese
½ cup grated Parmesan cheese
1 jar (28 oz.) spaghetti sauce

1. Preheat oven to 350°. Place eggs and bread crumbs in separate shallow bowls. Dip eggplant in eggs, then coat in crumbs. Place on baking sheets coated with cooking spray. Bake 15-20 minutes or until tender and golden brown, turning once.
2. In a small bowl, combine mushrooms, basil and oregano. In another small bowl, combine the cheeses.
3. Spread ½ cup sauce into a 13x9-in. baking dish coated with cooking spray. Layer with a third of the mushroom mixture, a third of the eggplant, ¾ cup sauce and a third of the cheese mixture. Repeat layers twice.
4. Bake, uncovered, for 25-30 minutes or until heated through and cheese is melted.
1 serving: 305 cal., 12g fat (5g sat. fat), 102mg chol., 912mg sod., 32g carb. (12g sugars, 9g fiber), 18g pro.

CORNBREAD CASSEROLE

My husband likes spicy foods, so I'll frequently sprinkle chopped jalapeno peppers over half of this casserole—just for him!
—Carrina Cooper, McAlpin, FL

PREP: 5 min. • **BAKE:** 30 min.
MAKES: 6 servings

1 can (15¼ oz.) whole kernel corn, drained
1 can (14¾ oz.) cream-style corn
1 pkg. (8½ oz.) cornbread/ muffin mix
1 large egg
2 Tbsp. butter, melted
¼ tsp. garlic powder
¼ tsp. paprika

Preheat oven to 400°. In a large bowl, combine all ingredients. Pour into a greased 11x7-in. baking dish. Bake, uncovered, for 25-30 minutes or until the top and edges are golden brown.
1 serving: 311 cal., 10g fat (4g sat. fat), 54mg chol., 777mg sod., 50g carb. (14g sugars, 3g fiber), 6g pro.

FREEZE IT

TURKEY CORDON BLEU CASSEROLE

We love everything about traditional cordon bleu, and this variation is so easy to make. It's a delicious way to eat Thanksgiving leftovers.
—Kristine Blauert, Wabasha, MN

PREP: 20 min. • **BAKE:** 25 min.

MAKES: 8 servings

 2 cups uncooked elbow macaroni
 2 cans (10¾ oz. each) condensed cream of chicken soup, undiluted
 ¾ cup 2% milk
 ¼ cup grated Parmesan cheese
 1 tsp. prepared mustard
 1 tsp. paprika
 ½ tsp. dried rosemary, crushed
 ¼ tsp. garlic powder
 ⅛ tsp. rubbed sage
 2 cups cubed cooked turkey
 2 cups cubed fully cooked ham
 2 cups shredded part-skim mozzarella cheese
 ¼ cup crushed Ritz crackers

1. Preheat oven to 350°. Cook macaroni according to package directions.

2. Meanwhile, whisk together the soup, milk, Parmesan cheese, mustard and seasonings. Stir in the turkey, ham and mozzarella cheese.

3. Drain the macaroni; add to the soup mixture and toss to combine. Transfer to a greased 13x9-in. baking dish or eight greased 8-oz. ramekins. Sprinkle with crushed crackers. Bake, uncovered, until bubbly, 25-30 minutes.

Freeze option: Cover and freeze unbaked in baking dish or ramekins. To use, partially thaw in the refrigerator overnight. Remove from refrigerator 30 minutes before baking. Bake as directed, increasing time as necessary to heat through and for a thermometer inserted in center to read 165°.

1 cup: 327 cal., 14g fat (6g sat. fat), 64mg chol., 1090mg sod., 23g carb. (3g sugars, 1g fiber), 27g pro.

"**Absolutely delicious! I added two shakes of Old Bay (my personal preference). This casserole was so good that my very picky husband had three helpings. I will be adding this to my recipe box.**"

—EMIZEE252, TASTEOFHOME.COM

NEW ENGLAND LAMB BAKE

This hearty dish is perfect for warming up on a chilly winter evening. The aroma is almost as delightful as the dish itself.
—Frank Grady, Fort Kent, ME

PREP: 25 min. • **BAKE:** 1½ hours
MAKES: 8 servings

- 1 Tbsp. canola oil
- 2 lbs. boneless leg of lamb, cut into 1-in. cubes
- 1 large onion, chopped
- ¼ cup all-purpose flour
- 3 cups chicken broth
- 2 large leeks (white portion only), cut into ½-in. slices
- 2 large carrots, sliced
- 2 Tbsp. minced fresh parsley, divided
- ½ tsp. dried rosemary, crushed
- ½ tsp. salt
- ¼ tsp. pepper
- ¼ tsp. dried thyme
- 3 large potatoes, peeled and sliced
- 3 Tbsp. butter, melted and divided

1. Preheat oven to 375°. In a Dutch oven, heat oil over medium heat. Add lamb and onion; cook and stir until meat is no longer pink. Stir in flour until blended. Gradually add the broth. Bring to a boil; cook until thickened, 1-2 minutes, stirring to loosen browned bits from pan. Add the leeks, carrots, 1 Tbsp. parsley, rosemary, salt, pepper and thyme.

2. Spoon into a greased 13x9-in. or 3-qt. baking dish. Cover with potato slices; brush with 2 Tbsp. melted butter. Bake 1 hour; brush potatoes with the remaining butter. Return to oven; bake until the meat is tender and potatoes are golden, 30 minutes to 1 hour more. Cool briefly; sprinkle with remaining parsley.

Freeze option: Remove baking dish from oven; cool completely. Before adding the remaining parsley, cover dish and freeze. Freeze parsley separately. To use, partially thaw lamb in refrigerator overnight. Remove from refrigerator 30 minutes before baking; thaw remaining parsley. Preheat oven to 350°. Reheat, covered, until a thermometer reads 165°, about 1 hour. Sprinkle with the remaining parsley.

1 piece: 356 cal, 13g fat (5g sat. fat), 82mg chol., 631mg sod., 34g carb. (4g sugars, 4g fiber), 25g pro. **Diabetic Exchanges:** 3 starch, 3 lean meat, 1½ fat.

TOP TIP

To prepare leeks, first remove any withered outer leaves and trim the root end. Cut off and discard the green upper leaves at the point where the pale green turns dark green. Leeks often contain sand between their many layers. For sliced or chopped leeks, cut the leek open lengthwise down one side and rinse well under cold running water, separating the leaves.

MOM'S TURKEY TETRAZZINI

If you're looking for stick-to-your-ribs comfort food, this hearty dish will meet your needs!
—Judy Batson, Tampa, FL

PREP: 25 min. • **BAKE:** 25 min. + standing
MAKES: 6 servings

- 1 pkg. (12 oz.) fettuccine
- ½ lb. sliced fresh mushrooms
- 1 medium onion, chopped
- ¼ cup butter, cubed
- 3 Tbsp. all-purpose flour
- 1 cup white wine or chicken broth
- 3 cups 2% milk
- 3 cups cubed cooked turkey
- ¾ tsp. salt
- ½ tsp. pepper
- ½ tsp. hot pepper sauce
- ½ cup shredded Parmesan cheese
  Paprika, optional

1. Preheat oven to 375°. Cook fettuccine according to the package directions.
2. Meanwhile, in a large skillet, saute the mushrooms and onion in butter until tender. Stir in flour until blended; whisk in wine until smooth, about 2 minutes. Slowly whisk in milk. Bring to a boil; cook and stir until thickened. Stir in turkey, salt, pepper and pepper sauce.
3. Drain the fettuccine. Layer half of the fettuccine, turkey mixture and cheese in a greased 13x9-in. baking dish. Repeat layers. Sprinkle with paprika if desired.
4. Cover and bake for 25-30 minutes or until heated through. Let casserole stand 10 minutes before serving.
1 cup: 516 cal., 17g fat (9g sat. fat), 87mg chol., 596mg sod., 53g carb. (10g sugars, 4g fiber), 37g pro.

BAKED MAC & CHEESE

Even people who have made their own macaroni and cheese for years ask for the recipe when they taste my buttery crumb-topped version. For even more flavor, make it with extra-sharp white cheddar cheese.
—Shelby Thompson, Dover, DE

PREP: 15 min. • **BAKE:** 30 min.
MAKES: 8 servings

- 1 pkg. (16 oz.) uncooked elbow macaroni
- ⅓ cup plus ¼ cup butter, divided
- ¾ cup finely chopped onion
- 6 Tbsp. all-purpose flour
- 1 tsp. ground mustard
- ¾ tsp. salt
- ¼ tsp. pepper
- 4½ cups 2% milk
- 4 cups shredded sharp cheddar cheese
- ¾ cup dry bread crumbs

1. Cook macaroni according to package directions for al dente; drain.
2. In a Dutch oven, heat ⅓ cup butter over medium heat; saute onion until tender. Stir in flour and seasonings until blended; gradually stir in milk. Bring to a boil, stirring constantly; cook and stir until thickened. Stir in cheese until melted. Stir in macaroni. Transfer mixture to a greased 13x9-in. baking dish.
3. In a microwave, melt remaining butter; toss with bread crumbs. Sprinkle over casserole. Bake, uncovered, at 350° until heated through, 30-35 minutes.
1 cup: 689 cal., 37g fat (22g sat. fat), 104mg chol., 834mg sod., 62g carb. (10g sugars, 3g fiber), 28g pro.

FOURTH OF JULY BEAN CASSEROLE

The outstanding barbecue flavor of these beans makes them a favorite for cookouts all summer and into the fall. It's a popular dish with adults and kids alike. Beef makes it much better than plain pork and beans.

—Donna Fancher, Lawrence, IN

PREP: 20 min. • **BAKE:** 1 hour
MAKES: 12 servings

- ½ lb. bacon strips, diced
- ½ lb. ground beef
- 1 cup chopped onion
- 1 can (28 oz.) pork and beans
- 1 can (16 oz.) kidney beans, rinsed and drained
- 1 can (15¼ oz.) lima beans, rinsed and drained
- ½ cup barbecue sauce
- ½ cup ketchup
- ½ cup sugar
- ½ cup packed brown sugar
- 2 Tbsp. prepared mustard
- 2 Tbsp. molasses
- 1 tsp. salt
- ½ tsp. chili powder

1. In a large skillet over medium heat, cook bacon, beef and onion until the meat is no longer pink; drain.

2. Transfer to a greased 2½-qt. baking dish; add all the beans and mix well. In a small bowl, combine the remaining ingredients; stir into beef and bean mixture.

3. Cover and bake at 350° for 45 minutes. Uncover; bake 15 minutes longer.

1 cup: 278 cal., 6g fat (2g sat. fat), 15mg chol., 933mg sod., 47g carb. (26g sugars, 7g fiber), 12g pro.

"This is the best bean recipe ever. I make it for our summer cookouts. I also make it for our Christmas dinner. Everyone loves it and looks forward to it."

—NENE1, TASTEOFHOME.COM

PUFF PASTRY CHICKEN POTPIE

When my wife is craving comfort food, I whip up my special chicken potpie. It's easy to make, sticks to your ribs and delivers soul-satisfying flavor.
—Nick Iverson, Denver, CO

PREP: 45 min. • **BAKE:** 45 min. + standing
MAKES: 8 servings

- 1 pkg. (17.3 oz.) frozen puff pastry, thawed
- 2 lbs. boneless skinless chicken breasts, cut into 1-in. pieces
- 1 tsp. salt, divided
- 1 tsp. pepper, divided
- 4 Tbsp. butter, divided
- 1 large onion, chopped
- 2 garlic cloves, minced
- 1 tsp. minced fresh thyme or ¼ tsp. dried thyme
- 1 tsp. minced fresh sage or ¼ tsp. rubbed sage
- ½ cup all-purpose flour
- 2 cups chicken broth
- 1 cup plus 1 Tbsp. half-and-half cream, divided
- 2 cups frozen mixed vegetables (about 10 oz.)
- 1 Tbsp. lemon juice
- 1 large egg yolk

1. Preheat oven to 400°. On a lightly floured surface, roll each pastry sheet into a 12x10-in. rectangle. Cut one sheet crosswise into six 2-in. strips; cut the remaining sheet lengthwise into five 2-in. strips. On a baking sheet, closely weave the strips to make a 12x10-in. lattice. Freeze the lattice while making filling.

2. Toss chicken with ½ tsp. each salt and pepper. In a large skillet, heat 1 Tbsp. butter over medium-high heat; saute chicken until browned, 5-7 minutes. Remove from pan.

3. In the same skillet, heat the remaining butter over medium-high heat; saute onion until tender, 5-7 minutes. Stir in garlic and herbs; cook 1 minute. Stir in flour until blended; cook and stir 1 minute. Gradually stir in broth and 1 cup cream. Bring to a boil, stirring constantly; cook and stir until thickened, about 2 minutes.

4. Stir in the vegetables, lemon juice, chicken and the remaining salt and pepper; return to a boil. Transfer to a greased 2-qt. oblong baking dish. Top with lattice, trimming to fit.

5. Whisk together the egg yolk and the remaining cream; brush over pastry. Bake, uncovered, until bubbly and golden brown, 45-55 minutes. Let stand for 15 minutes before serving.

1 serving: 523 cal., 25g fat (10g sat. fat), 118mg chol., 829mg sod., 42g carb. (4g sugars, 6g fiber), 30g pro.

REUBEN BREAD PUDDING

Our Aunt Renee always brought this casserole to family picnics in Chicago. When it became a big hit, she started bringing two or three. I have also made it using dark rye bread or marbled rye and ham instead of corned beef.
—Johnna Johnson, Scottsdale, AZ

PREP: 20 min. • **BAKE:** 35 min.
MAKES: 6 servings

- 4 cups cubed rye bread (about 6 slices)
- 2 Tbsp. butter, melted
- 2 cups cubed or shredded cooked corned beef (about ½ lb.)
- 1 can (14 oz.) sauerkraut, rinsed and well drained
- 1 cup shredded Swiss cheese, divided
- 3 large eggs
- 1 cup 2% milk
- ⅓ cup prepared Thousand Island salad dressing
- 1½ tsp. prepared mustard
- ¼ tsp. pepper

1. Preheat oven to 350°. In a large bowl, toss the bread cubes with butter. Stir in corned beef, sauerkraut and ½ cup of the cheese; transfer to a greased 11x7-in. baking dish.
2. In the same bowl, whisk eggs, milk, salad dressing, mustard and pepper; pour over top. Bake, uncovered, 30 minutes. Sprinkle with the remaining cheese. Bake 5-7 minutes longer or until golden and a knife inserted in the center comes out clean.
1 serving: 390 cal., 25g fat (10g sat. fat), 165mg chol., 1295mg sod., 21g carb. (7g sugars, 3g fiber), 19g pro.

BLT EGG BAKE

I created this recipe to combine classic BLT flavors and served it at a brunch for my church ladies group. I shared the recipe many times that day!
—Priscilla Detrick, Catoosa, OK

TAKES: 30 min. • **MAKES:** 4 servings

- ¼ cup mayonnaise
- 5 slices bread, toasted
- 4 slices process American cheese
- 12 bacon strips, cooked and crumbled
- 2 Tbsp. butter
- 2 Tbsp. all-purpose flour
- ¼ tsp. salt
- ⅛ tsp. pepper
- 1 cup 2% milk
- 4 large eggs
- 1 medium tomato, halved and sliced
- ½ cup shredded cheddar cheese
- 2 green onions, thinly sliced
  Shredded lettuce

1. Preheat oven to 325°. Spread the mayonnaise on one side of each slice of toast and cut into small pieces. Arrange toast, mayonnaise side up, in a greased 8-in. square baking dish. Top with cheese slices and bacon.
2. In a small saucepan, melt butter. Stir in the flour, salt and pepper until smooth. Gradually add milk. Bring to a boil; cook and stir 2 minutes or until thickened. Pour over bacon.
3. In a large skillet, fry eggs over medium heat until they reach desired doneness; place over bacon. Top with tomato slices; sprinkle with cheddar cheese and onions. Bake, uncovered, 10 minutes. Cut into squares; serve with lettuce.
1 serving: 594 cal., 42g fat (16g sat. fat), 251mg chol., 1262mg sod., 25g carb. (7g sugars, 1g fiber), 27g pro.

SIDES & SALADS

A TOP-NOTCH SIDE DISH MAKES A GOOD MEAL GREAT. TRY THESE ALL-TIME FAVORITES!

CRUNCHY BROCCOLI SALAD

I never liked broccoli when I was younger, but now I'm hooked on this salad's light, sweet taste. It gives broccoli a whole new look and personality.
—Jessica Conrey, Cedar Rapids, IA

TAKES: 25 min. • **MAKES:** 10 servings

- 8 cups fresh broccoli florets (about 1 lb.)
- 1 bunch green onions, thinly sliced
- ½ cup dried cranberries
- 3 Tbsp. canola oil
- 3 Tbsp. seasoned rice vinegar
- 2 Tbsp. sugar
- ¼ cup sunflower kernels
- 3 bacon strips, cooked and crumbled

In a large bowl, combine broccoli, green onions and cranberries. In a small bowl, whisk the oil, vinegar and sugar until blended; drizzle over broccoli mixture and toss to coat. Refrigerate salad until serving. Sprinkle with sunflower kernels and bacon before serving.

¾ cup: 121 cal., 7g fat (1g sat. fat), 2mg chol., 233mg sod., 14g carb. (10g sugars, 3g fiber), 3g pro. **Diabetic exchanges:** 1 vegetable, 1 fat, ½ starch.

Creamy Broccoli Salad: Omit oil and vinegar and reduce sugar to 1 Tbsp. Combine 1 cup mayonnaise, 2 Tbsp. cider vinegar and sugar. Pour over broccoli mixture and toss to coat.

Crunchy Cauliflower-Broccoli Salad: Substitute 4 cups fresh cauliflowerets for 4 cups of the broccoli florets.

SLOW COOKER
SLOW-COOKED RANCH POTATOES

Even after seven years, my family still asks for this tasty potato and bacon dish. Try it once and I'll bet your family will be hooked, too.
—Lynn Ireland, Lebanon, WI

PREP: 15 min. • **COOK:** 7 hours.
MAKES: 10 servings

- 6 bacon strips, chopped
- 2½ lbs. small red potatoes, cubed
- 1 pkg. (8 oz.) cream cheese, softened
- 1 can (10¾ oz.) condensed cream of potato soup, undiluted
- ¼ cup 2% milk
- 1 envelope buttermilk ranch salad dressing mix
- 3 Tbsp. thinly sliced green onions

1. In a large skillet, cook bacon over medium heat until crisp, stirring occasionally. Transfer the bacon with a slotted spoon to paper towels. Drain; reserve 1 Tbsp. of drippings in skillet.

2. Place potatoes in a 3-qt. slow cooker. In a bowl, beat cream cheese, soup, milk, dressing mix and the reserved drippings until blended; stir into potatoes. Sprinkle with bacon.

3. Cook, covered, on low for 7-8 hours or until the potatoes are tender. Top with green onions.

¾ cup: 230 cal., 12g fat (6g sat. fat), 33mg chol., 545mg sod., 25g carb. (2g sugars, 2g fiber), 6g pro.

5 INGREDIENTS

GARLIC MASHED RED POTATOES

These creamy garlic mashed potatoes are so good, you can serve them plain—no butter or gravy needed! This is the only way I make my mashed potatoes.
—Valerie Mitchell, Olathe, KS

TAKES: 30 min. • **MAKES:** 6 servings

8 medium red potatoes, quartered
3 garlic cloves, peeled
2 Tbsp. butter
½ cup fat-free milk, warmed
½ tsp. salt
¼ cup grated Parmesan cheese

Place potatoes and garlic in a large saucepan; cover with water. Bring to a boil. Reduce heat; cover and simmer for 15-20 minutes or until potatoes are very tender. Drain well. Add the butter, milk and salt; mash. Stir in cheese.

1 cup: 190 cal., 5g fat (3g sat. fat), 14mg chol., 275mg sod., 36g carb. (0 sugars, 4g fiber), 8g pro. **Diabetic exchanges:** 2 starch, ½ fat.

BONUS: COLCANNON POTATOES

Every Irish family has its own version or this classic dish. My recipe comes from my father's family and is part of my annual St. Pat's menu, along with lamb chops, carrots and soda bread.
—Marilou Robinson, Portland, OR

PREP: 25 min. • **COOK:** 35 min.
MAKES: 12 servings

1 medium head cabbage
   (about 2 lbs.), shredded
4 lbs. medium potatoes
   (about 8), peeled and quartered
2 cups whole milk
1 cup chopped green onions
1½ tsp. salt
½ tsp. pepper
¼ cup butter, melted
   Crumbled cooked bacon
   Minced fresh parsley, optional

1. Place cabbage and 2 cups water in a large saucepan; bring to a boil. Reduce heat; simmer, covered, until the cabbage is tender, about 10 minutes. Drain, reserving the cooking liquid; keep cabbage warm in separate dish.

2. In same pan, combine potatoes and the reserved cooking liquid. Add additional water to cover potatoes; bring to a boil. Reduce heat; cook, uncovered, until the potatoes are tender, 15-20 minutes. Meanwhile, place milk, green onions, salt and pepper in a small saucepan; bring just to a boil and remove from heat.

3. Drain the potatoes; place in a large bowl and mash. Add the milk mixture; beat just until blended. Stir in cabbage. To serve, drizzle mixture with butter; top with the parsley and bacon.

1 cup: 168 cal., 5g fat (3g sat. fat), 14mg chol., 361mg sod., 27g carb. (6g sugars, 4g fiber), 4g pro. **Diabetic exchanges:** 2 starch, 1 fat.

ELEGANT GREEN BEANS

Mushrooms and water chestnuts give new life to ordinary green bean casserole. Every time I make it for my friends, they ask for the recipe.
—Linda Poe, Sandstone, MN

PREP: 20 min. • **BAKE:** 50 min.
MAKES: 8 servings

- 1 **can (8 oz.) sliced water chestnuts, drained**
- 1 **small onion, chopped**
- 1 **jar (4½ oz.) sliced mushrooms, drained**
- 6 **Tbsp. butter, divided**
- ¼ **cup all-purpose flour**
- 1 **cup 2% milk**
- ½ **cup chicken broth**
- 1 **tsp. reduced-sodium soy sauce**
- ⅛ **tsp. hot pepper sauce**
  Dash salt
- 1 **pkg. (16 oz.) frozen French-style green beans, thawed**
- ½ **cup shredded cheddar cheese**
- 1 **cup crushed French-fried onions**

1. Preheat oven to 350°. In a small skillet, saute the water chestnuts, onion and sliced mushrooms in 2 Tbsp. of butter for 4-5 minutes or until the onion is crisp-tender; set aside.

2. In large skillet, melt remaining butter; stir in flour until smooth. Stir in the milk, broth, soy sauce, pepper sauce and salt. Bring to a boil; cook and stir sauce for 2 minutes or until thickened. Remove from heat; stir in green beans and cheese.

3. Spoon half of the bean mixture into a greased 1½-qt. baking dish. Layer with the water chestnut mixture and the remaining bean mixture.

4. Bake, uncovered, 45 minutes. Top with French-fried onions. Bake 5 minutes more or until heated through.

¾ cup: 218 cal., 15g fat (8g sat. fat), 35mg chol., 392mg sod., 17g carb. (5g sugars, 3g fiber), 5g pro.

TOP TIP

Traditionally, a pinch is thought to be the amount of a dry ingredient that can be held between the thumb and forefinger. A dash is a very small amount of seasoning added with a quick downward stroke of the hand, and measures between $\frac{1}{16}$ and a scant $\frac{1}{8}$ teaspoon.

TEXAS-STYLE SPANISH RICE

A Mexican friend gave me the original version of this fragrant rice dish, but I've modified the spices to suit my family's tastes. The golden color and warm flavor brightens up anything you put beside it.
—Melissa Pride, Plano, TX

PREP: 15 min. • **COOK:** 20 min.
MAKES: 6 servings

- ¼ cup chopped onion
- ¼ cup chopped green pepper
- 2 Tbsp. vegetable oil
- 1 cup uncooked long grain rice
- ½ cup tomatoes with green chilies
- ¼ tsp. ground turmeric
- 1 tsp. ground cumin
- ½ tsp. salt
- ¼ tsp. garlic powder
- 2 cups water
- 2 to 3 Tbsp. chopped fresh cilantro, optional

In a skillet, saute onion and green pepper in oil for about 2 minutes. Add rice and stir until coated with oil. Add tomatoes, turmeric, cumin, salt, garlic powder and water; bring to a boil. Reduce heat and simmer, covered, about 20 minutes or until the liquid is absorbed. Add cilantro if desired.

¾ cup: 166 cal., 5g fat (1g sat. fat), 0 chol., 279mg sod., 27g carb. (2g sugars, 1g fiber), 3g pro.

5 INGREDIENTS
ROASTED PARMESAN CARROTS

Mom always told us, "Eat your carrots, help your eyes." Rich in beta carotene, carrots not only support health but also taste amazing when roasted and tossed with Parmesan.
—*Taste of Home* Test Kitchen

TAKES: 25 min. • **MAKES:** 4 servings

- 1 lb. fresh carrots, peeled
- 1 tsp. olive oil
- ½ tsp. kosher salt
- ¼ tsp. freshly ground pepper
- ¼ tsp. dried thyme
- 3 Tbsp. grated Parmesan cheese

1. Preheat oven to 450°. Cut carrots crosswise in half and then lengthwise into ½-in.-thick sticks. Toss with oil, salt, pepper and thyme; spread evenly in a greased 15x10-in. baking pan.
2. Roast 12-15 minutes or until tender and lightly browned, stirring once. Toss with cheese.

1 serving: 72 cal., 2g fat (1g sat. fat), 3mg chol., 386mg sod., 11g carb. (5g sugars, 3g fiber), 2g pro. **Diabetic exchanges:** 1 vegetable, ½ fat.

PARMESAN RISOTTO

Risotto is a creamy Italian rice dish. In this version, the rice is briefly sauteed, then slowly cooked in wine and seasonings. You can cut back this recipe to make a smaller yield, but still add the broth ½ cup at a time.
—*Taste of Home* Test Kitchen

PREP: 15 min. • **COOK:** 30 min.
MAKES: 12 servings

- 8 cups chicken broth
- ½ cup finely chopped onion
- ¼ cup olive oil
- 3 cups arborio rice
- 2 garlic cloves, minced
- 1 cup dry white wine or water
- ½ cup shredded Parmesan cheese
- ¼ tsp. salt
- ¼ tsp. pepper
- 3 Tbsp. minced fresh parsley

1. In a large saucepan, heat broth, then reduce heat to low and keep warm. In a Dutch oven, saute onion in oil until tender. Add the rice and garlic; cook and stir for 2-3 minutes. Reduce the heat; stir in the wine. Cook and stir mixture until all the liquid is absorbed.

2. Add the heated broth, ½ cup at a time, stirring constantly. Allow the liquid to absorb between additions. Cook just until risotto is creamy and rice is almost tender. (Cooking time is about 20 minutes.) Add the remaining ingredients; cook and stir until heated through. Serve immediately.

¾ cup: 260 cal., 6g fat (1g sat. fat), 2mg chol., 728mg sod., 41g carb. (1g sugars, 1g fiber), 6g pro.

BALSAMIC GREEN BEAN SALAD

Serve up green beans in a whole new way! The tangy flavors and crunch of this tasty-looking side complement any special meal or potluck.
—Megan Spencer, Farmington Hills, MI

PREP: 30 min. + chilling • **MAKES:** 16 servings

- 2 lbs. fresh green beans, trimmed and cut into 1½-in. pieces
- ¼ cup olive oil
- 3 Tbsp. lemon juice
- 3 Tbsp. balsamic vinegar
- ¼ tsp. salt
- ¼ tsp. garlic powder
- ¼ tsp. ground mustard
- ⅛ tsp. pepper
- 1 large red onion, chopped
- 4 cups cherry tomatoes, halved
- 1 cup (4 oz.) crumbled feta cheese

1. Place beans in a 6-qt. stockpot; add water to cover. Bring to a boil. Cook, covered, for about 8-10 minutes or until crisp-tender. Drain and immediately place into ice water. Drain and pat dry.

2. In a small bowl, whisk oil, lemon juice, vinegar, salt, garlic powder, mustard and pepper. Drizzle over the beans. Add onion; toss to coat. Refrigerate, covered, for at least 1 hour. Just before serving, stir in tomatoes and cheese.

¾ cup: 77 cal., 5g fat (1g sat. fat), 4mg chol., 112mg sod., 7g carb. (3g sugars, 3g fiber), 3g pro. Diabetic exchanges: 1 vegetable, 1 fat.

CHEESY STUFFED BAKED POTATOES

These special potatoes are a hit with my whole family, from the smallest grandchild on up. I prepare them up to a week in advance, wrap them well and freeze them. Their flavorful filling is especially nice with juicy ham slices.
—Marge Clark, West Lebanon, IN

PREP: 1¼ hours • **BAKE:** 20 min.
MAKES: 6 servings

3	large baking potatoes (1 lb. each)
1½	tsp. canola oil, optional
½	cup sliced green onions
½	cup butter, cubed, divided
½	cup half-and-half cream
½	cup sour cream
1	tsp. salt
½	tsp. white pepper
1	cup shredded cheddar cheese
	Paprika

1. Scrub and pierce potatoes. Rub with oil if desired. Bake at 400° for 50-75 minutes or until tender. When cool enough to handle, cut each potato in half lengthwise. Scoop out the pulp, leaving a thin shell; set aside.

2. In a small skillet, saute onions in ¼ cup butter until tender. In a large bowl, mash potato pulp. Stir in onion mixture, cream, sour cream, salt and pepper. Fold in the cheese. Stuff into potato shells.

3. Place on a baking sheet. Melt remaining butter; drizzle over potatoes. Sprinkle with paprika. Bake at 375° for 20 minutes or until heated through.

Freeze option: Potatoes may be stuffed ahead of time and refrigerated or frozen. Allow additional time for reheating.

1 serving: 416 cal., 26g fat (17g sat. fat), 84mg chol., 693mg sod., 36g carb. (4g sugars, 3g fiber), 9g pro.

Ranch Stuffed Baked Potatoes: Stir 1 to 2 Tbsp. ranch salad dressing mix into the sour cream before adding to mashed potatoes. Fold in three crumbled cooked bacon strips with the cheese.

Tex-Mex Stuffed Baked Potatoes: Omit green onions and ¼ cup butter. Stir in 1 can (4 oz.) of chopped green chilies, drained. Substitute pepper jack cheese for the cheddar and chili powder for the paprika.

Herb-Stuffed Baked Potatoes: Add 2 Tbsp. each minced chives and fresh parsley with the onions. Substitute mozzarella for the cheddar.

Broccoli-Stuffed Baked Potatoes: Omit green onions. Saute 2 cups fresh broccoli florets and ½ cup chopped onion in ¼ cup butter. Stir into mashed potatoes.

BONUS:

5 INGREDIENTS

CREAMY TWICE-BAKED SWEET POTATOES

The addition of cream cheese makes these twice-baked sweet potatoes very creamy. Unlike some sweet potato dishes, they're not overly sweet. And they're convenient as well delicious. You can prepare them ahead of time, and it's easy to increase the quantity to serve a family or a crowd.

—Linda Call, Falun, KS

PREP: 15 min. • **BAKE:** 1 hour
MAKES: 2 servings

2	medium sweet potatoes (about 10 oz. each)
2	oz. cream cheese, softened
1	Tbsp. brown sugar
¼	tsp. ground cinnamon
2	Tbsp. chopped pecans

1. Preheat oven to 375°. Scrub potatoes; pierce several times with a fork. Bake on a foil-lined baking sheet until tender, 45-60 minutes. Cool slightly.

2. Cut off a thin slice from top of each potato. Scoop out pulp, leaving ¼-in.-thick shells. Mash the pulp with cream cheese, brown sugar and cinnamon. Spoon the pulp mixture into the shells; return to pan. Top with pecans. Bake the potatoes until heated through, 15-20 minutes.

1 stuffed potato: 297 cal., 16g fat (7g sat. fat), 32mg chol., 100mg sod., 36g carb. (18g sugars, 4g fiber), 5g pro.

5 INGREDIENTS
LEMON ROASTED FINGERLINGS & BRUSSELS SPROUTS

I've made this recipe with other veggie combinations, too—the key is choosing ones that roast in about the same amount of time. Try skinny green beans with thinly sliced onions, cauliflower florets with baby carrots, or okra with cherry tomatoes.

—Courtney Gaylord, Columbus, IN

PREP: 15 min. • **BAKE:** 20 min.
MAKES: 8 servings

- 1 lb. fingerling potatoes, halved
- 1 lb. Brussels sprouts, trimmed and halved
- 6 Tbsp. olive oil, divided
- ¾ tsp. salt, divided
- ¼ tsp. pepper
- 3 Tbsp. lemon juice
- 1 garlic clove, minced
- 1 tsp. Dijon mustard
- 1 tsp. honey

1. Preheat oven to 425°. Place potatoes and Brussels sprouts in a greased 15x10x1-in. baking pan. Drizzle with 2 Tbsp. oil; sprinkle with ½ tsp. salt and pepper. Toss to coat. Roast 20-25 minutes or until tender, stirring once.
2. In a small bowl, whisk the lemon juice, garlic, mustard, honey and the remaining oil and salt until blended. Transfer the vegetables to a large bowl; drizzle with vinaigrette and toss to coat. Serve warm.
¾ cup: 167 cal., 10g fat (1g sat. fat), 0 chol., 256mg sod., 17g carb. (3g sugars, 3g fiber), 3g pro. **Diabetic exchanges:** 2 fat, 1 starch, 1 vegetable.

CHERRY TOMATO SALAD

This recipe evolved from a need to use up the bumper crops of cherry tomatoes that we seem to grow each year. It's become a summer favorite, especially at cookouts.
—Sally Sibley, St. Augustine, FL

PREP: 15 min. + marinating
MAKES: 6 servings

- 1 qt. cherry tomatoes, halved
- ¼ cup canola oil
- 3 Tbsp. white vinegar
- ½ tsp. salt
- ½ tsp. sugar
- ¼ cup minced fresh parsley
- 1 to 2 tsp. minced fresh basil
- 1 to 2 tsp. minced fresh oregano

Place tomatoes in a shallow bowl. In a small bowl, whisk oil, vinegar, salt and sugar until blended; stir in herbs. Pour over the tomatoes; gently toss to coat. Refrigerate, covered, overnight.
¾ cup: 103 cal., 10g fat (1g sat. fat), 0 chol., 203mg sod., 4g carb. (3g sugars, 1g fiber), 1g pro. **Diabetic exchanges:** 2 fat, 1 vegetable.

CHEESY SLOW-COOKED CORN

Even those who usually don't eat much corn will ask for a second helping of this creamy, cheesy side dish. Folks love the flavor, but I love how easy it is to make with ingredients I usually have on hand.
—Mary Ann Truitt, Wichita, KS

PREP: 5 min. • **COOK:** 3 hours
MAKES: 12 servings

9½ cups (48 oz.) frozen corn
11 oz. cream cheese, softened
¼ cup butter, cubed
3 Tbsp. water
3 Tbsp. milk
2 Tbsp. sugar
6 slices process American cheese, cut into small pieces

In a 4- or 5-qt. slow cooker, combine all the ingredients. Cook, covered, on low, until heated through and the cheese is melted, 3-4 hours, stirring once.

1 cup: 265 cal., 16g fat (9g sat. fat), 39mg chol., 227mg sod., 27g carb. (6g sugars, 2g fiber), 7g pro.

BONUS:

5 INGREDIENTS
FREEZER SWEET CORN

With this preparation, the corn stays crisp-tender, so I can enjoy it any time of the year. The recipe came from my daughter's mother-in-law, who lives on a farm in Iowa and knows a lot about corn.
—Judy Oudekerk, St. Michael, MN

PREP: 30 min. • **COOK:** 15 min. • **MAKES:** 3 qt.

4 qt. fresh corn (cut from about 20 ears)
1 qt. hot water
⅔ cup sugar
½ cup butter, cubed
2 tsp. salt

In a stockpot, combine all the ingredients; bring to a boil. Reduce heat; simmer, uncovered, 5-7 minutes, stirring occasionally. Transfer to large shallow containers to cool quickly, stirring occasionally. Freeze in resealable plastic freezer bags or freezer containers, allowing headspace for expansion.

½ cup: 113 cal., 5g fat (2g sat. fat), 10mg chol., 245mg sod., 18g carb. (9g sugars, 2g fiber), 2g pro.

COBB SALAD

Made on the fly in 1937 by Hollywood restaurateur Bob Cobb, the Cobb salad now is a world-famous American dish. Here's our fresh take, with all the original appeal and an extra-special presentation. Add your own touches and make it yours.
—*Taste of Home* Test Kitchen

TAKES: 40 min.
MAKES: 6 servings (1¼ cups dressing)

- ¼ cup red wine vinegar
- 2 tsp. salt
- 1 tsp. lemon juice
- 1 small garlic clove, minced
- ¾ tsp. coarsely ground pepper
- ¾ tsp. Worcestershire sauce
- ¼ tsp. sugar
- ¼ tsp. ground mustard
- ¾ cup canola oil
- ¼ cup olive oil

SALAD
- 6½ cups torn romaine
- 2½ cups torn curly endive
- 1 bunch watercress (4 oz.), trimmed, divided
- 2 cooked chicken breasts, chopped
- 2 medium tomatoes, seeded and chopped
- 1 medium ripe avocado, peeled and chopped
- 3 hard-boiled large eggs, chopped
- ½ cup crumbled blue or Roquefort cheese
- 6 bacon strips, cooked and crumbled
- 2 Tbsp. minced fresh chives

1. For the dressing: In a blender, combine the first eight ingredients. While dressing processes, gradually add the canola and olive oils in a steady stream.

2. In a large bowl, combine the romaine, endive and half of the watercress; toss lightly. Transfer to a serving platter. Arrange the chicken, tomatoes, avocado, eggs, cheese and bacon over the greens; sprinkle with chives. Top with remaining watercress. Cover and chill until serving.

3. To serve, drizzle 1 cup dressing over salad. Serve with the remaining dressing if desired.

1 serving: 575 cal., 52g fat (8g sat. fat), 147mg chol., 1171mg sod., 10g carb. (3g sugars, 5g fiber), 20g pro.

"One of my favorite salads. The dressing is light and tasty. Exactly what Cobb salad dressing should be."

—EBRAMKAMP, TASTEOFHOME.COM

MUSHROOM & SPINACH SAUTE

Mushrooms and spinach make a superfast combination that's perfect for two. This recipe is also easy to double or triple for a crowd.
—Pauline Howard, Lago Vista, TX

TAKES: 10 min. • **MAKES:** 2 servings

- 2 tsp. olive oil
- 2 cups sliced fresh mushrooms
- 2 garlic cloves, minced
- 1 pkg. (5 to 6 oz.) fresh baby spinach
- ⅛ tsp. salt
- ⅛ tsp. pepper

In a large skillet, heat oil over medium-high heat. Add mushrooms; saute until tender, about 2 minutes. Add garlic; cook 1 minute longer. Add spinach in batches; cook and stir until wilted, about 1 minute. Season with salt and pepper. Serve immediately.

¾ cup: 76 cal., 5g fat (1g sat. fat), 0 chol., 208mg sod., 6g carb. (2g sugars, 2g fiber), 4g pro. **Diabetic exchanges:** 1 vegetable, 1 fat.

GLAZED SWEET POTATOES

The fresh sweet potatoes Mom grew disappeared fast at our family table when she served them with this easy, flavorful glaze. You can use two 15½ oz. cans of sweet potatoes for this recipe instead of fresh ones; just drain them and skip the first step.
—Rosemary Pryor, Pasadena, MD

PREP: 30 min. • **BAKE:** 30 min.
MAKES: 5 servings

- 2 lbs. sweet potatoes
- ¼ cup butter, cubed
- ¼ cup maple syrup
- ¼ cup packed brown sugar
- ¼ tsp. ground cinnamon

1. Place fresh sweet potatoes in a large saucepan or Dutch oven; cover with water. Bring to a boil. Reduce heat; cover and cook 25-40 minutes or until tender. Drain; cool slightly and peel. Cut potatoes into chunks.

2. Preheat oven to 350°. Place sweet potatoes in a 2-qt. baking dish. In a small saucepan, combine butter, syrup, brown sugar and cinnamon; bring to a boil, stirring constantly. Pour over potatoes.

3. Bake, uncovered, 30-40 minutes or until heated through.

1 cup: 352 cal., 9g fat (6g sat. fat), 24mg chol., 96mg sod., 66g carb. (39g sugars, 6g fiber), 3g pro.

COUNTRY POTATO PANCAKES

These potato pancakes are really versatile. They can be a side dish for just about any meal—they go particularly well with pork—or the main course for a lighter meal. We have them often at our house.
—Lydia Robotewskyj, Franklin, WI

TAKES: 30 min. • **MAKES:** about 24 pancakes

- 3 large potatoes (about 2 lbs.), peeled
- 2 large eggs, lightly beaten
- 1 Tbsp. grated onion
- 2 Tbsp. all-purpose flour
- 1 tsp. salt
- ½ tsp. baking powder
  Vegetable oil
  Chives, finely chopped, optional

1. Finely grate the potatoes. Drain any liquid. Add eggs, onion, flour, salt and baking powder. In a frying pan, add oil to the depth of ⅛ in.; heat over medium-high until a thermometer reads 375°.
2. Drop batter by heaping tablespoonfuls in the hot oil. Flatten into patties. Fry until golden brown, turning once. Sprinkle with finely chopped chives, if desired. Serve immediately.

2 pancakes: 257 cal., 8g fat (1g sat. fat), 31mg chol., 242mg sod., 41g carb. (2g sugars, 5g fiber), 6g pro.

TOP TIP
During the prep stage, get as much of the starchy liquid out of the potatoes as possible. Use a grater instead of a food processor, which leaves more liquid behind. After draining, wrap the shredded potatoes in a paper or cloth towel and squeeze out excess liquid.

POTLUCK TACO SALAD

I found this recipe in an old school cookbook, and I've taken it to many potlucks since then. The layers look so pretty in a glass bowl.
—Sandy Fynaardt, New Sharon, IA

TAKES: 25 min.
MAKES: 8 servings (1 cup dressing)

1 lb. ground beef
1 envelope taco seasoning, divided
1 medium head iceberg lettuce, torn
1 can (16 oz.) kidney beans, rinsed and drained
1 large red onion, chopped
4 medium tomatoes, seeded and finely chopped
2 cups shredded cheddar cheese
4 cups crushed tortilla chips (about 8 oz.)
1 bottle (8 oz.) Thousand Island salad dressing
2 Tbsp. taco sauce

1. In a large skillet, cook beef over medium heat for 6-8 minutes or until no longer pink, breaking into crumbles; drain. Stir in 3 Tbsp. taco seasoning.

2. In a large bowl, layer the beef mixture, lettuce, beans, onion, tomatoes, cheese and crushed chips. In a small bowl, mix the salad dressing, taco sauce and the remaining taco seasoning; serve dressing with the salad.

1½ cups salad with 2 Tbsp. dressing: 574 cal., 34g fat (11g sat. fat), 66mg chol., 1109mg sod., 44g carb. (9g sugars, 5g fiber), 23g pro.

"I've made this for years now—for my family, lunches for my colleagues, and parties. Everyone raves about it and wants the recipe."
—MAGICKAT_CT, TASTEOFHOME.COM

MAMA'S POTATO SALAD

This old-fashioned potato salad recipe doesn't have many ingredients, so it isn't as colorful as many you find nowadays. But Mama made it the way her mother did, and that's the way I make it today. See if it isn't one of the best potato salads you've ever eaten!
—Sandra Anderson, New York, NY

TAKES: 30 min. • **MAKES:** 12 servings

- 3 to 3½ lbs. potatoes (about 10 medium)
- 6 hard-boiled large eggs
- 1 medium onion, finely chopped
- ½ cup mayonnaise
- ½ cup evaporated milk
- 3 Tbsp. white vinegar
- 2 Tbsp. prepared mustard
- ¼ cup sugar
- 1 tsp. salt
- ¼ tsp. pepper
  Additional hard-boiled large eggs, sliced
  Paprika

1. In a large kettle, cook potatoes in boiling salted water until tender. Drain and cool. Peel potatoes; cut into chunks. Separate egg yolks from whites. Set the yolks aside. Chop the egg whites and add to potatoes with onion.
2. In a small bowl, mash the yolks. Stir in mayonnaise, milk, vinegar, mustard, sugar, salt and pepper. Pour over potatoes; toss well. Adjust seasonings if necessary. Spoon into a serving bowl. Garnish with egg slices and paprika. Chill until serving.
1 cup: 231 cal., 11g fat (2g sat. fat), 113mg chol., 323mg sod., 27g carb. (8g sugars, 2g fiber), 6g pro.

BONUS: GERMAN POTATO SALAD

I'd always loved the potato salad my German grandmother made. So when I married a potato farmer and had spuds in abundance, I played with recipes that sounded similar until I came up with this salad that reminds me of hers.
—Sue Hartman, Parma, ID

TAKES: 25 min. • **MAKES:** 8 servings

- 5 bacon strips
- ¾ cup chopped onion
- 2 Tbsp. all-purpose flour
- 1 tsp. salt
- ⅛ tsp. pepper
- 1⅓ cups water
- ⅔ cup cider vinegar
- ¼ cup sugar
- 6 cups sliced cooked peeled potatoes

1. In a large skillet, fry bacon until crisp; remove and set aside. Drain all but 2-3 Tbsp. of the drippings; cook onion in the remaining drippings until tender. Stir in the flour, salt and pepper until blended. Add water and vinegar; cook and stir for 1 minute or until slightly thickened.
2. Stir in sugar until dissolved. Crumble bacon; gently stir in bacon and potatoes. Heat through, stirring lightly to coat potatoes. Serve warm.
1 cup: 119 cal., 8g fat (3g sat. fat), 9mg chol., 399mg sod., 10g carb. (8g sugars, 0 fiber), 2g pro.

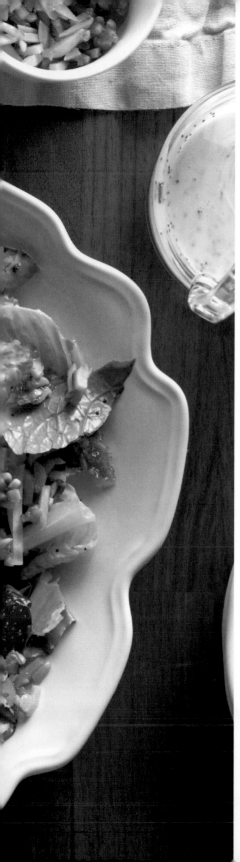

STRAWBERRY SALAD WITH POPPY SEED DRESSING

My family is always happy to see this fruit and veggie salad. If strawberries aren't available, use mandarin oranges and dried cranberries. To make this into a main dish, grill 2 lbs. of boneless, skinless chicken breasts, then slice and add them to the salad.
—Irene Keller, Kalamazoo, MI

TAKES: 30 min. • **MAKES:** 10 servings

- ¼ cup sugar
- ⅓ cup slivered almonds
- 1 bunch romaine, torn (about 8 cups)
- 1 small onion, halved and thinly sliced
- 2 cups halved fresh strawberries

DRESSING
- ¼ cup mayonnaise
- 2 Tbsp. sugar
- 1 Tbsp. sour cream
- 1 Tbsp. 2% milk
- 2¼ tsp. cider vinegar
- 1½ tsp. poppy seeds

1. Place the sugar in a small heavy skillet; cook and stir over medium-low heat until melted and caramel colored, about 10 minutes. Stir in almonds until coated. Spread on foil to cool.
2. Place romaine, onion and strawberries in a large bowl. Whisk together dressing ingredients; toss with the salad. Break candied almonds into pieces; sprinkle over the salad. Serve immediately.
¾ cup: 110 cal., 6g fat (1g sat. fat), 1mg chol., 33mg sod., 13g carb. (10g sugars, 2g fiber), 2g pro. **Diabetic exchanges:** ½ starch, 1 vegetable, 1 fat.

BONUS: BASIC BUTTERMILK SALAD DRESSING

When serving salad to a crowd, this recipe comes in handy. It makes a full quart of creamy, delicious dressing to toss with favorite greens and veggies.
—Patricia Mele, Lower Burrell, PA

TAKES: 5 min. • **MAKES:** 32 servings (2 Tbsp. each)

- 2 cups mayonnaise
- 2 cups buttermilk
- 1 Tbsp. onion powder
- 1 Tbsp. dried parsley flakes
- 1½ tsp. garlic powder
- ½ tsp. salt
- ½ tsp. celery salt
- ¼ tsp. pepper

Whisk together all ingredients. Refrigerate, covered, until serving.
2 Tbsp.: 98 cal., 10g fat (2g sat. fat), 2mg chol., 155mg sod., 1g carb. (1g sugars, 0 fiber), 1g pro. **Diabetic exchanges:** 2 fat

EASY MACARONI SALAD

This hearty pasta salad is sure to please appetites of all ages. It serves a lot of folks, but it's easy to cut down if you want it for a smaller gathering.
—LaVerna Mjones, Moorhead, MN

PREP: 15 min. + chilling
MAKES: 34 servings

- 2   lbs. uncooked elbow macaroni
- 12   hard-boiled large eggs, chopped
- 2½   lbs. fully cooked ham, cubed
- 1   pkg. (16 oz.) frozen peas, thawed
- 3   cups sliced celery
- 1   large green pepper, chopped
- ½   cup chopped onion
- 1   jar (4 oz.) diced pimientos, drained
- 4   cups mayonnaise

1. Cook macaroni according to package directions. Rinse in cold water; drain and cool completely.
2. Place the macaroni in a large bowl; stir in all of the remaining ingredients. Cover and refrigerate salad for at least 3 hours before serving.
1 cup: 380 cal., 26g fat (4g sat. fat), 102mg chol., 615mg sod., 23g carb. (2g sugars, 2g fiber), 13g pro.

FREEZE IT
JEN'S BAKED BEANS

My daughters wanted baked beans, so I gave homemade ones a shot. With mustard, molasses and a dash of heat, these beans are absolutely irresistible.
—Jennifer Heasley, York, PA

PREP: 20 min. • **BAKE:** 50 min.
MAKES: 8 servings

- 6   bacon strips, chopped
- 4   cans (15½ oz. each) great northern beans, rinsed and drained
- 1⅓   cups ketchup
- ⅔   cup packed brown sugar
- ⅓   cup molasses
- 3   Tbsp. yellow mustard
- 2½   tsp. garlic powder
- 1½   tsp. hot pepper sauce
- ¼   tsp. crushed red pepper flakes

1. Preheat oven to 325°. In an ovenproof Dutch oven, cook bacon over medium heat until crisp, stirring occasionally. Remove with a slotted spoon; drain on paper towels. Discard drippings.
2. Return bacon to the pan. Stir in the remaining ingredients; bring to a boil. Place in oven; bake beans, covered, for 50-60 minutes to allow flavors to blend.
Freeze option: Freeze cooled baked beans in freezer containers. To use, partially thaw in refrigerator overnight. Heat through in a saucepan, stirring occasionally; add broth or water if necessary.
¾ cup: 362 cal., 3g fat (1g sat. fat), 6mg chol., 1000mg sod., 71g carb. (39g sugars, 11g fiber), 13g pro.

THANKSGIVING STUFFING

This nicely seasoned stuffing is our favorite for holiday turkeys. It doesn't require a lot of prep time, which I like, and it tastes good whether it's stuffed in the bird or baked separately.
—Denise Goedeken, Platte Center, NE

PREP: 25 min. • **BAKE:** 30 min.
MAKES: about 12 cups

3 large onions, chopped
6 celery ribs, chopped
½ cup butter, cubed
3 garlic cloves, minced
4½ cups chicken or vegetable broth
½ cup minced fresh parsley
1 Tbsp. rubbed sage
1½ tsp. poultry seasoning
1½ tsp. salt
¾ tsp. pepper
1½ lbs. day-old French bread, cubed (27 cups)

1. Preheat oven to 350°. In a large skillet, saute the onions and celery in butter until tender; add garlic, cook 1 minute longer. Transfer to a large bowl; add the broth, parsley, sage, poultry seasoning, salt and pepper. Gently stir in the bread cubes until mixed.
2. Spoon into a greased 13x9-in. baking dish (dish will be full). Bake, uncovered, for 30-35 minutes or until lightly browned and heated through.
1 cup: 249 cal., 10g fat (5g sat. fat), 20mg chol., 1086mg sod., 34g carb. (4g sugars, 3g fiber), 7g pro.

BONUS: OYSTER STUFFING

This recipe came from my mother. She made it every Thanksgiving for my father, who absolutely loves it.
—Amy Daniels, Brodhead, WI

PREP: 30 min. • **BAKE:** 30 min.
MAKES: 4 servings

1 celery rib, chopped
1 small onion, chopped
¼ cup butter, cubed
2 Tbsp. minced fresh parsley
¼ tsp. poultry seasoning
⅛ tsp. rubbed sage
⅛ tsp. pepper
3 cups cubed day-old bread
1 large egg, beaten
⅔ cup chicken broth
1 cup shucked oysters, drained and coarsely chopped

1. Preheat oven to 350°. In a small skillet, saute the celery and onion in butter until tender; transfer to a large bowl. Stir in the parsley, poultry seasoning, sage and pepper. Add the bread cubes. Combine the egg, broth and oysters; add to the bread mixture, stirring gently to combine.
2. Transfer to a greased 1-qt. baking dish. Cover and bake for 20 minutes. Uncover; bake about 10-15 minutes longer or until a thermometer reads 160° and the stuffing is lightly browned.
¾ cup: 228 cal., 15g fat (8g sat. fat), 106mg chol., 495mg sod., 17g carb. (2g sugars, 1g fiber), 7g pro.

5 INGREDIENTS

LEMON PARMESAN ORZO

A splash of lemon and a sprinkle of chopped parsley brighten this orzo, It's fantastic with chicken, pork and fish, or on its own as a light lunch.
—Leslie Palmer, Swampscott, MA

TAKES: 20 min. • **MAKES:** 4 servings

- 1 **cup uncooked whole wheat orzo pasta**
- 1 **Tbsp. olive oil**
- ¼ **cup grated Parmesan cheese**
- 2 **Tbsp. minced fresh parsley**
- ½ **tsp. grated lemon zest**
- ¼ **tsp. salt**
- ¼ **tsp. pepper**

Cook orzo according to the package directions; drain. Transfer to a small bowl; drizzle with olive oil. Stir in the remaining ingredients.

½ cup: 191 cal., 6g fat (1g sat. fat), 4mg chol., 225mg sod., 28g carb. (0 sugars, 7g fiber), 7g pro. **Diabetic exchanges:** 2 starch, ½ fat.

NOTES

BREADS & ROLLS

FOR BREAKFAST, LUNCH OR DINNER, FRESHLY BAKED BREAD IS ALWAYS A WINNER!

FLAVORFUL HERB BREAD

Made in a bread machine, this loaf is one of my favorites because it has a wonderful texture and slices beautifully. The flavor of the herbs really comes through. It makes super sandwiches.
—Gerri Hamilton, Kingsville, ON

PREP: 15 min. • **BAKE:** 3-4 hours
MAKES: 1 loaf (2 lbs.)

- 1 cup warm milk (70° to 80°)
- 1 large egg, room temperature
- 2 Tbsp. butter, softened
- ¼ cup dried minced onion
- 2 Tbsp. sugar
- 1½ tsp. salt
- 2 Tbsp. dried parsley flakes
- 1 tsp. dried oregano
- 3½ cups bread flour
- 2 tsp. active dry yeast

Place all the ingredients in a bread machine pan in the order suggested by the manufacturer. Select the basic bread setting. Choose crust color and loaf size if available. Bake according to the bread machine directions (check dough after 5 minutes of mixing; add 1 to 2 Tbsp. water or flour if needed).

Note: We recommend you do not use a bread machine's time-delay feature for this recipe.

1 slice: 125 cal., 2g fat (1g sat. fat), 19mg chol., 248mg sod., 23g carb. (3g sugars, 1g fiber), 5g pro.

DILLY ROLLS

These versatile rolls are perfect to serve warm alongside any dinner. I always make a big batch since my family enjoys the rolls when they're cool, too, stuffed with filling like egg salad or ham salad.
—Mary Bickel, Terre Haute, IN

PREP: 25 min. + rising • **BAKE:** 20 min.
MAKES: 2 dozen

- 2 cups 4% cottage cheese
- 2 Tbsp. butter
- 2 pkg. (¼ oz. each) active dry yeast
- ½ cup warm water (110° to 115°)
- 2 large eggs, room temperature
- ¼ cup sugar
- 2 Tbsp. dried minced onion
- 1 to 2 Tbsp. dill weed
- 1 Tbsp. salt
- ½ tsp. baking soda
- 4½ to 5 cups all-purpose flour

1. In a large saucepan over medium heat, cook cottage cheese and butter until butter is melted. Cool to 110° to 115°. In a large bowl, dissolve yeast in water. Add eggs, sugar, onion, dill, salt, baking soda and cottage cheese mixture. Add 3 cups of flour; beat until smooth. Add enough remaining flour to form a soft dough.

2. Turn onto a floured surface; knead until smooth and elastic, 6-8 minutes. Place in a greased bowl, turning once to grease the top. Cover and let rise in a warm place until doubled, about 1 hour.

3. Punch dough down. Form into 24 balls; place in a 13x9-in. baking pan that has been sprayed with cooking spray. Cover and let the rolls rise until doubled, about 45 minutes.

4. Bake at 350° for 20-25 minutes.

1 roll: 130 cal., 2g fat (1g sat. fat), 24mg chol., 404mg sod., 21g carb. (3g sugars, 1g fiber), 5g pro.

HONEY BAGELS

Who has time to make from-scratch bagels? You do, with this easy recipe! The chewy golden bagels offer a hint of honey and are sure to impress the pickiest of palates.
—Taste of Home Test Kitchen

PREP: 1 hour + standing • **BAKE:** 20 min.
MAKES: 1 dozen

1	Tbsp. active dry yeast
1¼	cups warm water (110° to 115°)
3	Tbsp. canola oil
3	Tbsp. sugar
3	Tbsp. plus ¼ cup honey, divided
1	tsp. brown sugar
1½	tsp. salt
1	large egg
4	to 5 cups bread flour
1	Tbsp. dried minced onion
1	Tbsp. sesame seeds
1	Tbsp. poppy seeds

1. In a large bowl, dissolve yeast in warm water. Add the oil, sugar, 3 Tbsp. honey, brown sugar, salt and egg; mix well. Stir in enough flour to form a soft dough.

2. Turn onto a floured surface; knead until a smooth firm dough forms, for about 8-10 minutes. Cover and let rest for 10 minutes.

3. Punch dough down. Shape into 12 balls. Push thumb through centers to form a 1½-in. hole. Stretch and shape the dough to form an even ring. Place on a floured surface. Cover and let rest for 10 minutes; flatten bagels slightly.

4. In a large saucepan or Dutch oven, bring 8 cups water and the remaining honey to a boil. Drop the bagels, one at a time, into the boiling water. Cook for 45 seconds; turn and cook 45 seconds longer. Remove with a slotted spoon; drain and sprinkle with onion, sesame and poppy seeds.

5. Place bagels 2 in. apart on baking sheets lined with parchment paper. Bake at 425° for 12 minutes. Turn and bake until golden brown, about 5 minutes longer.

1 bagel: 265 cal., 5g fat (1g sat. fat), 16mg chol., 303mg sod., 48g carb. (14g sugars, 2g fiber), 7g pro.

BONUS:

5 INGREDIENTS

HONEY CINNAMON BUTTER

This is a simple but special spread for toast, muffins and bagels. The sweetness of the honey and warm cinnamon spice pair well together.
—Sue Seymour, Valatie, NY

TAKES: 5 min. • **MAKES:** about 1⅓ cups

1	cup butter, softened
½	cup honey
1	tsp. ground cinnamon

Beat all ingredients until smooth. Store tightly covered in the refrigerator.

1 Tbsp.: 107 cal., 9g fat (6g sat. fat), 24mg chol., 73mg sod., 7g carb. (7g sugars, 0 fiber), 0 pro.

PULL-APART BACON BREAD

I stumbled across this recipe while looking for something different to take to a brunch. Boy, am I glad I did! Everyone asked for the recipe and was surprised it called for only five ingredients. It can't be beat as treat to bake and take to any informal get-together.
—Traci Collins, Cheyenne, WY

PREP: 20 min. + rising • **BAKE:** 55 min.
MAKES: 16 servings

- 12 **bacon strips, diced**
- 1 **loaf (1 lb.) frozen bread dough, thawed**
- 2 **Tbsp. olive oil, divided**
- 1 **cup shredded part-skim mozzarella cheese**
- 1 **envelope (1 oz.) ranch salad dressing mix**

1. In a large skillet, cook the bacon over medium heat for 5 minutes or until partially cooked; drain on paper towels. Roll out dough to ½-in. thickness; brush with 1 Tbsp. of oil. Cut into 1-in. pieces; place in a large bowl. Add the bacon, cheese, dressing mix and the remaining oil; toss to coat.

2. Arrange dough pieces in a 9x5-in. oval on a parchment-lined baking sheet, layering as needed. Cover and let rise in a warm place for 30 minutes or until the dough has doubled.

3. Bake at 350° for 40 minutes. Cover with foil; bake bread 15 minutes longer or until golden brown.

1 serving: 149 cal., 6g fat (2g sat. fat), 8mg chol., 621mg sod., 17g carb. (1g sugars, 1g fiber), 6g pro.

▬ NOTES

_____
_____
_____
_____
_____
_____
_____
_____
_____
_____
_____

EASY CHEESY BISCUITS

I'm a big fan of homemade biscuits...but not the rolling and cutting that goes into making them. The drop biscuit method solves everything.
—Christina Addison, Blanchester, OH

TAKES: 30 min. • **MAKES:** 1 dozen

- 3 cups all-purpose flour
- 3 tsp. baking powder
- 1 Tbsp. sugar
- 1 tsp. salt
- ¾ tsp. cream of tartar
- ½ cup cold butter
- 1 cup shredded sharp cheddar cheese
- 1 garlic clove, minced
- ¼ to ½ tsp. crushed red pepper flakes
- 1¼ cups 2% milk

1. Preheat oven to 450°. In a large bowl, whisk flour, baking powder, sugar, salt and cream of tartar. Cut in butter until mixture resembles coarse crumbs. Stir in cheese, garlic and pepper flakes. Add milk; stir just until moistened.

2. Drop dough by heaping ¼ cupfuls 2 in. apart onto a greased baking sheet. Bake until golden brown, 18-20 minutes. Serve biscuits warm.

1 biscuit: 237 cal., 12g fat (7g sat. fat), 32mg chol., 429mg sod., 26g carb. (2g sugars, 1g fiber), 7g pro.

GARLIC HERB BUBBLE LOAF

I adapted an old sour cream bread recipe for this deliciously different pull-apart loaf. It has a light crust, tender interior and lots of herb and butter flavor. It's wonderful served next to a hot bowl of potato soup.
—Katie Crill, Priest River, ID

PREP: 25 min. + rising • **BAKE:** 35 min.
MAKES: 18 servings

- ½ cup water (70° to 80°)
- ½ cup sour cream
- 2 Tbsp. butter, softened
- 3 Tbsp. sugar
- 1½ tsp. salt
- 3 cups bread flour
- 2¼ tsp. active dry yeast

GARLIC HERB BUTTER
- ¼ cup butter, melted
- 4 garlic cloves, minced
- ¼ tsp. each dried oregano, thyme and rosemary, crushed

1. Place the first seven ingredients in a bread machine pan, in the order suggested by the manufacturer. Select the dough setting (check dough after 5 minutes of mixing; add 1-2 Tbsp. of water or flour if needed).

2. When cycle is completed, turn dough onto a lightly floured surface. Cover and let rest for 15 minutes. Divide dough into 36 pieces. Shape each piece into a ball. In a shallow bowl, combine butter, garlic and herbs. Dip each ball in the butter mixture; place in an ungreased 9x5-in. loaf pan. Cover and let rise in a warm place until doubled, about 45 minutes.

3. Bake at 375° for 35-40 minutes or until golden brown (cover loosely with foil if bread browns too quickly). Remove from pan to a wire rack. Serve warm.

Note: We recommend you do not use a bread machine's time-delay feature for this recipe.

1 serving: 141 cal., 6g fat (3g sat. fat), 12mg chol., 230mg sod., 19g carb. (2g sugars, 1g fiber), 3g pro.

BEST EVER BANANA BREAD

Whenever I pass a display of bananas in the grocery store, I can almost smell the wonderful aroma of this bread. It really is that good!
—Gert Kaiser, Kenosha, WI

PREP: 15 min. • **BAKE:** 1¼ hours + cooling
MAKES: 1 loaf (16 slices)

1¾ cups all-purpose flour
1½ cups sugar
1 tsp. baking soda
½ tsp. salt
2 large eggs, room temperature
2 medium ripe bananas, mashed (1 cup)
½ cup canola oil
¼ cup plus 1 Tbsp. buttermilk
1 tsp. vanilla extract
1 cup chopped walnuts

1. Preheat oven to 325°. Grease a 9x5-in. loaf pan; set aside. In a large bowl, stir together the flour, sugar, baking soda and salt. In another bowl, combine eggs, bananas, oil, buttermilk and vanilla; add to the flour mixture, stirring just until combined. Fold in nuts.
2. Pour into prepared loaf pan. Bake for 1¼ to 1½ hours or until a toothpick comes out clean. Cool on a wire rack.
1 slice: 255 cal., 12g fat (1g sat. fat), 27mg chol., 166mg sod., 34g carb. (21g sugars, 1g fiber), 4g pro.

BONUS:
ZUCCHINI NUT BREAD

Lighter and fluffier than most zucchini breads, this recipe is a great way to put surplus zucchini to good use.
—Kevin Bruckerhoff, Columbia, MO

PREP: 15 min. • **BAKE:** 55 min. + cooling
MAKES: 2 loaves (12 slices each)

2 cups sugar
1 cup canola oil
3 large eggs, room temperature
2 tsp. vanilla extract
3 cups all-purpose flour
1 tsp. salt
1 tsp. baking soda
1 tsp. grated lemon zest
1 tsp. ground cinnamon
¼ tsp. baking powder
2 cups shredded zucchini (about 2 medium)
½ cup chopped walnuts or pecans

1. Preheat oven to 350°. Grease two 8x4-in. loaf pans; set aside. In a large bowl, beat sugar, oil, eggs and vanilla until well blended. In another bowl, whisk flour, salt, baking soda, lemon zest, cinnamon and baking powder; gradually beat into sugar mixture, mixing just until moistened. Stir in zucchini and walnuts.
2. Transfer batter to prepared pans. Bake for 55-65 minutes or until a toothpick inserted in center comes out clean. Cool 10 minutes before removing from pans to wire racks to cool.
1 slice: 229 cal., 11g fat (1g sat. fat), 26mg chol., 165mg sod., 29g carb. (17g sugars, 1g fiber), 3g pro.

CARAMEL-PECAN STICKY BUNS

My mother made delicious cinnamon rolls when I was a child. Later, she taught my sister and me to make them. I've since added the caramel and pecans. These scrumptious, fragrant buns are a huge hit wherever I take them.
—Judy Powell, Star, ID

PREP: 30 min. + rising • **BAKE:** 30 min.
MAKES: 1 dozen

- 1 pkg. (¼ oz.) active dry yeast
- ¾ cup warm water (110° to 115°)
- ¾ cup warm milk (110° to 115°)
- ¼ cup sugar
- 3 Tbsp. canola oil
- 2 tsp. salt
- 3¾ to 4¼ cups all-purpose flour

FILLING
- ¼ cup butter, softened
- ¼ cup sugar
- 3 tsp. ground cinnamon
- ¾ cup packed brown sugar
- ½ cup heavy whipping cream
- 1 cup coarsely chopped pecans

1. In a large bowl, dissolve yeast in warm water. Add the milk, sugar, oil, salt and 1¼ cups flour. Beat on medium speed for 2-3 minutes or until smooth. Stir in enough of the remaining flour to form a soft dough.

2. Turn onto a floured surface; knead until smooth and elastic, 6-8 minutes. Place in a greased bowl, turning once to grease top. Cover and let rise in a warm place until doubled, about 1 hour.

3. Punch dough down. Turn onto a lightly floured surface. Roll into an 18x12-in. rectangle. Spread butter to within ½ in. of edges. Combine sugar and cinnamon; sprinkle over butter. Roll up jelly-roll style, starting with a long side; pinch seam to seal. Cut into 12 slices.

4. Combine the brown sugar and cream; pour into a greased 13x9-in. baking pan. Sprinkle with pecans. Place rolls cut side down over the pecans. Cover and let rise until doubled, about 1 hour.

5. Bake at 350° for 30-35 minutes or until well browned. Cool for 1 minute before inverting onto a serving platter.

1 sticky bun: 405 cal., 19g fat (6g sat. fat), 26mg chol., 450mg sod., 55g carb. (23g sugars, 2g fiber), 6g pro.

TOP TIP

Quick-rise yeast can be used instead of active dry yeast in recipes. However, quick-rise yeast doesn't need to be dissolved in water before mixing, and it requires only one rise. In place of its first rise, cover the dough and let it rest for 10 minutes before shaping it. Once you have shaped it, the rise should take about half the time listed for active dry yeast.

CRANBERRY ORANGE SCONES

Moist and scrumptious, these scones come out perfect every time. There's nothing better than serving these remarkable scones warm with the delicate orange butter.
—Karen McBride, Indianapolis, IN

PREP: 20 min. • **BAKE:** 15 min.
MAKES: 10 scones

- 2 cups all-purpose flour
- 10 tsp. sugar, divided
- 1 Tbsp. grated orange zest
- 2 tsp. baking powder
- ½ tsp. salt
- ¼ tsp. baking soda
- ⅓ cup cold butter
- 1 cup dried cranberries
- ¼ cup orange juice
- ¼ cup half-and-half cream
- 1 large egg, room temperature
- 1 Tbsp. whole milk

GLAZE (OPTIONAL)
- ½ cup confectioners' sugar
- 1 Tbsp. orange juice

ORANGE BUTTER
- ½ cup butter, softened
- 2 to 3 Tbsp. orange marmalade

1. Preheat oven to 400°. In a large bowl, combine flour, 7 tsp. sugar, the orange zest, baking powder, salt and baking soda. Cut in butter until the mixture resembles coarse crumbs; set aside. In a small bowl, combine the cranberries, orange juice, cream and egg. Add to the flour mixture and stir until a soft dough forms.

2. On a floured surface, gently knead dough 6-8 times. Pat into an 8-in. circle. Cut into 10 wedges. Separate wedges and place on a greased baking sheet. Brush with milk; sprinkle with remaining sugar.

3. Bake for 12-15 minutes or until lightly browned. Remove to a wire rack.

4. Combine glaze ingredients if desired; drizzle over scones. Combine the orange butter ingredients; serve butter with the warm scones.

1 scone: 331 cal., 17g fat (10g sat. fat), 65mg chol., 396mg sod., 43g carb. (22g sugars, 1g fiber), 4g pro.

BUTTERY CORNBREAD

A friend gave me this recipe several years ago, and it's my favorite. I love to serve the melt-in-your mouth bread hot from the oven with butter and syrup. It gets rave reviews on holidays and at potluck dinners—and around the kitchen table.
—Nicole Callen, Auburn, CA

PREP: 15 min. • **BAKE:** 25 min.
MAKES: 15 servings

- ⅔ cup butter, softened
- 1 cup sugar
- 3 large eggs, room temperature
- 1⅔ cups 2% milk
- 2⅓ cups all-purpose flour
- 1 cup cornmeal
- 4½ tsp. baking powder
- 1 tsp. salt

1. Preheat oven to 400°. Grease a 13x9-in. baking pan; set aside. In a large bowl, cream butter and sugar until light and fluffy. Combine eggs and milk. Combine flour, cornmeal, baking powder and salt; add to the creamed mixture alternately with the egg mixture.

2. Pour batter into prepared pan. Bake 22-27 minutes or until a toothpick inserted in the center comes out clean. Cut into squares; serve warm.

1 slice: 259 cal., 10g fat (6g sat. fat), 68mg chol., 386mg sod., 37g carb. (15g sugars, 1g fiber), 5g pro.

ICEBOX BUTTERHORNS

If you like a roll that melts in your mouth, try my Mom's recipe. She had a way with the dough, giving it just the right touch to turn out beautiful buttery rolls every time. With this recipe, you can too.

— Judy Clark, Elkhart, IN

PREP: 15 min. + chilling • **BAKE:** 15 min.
MAKES: 2 dozen

- 2 pkg. (¼ oz. each) active dry yeast
- ¼ cup warm water (110° to 115°)
- 2 cups warm whole milk (110° to 115°)
- ¾ cup butter, melted
- ½ cup sugar
- 1 large egg, room temperature
- 1 tsp. salt
- 6½ cups all-purpose flour
  Additional melted butter

1. In a small bowl, dissolve yeast in warm water. In a large bowl, combine the milk, butter, sugar, egg, salt, the yeast mixture and 3 cups flour; beat on medium speed until smooth. Stir in enough remaining flour to form a soft dough (the dough will be sticky).

2. Do not knead. Place in a greased bowl, turning once to grease the top. Cover with plastic wrap and refrigerate overnight.

3. Punch down dough. Turn onto a lightly floured surface; divide in half. Roll each portion into a 12-in. circle; cut each circle into 12 wedges. Roll up wedges from the wide end. Place 2 in. apart on greased baking sheets, point side down. Cover with kitchen towels; let rise in a warm place until doubled, about 1 hour.

4. Bake at 350° for 15-20 minutes or until golden brown. Immediately brush with additional melted butter. Remove from pans to wire racks to cool.

1 roll: 206 cal., 7g fat (4g sat. fat), 27mg chol., 170mg sod., 31g carb. (6g sugars, 1g fiber), 5g pro.

NOTES

_____
_____
_____
_____
_____
_____
_____
_____
_____
_____
_____
_____

PARMESAN-BACON BUBBLE BREAD

When I needed to put some leftover bread dough to good use, I started with a recipe I often use for bubble bread and substituted savory ingredients for the usual sweet ones.

—Lori McLain, Denton, TX

PREP: 20 min. + rising • **BAKE:** 20 min.
MAKES: 16 servings

1	loaf frozen bread dough, thawed (16 oz.)
¼	cup butter, melted
¾	cup shredded Parmesan cheese
6	bacon strips, cooked and finely crumbled
⅓	cup finely chopped green onions
2	Tbsp. grated Parmesan cheese
2	Tbsp. salt-free herb seasoning blend
1½	tsp. sugar
	Alfredo sauce, optional

1. Turn the dough onto a lightly floured surface; divide and shape into 16 rolls.
2. Place butter in a shallow bowl. In a second large bowl, combine the next six ingredients. Dip the dough pieces in the melted butter, then toss with the cheese mixture to coat. Stack pieces in a greased 9-in. cast-iron skillet.
3. Cover with a kitchen towel and let rise in a warm place until almost doubled, about 45 minutes. Bake at 350° until golden brown, for 20-25 minutes. Serve warm, with Alfredo sauce if desired.

1 piece: 140 cal., 6g fat (3g sat. fat), 14mg chol., 311mg sod., 14g carb. (2g sugars, 1g fiber), 6g pro.

"This bread is easy and delicious— it gets so light and crispy. And my family really enjoyed it. I will definitely make it again!"

—CATBIRD513, TASTEOFHOME.COM

TOP TIP

Instead of the Alfredo sauce suggested, you can serve this bread with marinara sauce or pesto. Better still, set out all three and let guests choose their favorite! You can also bake the dough in a greased 9x5-in. loaf pan.

AMISH POTATO BREAD

A mix of whole wheat and all-purpose flour, plus mashed potatoes, gives this golden bread its wonderful texture.
—Sue Violette, Neillsville, WI

PREP: 30 min. + rising
BAKE: 40 min. + cooling
MAKES: 1 loaf (16 slices)

 1   pkg. (¼ oz.) active dry yeast
 ¼   cup warm water (110° to 115°)
 1¾ cups warm fat-free
     milk (110° to 115°)
 ⅓   cup butter, softened
 ¼   cup mashed potatoes (without
     added milk and butter)
 3   Tbsp. sugar
 1½ tsp. salt
 1½ cups whole wheat flour
 3½ to 4 cups all-purpose flour

1. In a large bowl, dissolve yeast in warm water. Add the milk, butter, potatoes, sugar, salt, whole wheat flour and ½ cup all-purpose flour. Beat until smooth. Stir in enough of the remaining flour to form a firm dough.

2. Turn onto a lightly floured surface; knead until smooth and elastic, for about 6-8 minutes. Place in a bowl coated with cooking spray, turning once to coat the top. Cover and let rise in a warm place until doubled, about 1 hour.

3. Punch dough down and turn onto a floured surface; shape into a loaf. Place in a 9x5-in. loaf pan coated with cooking spay. Cover and let rise until doubled, about 30 minutes.

4. Bake at 350° for 40-45 minutes or until golden brown. Remove from pan to wire rack to cool.

1 slice: 193 cal., 4g fat (2g sat. fat), 11mg chol., 276mg sod., 33g carb. (4g sugars, 2g fiber), 6g pro. **Diabetic exchanges:** 2 starch, 1 fat.

CLASSIC IRISH SODA BREAD

This traditional Irish soda bread can be made with an assortment of mix-ins such as dried fruit and nuts; I like it with a handful of raisins. It's the perfect change-of-pace item to bring to a get-together.
—Gloria Warczak, Cedarburg, WI

PREP: 15 min. • **BAKE:** 30 min.
MAKES: 8 servings

 2   cups all-purpose flour
 2   Tbsp. brown sugar
 1   tsp. baking powder
 1   tsp. baking soda
 ½   tsp. salt
 3   Tbsp. cold butter, cubed
 2   large eggs, divided use,
     room temperature
 ¾   cup buttermilk
 ⅓   cup raisins

1. Preheat oven to 375°. Grease a baking sheet; set aside. Whisk together first five ingredients. Cut in butter until the mixture resembles coarse crumbs. In another bowl, whisk together one egg and the buttermilk. Add to the flour mixture; stir just until moistened. Stir in raisins.

2. Turn dough onto a lightly floured surface; knead gently 6-8 times. Shape into a 6½-in. round loaf; place loaf on prepared baking sheet. Using a sharp knife, make a shallow cross in the top of the loaf. Whisk the remaining egg; brush over top.

3. Bake 30-35 minutes or until golden brown. Remove from pan to a wire rack. Serve warm.

1 piece: 210 cal., 6g fat (3g sat. fat), 59mg chol., 463mg sod., 33g carb. (8g sugars, 1g fiber), 6g pro.

BEST EVER BREADSTICKS

Present these breadsticks alongside an Italian favorite like lasagna or spaghetti. They're an attractive and edible addition to the table setting.
—Carol Wolfer, Lebanon, OR

PREP: 20 min. + rising
BAKE: 10 min. + cooling
MAKES: about 24 breadsticks

3	to 3¼ **cups all-purpose flour**
1	**pkg. (¼ oz.) quick-rise yeast**
1	**Tbsp. sugar**
1	**tsp. salt**
¾	**cup whole milk**
¼	**cup plus 1 Tbsp. water, divided**
1	**Tbsp. butter**
1	**large egg white**
	Coarse salt

1. Combine 1½ cups flour, yeast, sugar and salt. In a small saucepan, heat milk, ¼ cup water and butter to 120°-130°. Add to dry ingredients; beat on medium speed just until moistened. Stir in enough of the remaining flour to form a stiff dough.

2. Turn dough onto a lightly floured surface; knead until smooth and elastic, 6-8 minutes. Place in a greased bowl, turning once to grease top. Cover with plastic; let rise in a warm place until doubled, about 30 minutes. Punch down dough. Pinch off golf ball-size pieces. On a lightly floured surface, shape each piece into a 6-in. rope. Place on greased baking sheets 1 in. apart. Cover and let rise for 15 minutes.

3. Preheat oven to 400°. Beat egg white and remaining water; brush over the breadsticks. Sprinkle with coarse salt. Bake until golden, about 10 minutes. Remove from pans to wire racks to cool.

1 breadstick: 93 cal., 1g fat (1g sat. fat), 3mg chol., 144mg sod., 17g carb. (1g sugars, 1g fiber), 3g pro. **Diabetic exchanges:** 1 starch.

HOW TO PROOF YEAST

If you have doubts about the age of your yeast, proof it. This just means waiting to see if it produces fermentation activity before you continue with the recipe steps.

1. **In a large bowl, dissolve yeast and 1 tsp. sugar in ½ cup water.**

2. **After 10 minutes of standing, the yeast mixture should be foamy and bubbly.**

1.

2.

HONEY-OAT PAN ROLLS

These tender rolls are a welcome addition to any meal. Whole wheat flour and oats make them nutritious, too.
—Arlene Butler, Ogden, UT

PREP: 45 min. + rising • **BAKE:** 20 min.
MAKES: 2 dozen

- 2½ to 2¾ cups all-purpose flour
- ¾ cup whole wheat flour
- ½ cup old-fashioned oats
- 2 pkg. (¼ oz. each) active dry yeast
- 1 tsp. salt
- 1 cup water
- ¼ cup honey
- 5 Tbsp. butter, divided
- 1 large egg, room temperature

1. In a large bowl, mix 1 cup all-purpose flour, whole wheat flour, oats, yeast and salt. In a small saucepan, heat water, honey and 4 Tbsp. butter to 120°-130°. Add to dry ingredients; beat on medium speed 2 minutes. Add egg; beat on high 2 minutes. Stir in enough of the remaining all-purpose flour to form a soft dough (dough will be sticky).

2. Turn dough onto a floured surface; knead until smooth and elastic, about 6-8 minutes. Place in a greased bowl, turning once to grease the top. Cover with plastic wrap and let rise in a warm place until doubled, about 1 hour.

3. Punch down dough. Turn onto a lightly floured surface; divide and shape into 24 balls. Place in a greased 13x9-in. baking pan. Cover with a kitchen towel; let rise in a warm place until doubled, about 30 minutes.

4. Preheat oven to 375°. Bake 20-22 minutes or until golden brown. Melt the remaining butter; brush over the hot rolls. Remove from pan to a wire rack.

1 roll: 103 cal., 3g fat (2g sat. fat), 15mg chol., 126mg sod., 17g carb. (3g sugars, 1g fiber), 3g pro. **Diabetic exchanges:** 1 starch, ½ fat.

HOMEMADE EGG BREAD

People rave about this tender, delicate bread every time I serve it. The egg gives it a delightful richness.
—June Mullins, Livonia, MO

PREP: 30 min. + rising • **BAKE:** 30 min.
MAKES: 2 loaves (16 slices each)

- 2 pkg. (¼ oz. each) active dry yeast
- ½ cup warm water (110° to 115°)
- 1½ cups warm whole milk
     (110° to 115°)
- 3 large eggs, room temperature
- ¼ cup butter, softened
- ¼ cup sugar
- 1 Tbsp. salt
- 7 to 7½ cups all-purpose flour
- 1 large egg yolk, room temperature
- 2 Tbsp. water
     Sesame seeds

1. In a large bowl, dissolve yeast in warm water. Add milk, eggs, butter, sugar, salt and 3 cups flour; beat on medium speed until smooth. Stir in enough of the remaining flour to form a soft dough.
2. Turn onto a floured surface, knead until smooth and elastic, 6-8 minutes. Place in a greased bowl, turning once to grease the top. Cover with plastic wrap; let rise in warm place until doubled, 1½ to 2 hours.
3. Punch down dough. Turn onto a lightly floured surface; divide into six portions. Roll each into a 14-in.-long rope. For each loaf, braid three ropes together on a greased baking sheet; pinch ends to seal and tuck under. Cover with kitchen towels; let rise until doubled, about 50 minutes.
4. Beat together egg yolk and water; brush over loaves. Sprinkle with sesame seeds. Bake at 375° until golden brown, 30-35 minutes. Remove from pans to wire racks.
1 slice: 135 cal., 3g fat (1g sat. fat), 28mg chol., 245mg sod., 23g carb. (2g sugars, 1g fiber), 4g pro.

ROLLED BUTTERMILK BISCUITS

I scribbled down this recipe when our family visited the Cooperstown Farm Museum more than 25 years ago. I must have gotten it right, because the biscuits turn out great every time!
—Patricia Kile, Elizabethtown, PA

PREP: 20 min. • **BAKE:** 15 min.
MAKES: 8 biscuits

- 2 cups all-purpose flour
- 3 tsp. baking powder
- ½ tsp. baking soda
- ¼ tsp. salt
- 3 Tbsp. cold butter
- ¾ to 1 cup buttermilk
- 1 Tbsp. fat-free milk

1. Preheat oven to 450°. Coat a baking sheet with cooking spray; set aside. In a large bowl, combine the flour, baking powder, baking soda and salt; cut in the butter until the mixture resembles coarse crumbs. Stir in enough buttermilk just to moisten dough.
2. Turn the dough onto a lightly floured surface; knead 3-4 times. Pat or roll to ¾-in. thickness. Cut with a floured 2½-in. biscuit cutter. Place cutouts on prepared baking sheet.
3. Brush with milk. Bake biscuits until golden brown, 12-15 minutes.
1 serving: 164 cal., 5g fat (3g sat. fat), 13mg chol., 382mg sod., 25g carb. (0 sugars, 1g fiber), 4g pro. **Diabetic exchanges:** 1½ starch, 1 fat.

5 INGREDIENTS
MOM'S ITALIAN BREAD

I think Mom used to bake at least four of these tender loaves at once, and they never lasted long. She served bread with every Italian meal. I love it toasted, too.
—Linda Harrington, Windham, NH

PREP: 30 min. + rising
BAKE: 20 min. + cooling
MAKES: 2 loaves (12 slices each)

- 1 pkg. (¼ oz.) active dry yeast
- 2 cups warm water (110° to 115°)
- 1 tsp. sugar
- 2 tsp. salt
- 5½ cups all-purpose flour

1. In a large bowl, dissolve yeast in warm water. Add the sugar, salt and 3 cups flour. Beat on medium speed for 3 minutes. Stir in remaining flour to form a soft dough.

2. Turn dough onto a floured surface; knead until smooth and elastic, about 6-8 minutes. Place in a greased bowl, turning once to grease the top. Cover and let rise in a warm place until doubled, about 1 hour.

3. Punch dough down. Turn onto a floured surface; divide in half. Shape each portion into a loaf. Place each loaf seam side down on a greased baking sheet. Cover and let rise until doubled, about 30 minutes.

4. Meanwhile, preheat oven to 400°. With a sharp knife, make four shallow slashes across the top of each loaf. Bake until golden brown, 20-25 minutes. Remove from pans to wire racks to cool.

1 slice: 106 cal., 0 fat (0 sat. fat), 0 chol., 197mg sod., 22g carb. (1g sugars, 1g fiber), 3g pro. **Diabetic exchanges:** 1½ starch.

BONUS: GARLIC BASIL BUTTER

Instead of serving plain butter alongside your fresh homemade bread, offer up this herb-laden whipped butter.
—*Taste of Home* Test Kitchen

TAKES: 10 min. • **MAKES:** ½ cup

- ½ cup butter, softened
- 4 tsp. minced fresh basil
- 1½ tsp. minced fresh parsley
- ½ tsp. garlic powder
  Fresh sage and thyme

In a small bowl, combine the butter, basil, parsley and garlic powder. Beat on medium-low speed until mixture is combined. Garnish with sage and thyme.

1 tsp.: 101 cal., 11g fat (7g sat. fat), 31mg chol., 116mg sod., 0 carb. (0 sugars, 0 fiber), 0 pro.

BEST CINNAMON ROLLS

Surprise a neighbor with a batch of oven-fresh cinnamon rolls slathered in cream cheese frosting. These breakfast treats make Christmas morning or any special occasion even more memorable.
—Shenai Fisher, Topeka, KS

PREP: 40 min. + rising
BAKE: 20 min. + cooling • **MAKES:** 16 rolls

- 1 pkg. (¼ oz.) active dry yeast
- 1 cup warm whole milk (110° to 115°)
- ½ cup sugar
- ⅓ cup butter, melted
- 2 large eggs, room temperature
- 1 tsp. salt
- 4 to 4½ cups all-purpose flour

FILLING
- ¾ cup packed brown sugar
- 2 Tbsp. ground cinnamon
- ¼ cup butter, melted, divided

FROSTING
- ½ cup butter, softened
- ¼ cup cream cheese, softened
- ½ tsp. vanilla extract
- ⅛ tsp. salt
- 1½ cups confectioners' sugar

1. Dissolve yeast in warm milk. In another bowl, combine sugar, butter, eggs, salt, yeast mixture and 2 cups flour; beat on medium speed until smooth. Stir in enough remaining flour to form a soft dough (dough will be sticky).

2. Turn dough onto a floured surface; knead until smooth and elastic, about 6-8 minutes. Place in a greased bowl, turning once to grease the top. Cover and let rise in a warm place until doubled, about 1 hour.

3. Mix brown sugar and cinnamon. Punch down dough; divide in half. On a lightly floured surface, roll one portion into an 11x8-in. rectangle. Brush with 2 Tbsp. butter; sprinkle with half of the brown sugar mixture to within ½ in. of edges. Roll up jelly-roll style, starting with a long side; pinch seam to seal. Cut into eight slices; place in a greased 13x9-in. pan, cut side down. Cover with a kitchen towel. Repeat with remaining dough and filling. Let rise in a warm place until doubled, about 1 hour. Preheat oven to 350°.

4. Bake 20-25 minutes or until golden brown. Cool on wire racks.

5. For frosting, beat butter, cream cheese, vanilla and salt until blended; gradually beat in confectioners' sugar. Spread over tops of rolls. Refrigerate leftovers.

1 roll: 364 cal., 15g fat (9g sat. fat), 66mg chol., 323mg sod., 53g carb. (28g sugars, 1g fiber), 5g pro.

TOP TIP

To save time in the morning, cinnamon roll dough can be made in advance and kept in the refrigerator. After the dough has risen and is shaped, cover tightly and refrigerate for up to 24 hours. When ready to bake, remove from the refrigerator, partially unwrap and let rise until doubled. Then bake according to the recipe directions.

EASY POTATO ROLLS

After I discovered this recipe, it became a mainstay for me. I make the dough ahead of time when company is coming, and I keep some in the refrigerator to bake for our ranch hands. Any leftover mashed potatoes are sure to go into these rolls.
—Jeanette McKinney, Belleview, MO

PREP: 20 min. + rising • **BAKE:** 20 min.
MAKES: 45 rolls

- 2 pkg. (¼ oz. each) active dry yeast
- 1⅓ cups warm water (110° to 115°), divided
- 1 cup warm mashed potatoes (without added milk and butter)
- ⅔ cup sugar
- ⅔ cup shortening
- 2 large eggs, room temperature
- 2½ tsp. salt
- 6 to 6½ cups all-purpose flour

1. In a small bowl, dissolve yeast in ⅔ cup warm water. In a large bowl, combine mashed potatoes, sugar, shortening, eggs, salt, remaining ⅔ cup water, yeast mixture and 2 cups of the flour; beat until smooth. Stir in enough of the remaining flour to form a soft dough.
2. Do not knead. Shape into a ball; place in a greased bowl, turning once to grease the top. Cover and let rise in a warm place until doubled, about 1 hour.
3. Punch down dough; divide into thirds. Divide and shape one portion into 15 balls; place in a greased 9-in. round baking pan. Cover with a kitchen towel. Repeat with the remaining dough. Let rise in a warm place until doubled, about 30 minutes.
4. Bake at 375° for 20-25 minutes or until golden brown. Remove from pans to wire racks. Serve warm.
1 roll: 106 cal., 3g fat (1g sat. fat), 8mg chol., 136mg sod., 17g carb. (3g sugars, 1g fiber), 2g pro.

GARLIC-CHEESE FLAT BREAD

Unless you plan to double the recipe, don't count on leftovers. As an appetizer or a side dish, this cheesy flat bread will be devoured in less time than it takes to bake. And that's not long!
—Suzanne Zick, Maiden, NC

TAKES: 25 min. • **MAKES:** 12 servings

- 1 tube (11 oz.) refrigerated thin pizza crust
- 2 Tbsp. butter, melted
- 1 Tbsp. minced fresh basil
- 4 garlic cloves, minced
- ¾ cup shredded cheddar cheese
- ½ cup grated Romano cheese
- ¼ cup grated Parmesan cheese

1. Preheat oven to 425°. Unroll dough into a greased 15x10x1-in. baking pan; flatten dough to 13x9-in. rectangle and build up edges slightly.
2. Drizzle dough with butter. Sprinkle with basil, garlic and cheeses.
3. Bake for 11-14 minutes or until crisp. Cut into squares; serve warm.
1 piece: 146 cal., 8g fat (4g sat. fat), 19mg chol., 317mg sod., 13g carb. (1g sugars, 0 fiber), 6g pro.

DESSERTS

SATISFY YOUR SWEET TOOTH WITH CLASSIC CAKES, COOKIES AND MORE!

SOUR CREAM POUND CAKE

Because I'm our town's postmaster, I don't have much spare time to bake. But when I do, I enjoy making desserts like this one. It tastes great as is, or tucked under a layer of ice cream and chocolate syrup as a super hot fudge sundae!
—Karen Conrad, East Troy, WI

PREP: 15 min. • **BAKE:** 1¼ hours + cooling
MAKES: 20 servings

- 1 **cup butter, softened**
- 3 **cups sugar**
- 6 **large eggs, room temperature**
- 3 **cups all-purpose flour**
- ¼ **tsp. baking soda**
- ¼ **tsp. salt**
- 1 **cup sour cream**
- 2 **tsp. vanilla extract**
  Confectioners' sugar, optional

1. Preheat oven to 325°. In a bowl, cream butter and sugar until light and fluffy, about 5-7 minutes. Add eggs, one at a time, beating well after each addition. Combine flour, baking soda and salt; add to creamed mixture alternately with sour cream and vanilla. Beat on low just until blended. Pour into a greased and floured 10-in. fluted tube pan.
2. Bake for 1¼ to 1½ hours or until a toothpick comes out clean. Cool in pan for 15 minutes before removing to a wire rack to cool completely. Sprinkle with confectioners' sugar if desired.
1 piece: 311 cal., 13g fat (7g sat. fat), 96mg chol., 163mg sod., 45g carb. (30g sugars, 1g fiber), 4g pro.

OATMEAL RAISIN COOKIES

A friend gave me this recipe many years ago, and these cookies are as delicious as the ones Mom used to make. The secret is to measure exactly (no guessing on the amounts) and to not overbake.
—Wendy Coalwell, Abbeville, GA

TAKES: 30 min. • **MAKES:** about 3½ dozen

- 1 **cup shortening**
- 1 **cup sugar**
- 1 **cup packed light brown sugar**
- 3 **large eggs, room temperature**
- 1 **tsp. vanilla extract**
- 2½ **cups all-purpose flour**
- 2 **tsp. baking soda**
- 1 **tsp. salt**
- 1 **tsp. ground cinnamon**
- 2 **cups old-fashioned oats**
- 1 **cup raisins**
- 1 **cup coarsely chopped pecans, optional**

1. Preheat oven to 350°. In a large bowl, cream shortening and sugars until light and fluffy. Beat in eggs, one at a time, beating well after each addition. Beat in vanilla. Combine the flour, baking soda, salt and cinnamon. Add to the creamed mixture, stirring just until combined. Stir in the oats, raisins and pecans if desired.
2. Shape into 1-in. balls. Place 2 in. apart on ungreased baking sheets. Flatten with a greased glass bottom.
3. Bake until golden brown, 10-11 minutes. Do not overbake. Remove to a wire rack.
1 cookie: 138 cal., 5g fat (1g sat. fat), 13mg chol., 123mg sod., 21g carb. (12g sugars, 1g fiber), 2g pro.

MRS. THOMPSON'S CARROT CAKE

I received this recipe in St. Paul from the mother of a patient I cared for back in 1972. It was, and still is, the best carrot cake I have ever tasted.
—Becky Wachob, Laramie, WY

PREP: 30 min. • **BAKE:** 35 min.
MAKES: 15 servings

- 3 cups shredded carrots
- 1 can (20 oz.) crushed pineapple, well drained
- 2 cups sugar
- 1 cup canola oil
- 4 large eggs, room temperature
- 2 cups all-purpose flour
- 2 tsp. baking soda
- 2 tsp. ground cinnamon

FROSTING
- 1 pkg. (8 oz.) cream cheese, softened
- ¼ cup butter, softened
- 2 tsp. vanilla extract
- 3¾ cups confectioners' sugar

1. Preheat oven to 350°. In a large bowl, beat the first five ingredients until well blended. In another bowl, mix the flour, baking soda and cinnamon; gradually beat into carrot mixture.

2. Transfer to a greased 13x9-in. baking pan. Bake for 35-40 minutes or until a toothpick inserted in the center comes out clean. Cool completely in pan on a wire rack.

3. For frosting, in a large bowl, beat the cream cheese, butter and vanilla until blended. Gradually beat in confectioners' sugar until smooth. Spread over cake. Store in refrigerator.

1 piece: 552 cal., 25g fat (7g sat. fat), 81mg chol., 269mg sod., 80g carb. (63g sugars, 2g fiber), 5g pro.

"This is the best carrot cake ever! I have made this cake for two weddings in the last two years. My son-in-law requests it as a Christmas present every year—I make it as cupcakes for him."

—MILLIEK, TASTEOFHOME.COM

EASY BOURBON PECAN PIE

Crunchy, chewy, not too sweet—and simple to make...just what you want in a pecan pie! The bourbon flavor is very mellow, not overpowering.
—Nick Iverson, Denver, CO

PREP: 10 min. + freezing
BAKE: 1¼ hours + cooling • **MAKES:** 10 servings

- 12 oz. toasted pecan halves, divided
- 4 large eggs, room temperature
- ½ cup packed dark brown sugar
- ¼ cup sugar
- 1 cup dark corn syrup
- 8 Tbsp. unsalted butter, melted
- ¼ cup bourbon
- 2 tsp. vanilla extract
- ¼ tsp. salt
- 1 sheet refrigerated pie crust
     Vanilla ice cream, optional

1. In a food processor, pulse half the pecans until coarsely chopped; reserve remaining pecans. Combine eggs and sugars until well mixed. Add the next five ingredients and the chopped pecans.

2. Unroll crust into a 9-in. metal pie plate; flute edge. Pour filling into crust. Arrange the reserved pecan halves over the filling. Place filled pie in freezer for 30 minutes.

3. Bake at 425° until crust is set, about 15 minutes. Reduce oven to 350°; continue baking until pie is puffed and set in the middle, about 1 hour (tent loosely with foil if needed to prevent overbrowning). Cool. If desired, serve with ice cream.

Note: To toast nuts, bake in a shallow pan in a 350° oven for 5-10 minutes or cook in a skillet over low heat until lightly browned, stirring occasionally.

1 slice: 600 cal., 41g fat (11g sat. fat), 103mg chol., 221mg sod., 56g carb. (43g sugars, 3g fiber), 7g pro.

TOP TIP

Dark brown sugar adds a nice caramel flavor to this pie, but don't worry if you only have light brown sugar—you'll get less caramel flavor but more bourbon flavor. We love the pairing of pecans and bourbon, but don't let that stop you from trying other nuts. Almonds and hazelnuts would both work nicely.

BUTTERMILK POUND CAKE

Now that I've retired from teaching, I have more time to bake. This cake is the one I make most often. It is a truly southern recipe, and one I think can't be topped—once you taste it, you won't go back to your other pound cake recipes.
—Gracie Hanchey, DeRidder, LA

PREP: 10 min. • **BAKE:** 70 min. + cooling
MAKES: 20 servings

- 1 **cup butter, softened**
- 2½ **cups sugar**
- 4 **large eggs, room temperature**
- 1 **tsp. vanilla extract**
- 3 **cups all-purpose flour**
- ¼ **tsp. baking soda**
- 1 **cup buttermilk**
  Confectioners' sugar, optional

1. Preheat oven to 325°. In a large bowl, cream butter and sugar until light and fluffy. Add eggs, one at a time, beating well after each addition. Beat in vanilla. Combine flour and baking soda; add alternately with buttermilk and beat well.
2. Pour into a greased and floured 10-in. fluted tube pan. Bake for 70 minutes or until a toothpick inserted in the center comes out clean. Let cake cool in pan for 15 minutes before removing to a wire rack to cool completely. Dust the cake with confectioners' sugar if desired.
1 slice: 285 cal., 10g fat (6g sat. fat), 68mg chol., 134mg sod., 45g carb. (30g sugars, 1g fiber), 4g pro.

STRAWBERRY SHORTCAKE

I grew up helping my mom cook and bake in our farmhouse kitchen. This sunny, traditional strawberry shortcake recipe brings back those happy memories
—Janet Becker, Anacortes, WA

PREP: 25 min. • **BAKE:** 20 min. + cooling
MAKES: 9 servings

- ⅔ **cup sugar**
- ¼ **cup shortening**
- 1 **large egg, room temperature**
- 1 **tsp. vanilla extract**
- ¼ **tsp. salt**
- 1½ **cups all-purpose flour**
- 2 **tsp. baking powder**
- ½ **cup whole milk**
- 1 **cup heavy whipping cream, whipped**
- 1½ **qt. fresh or frozen strawberries, sliced**

Preheat oven to 350°. In a bowl, cream the sugar and shortening. Add the egg and vanilla; beat well. Combine the dry ingredients and add alternately with milk to the creamed mixture. Spread in a greased 9-in. square baking pan. Bake for 20-25 minutes. Cool on wire rack. Cut into nine servings. Split each serving horizontally and fill with whipped cream and strawberries. Replace top of the cake; garnish with a dollop of whipped cream and more strawberries. Serve the shortcake immediately.
1 piece: 321 cal., 16g fat (8g sat. fat), 52mg chol., 195mg sod., 40g carb. (21g sugars, 2g fiber), 5g pro.

CHOCOLATE CAKE WITH CHOCOLATE FROSTING

When I made this rich chocolate cake to send to my kids' teachers, it vanished, so I had to make another one!
—Megan Moelbert, Springville, NY

PREP: 40 min. • **BAKE:** 30 min. + cooling
MAKES: 16 servings

- 2 cups sugar
- 2 cups water
- ⅔ cup canola oil
- 2 Tbsp. white vinegar
- 2 tsp. vanilla extract
- 3 cups all-purpose flour
- ⅓ cup plus 1 Tbsp. baking cocoa, sifted
- 2 tsp. baking soda
- 1 tsp. salt

FROSTING

- 3¾ cups confectioners' sugar
- ⅓ cup baking cocoa
- 1 cup butter, softened
- 1 tsp. vanilla extract
- 3 to 5 Tbsp. 2% milk

1. Preheat oven to 350°. Line bottoms of two greased 9-in. round baking pans with parchment; grease paper. Set aside.
2. In a large bowl, beat sugar, water, oil, vinegar and vanilla until well blended. In a large bowl, whisk flour, sifted cocoa, baking soda and salt; gradually add to sugar mixture, beating until smooth.
3. Transfer batter to prepared pans. Bake 30-35 minutes or until a toothpick inserted in the center comes out clean. Cool in pans for 10 minutes before removing to wire racks; remove paper. Cool completely.
4. For frosting, sift confectioners' sugar and cocoa together. In a large bowl, beat butter and vanilla until blended. Beat in confectioners' sugar mixture alternately with enough milk to reach desired consistency. Spread frosting between layers and over top and sides of cake.
1 slice: 491 cal., 22g fat (8g sat. fat), 31mg chol., 399mg sod., 74g carb. (53g sugars, 1g fiber), 3g pro.

NOTES

_____
_____
_____
_____
_____
_____
_____
_____
_____
_____
_____

LEMON-BLUEBERRY POUND CAKE

This moist cake is a staple at our family barbecues. We love it with a scoop of vanilla ice cream!
—Rebecca Little, Park Ridge, IL

PREP: 25 min. • **BAKE:** 55 min. + cooling
MAKES: 12 servings

- ⅓ cup butter, softened
- 4 oz. cream cheese, softened
- 2 cups sugar
- 3 large eggs, room temperature
- 1 large egg white, room temperature
- 1 Tbsp. grated lemon zest
- 2 tsp. vanilla extract
- 2 cups fresh or frozen unsweetened blueberries
- 3 cups all-purpose flour, divided
- 1 tsp. baking powder
- ½ tsp. baking soda
- ½ tsp. salt
- 1 cup (8 oz.) lemon yogurt

GLAZE
- 1¼ cups confectioners' sugar
- 2 Tbsp. lemon juice

1. Preheat oven to 350°. Grease and flour a 10-in. fluted tube pan. In a large bowl, cream the butter, cream cheese and sugar until blended. Add eggs and egg white, one at a time, beating well after each addition. Beat in lemon zest and vanilla.
2. Toss blueberries with 2 Tbsp. flour. In another bowl, mix the remaining flour with baking powder, baking soda and salt; add to creamed mixture alternately with yogurt, beating after each addition just until combined. Fold in blueberry mixture.
3. Transfer batter to prepared pan. Bake for 55-60 minutes or until a toothpick inserted in center comes out clean. Cool in pan 10 minutes before removing to wire rack; cool completely.
4. In a small bowl, mix confectioners' sugar and lemon juice until smooth. Drizzle over cake.

Note: For easier removal of cake, use solid shortening when greasing a fluted or plain tube pan.

1 slice: 434 cal., 10g fat (6g sat. fat), 78mg chol., 281mg sod., 80g carb. (54g sugars, 1g fiber), 7g pro.

TOP TIP

The hole in the center of a tube pan permits more surface area to be in contact with the heat. This allows cakes with high sugar or butter content to fully cook in the center without the edges overbrowning. To find the diameter of your fluted tube pan, measure across the open top.

HARVEST SWEET POTATO PIE

My father called this sweet potato pie recipe "royal pie," because he thought it was fit for a king. It's a most treasured hand-me-down family recipe.
—Fae Fisher, Callao, VA

PREP: 15 min. • **BAKE:** 45 min.
MAKES: 16 servings (2 pies)

- 4 large eggs, room temperature
- 1 can (12 oz.) evaporated milk
- 1¼ cups sugar
- ¾ cup butter, melted
- 2 tsp. ground cinnamon
- 2 tsp. pumpkin pie spice
- 1 tsp. vanilla extract
- 1 tsp. lemon extract
- ½ tsp. ground nutmeg
- ½ tsp. salt
- 4 cups mashed cooked sweet potatoes
- 2 unbaked pie shells (9 in.)
  Whipped cream, optional

Preheat oven to 425°. In a bowl, combine the first 10 ingredients; mix well. Beat in sweet potatoes. Pour into the pie shells. Bake for 15 minutes. Reduce heat to 350°; bake 30-35 minutes longer or until a knife inserted in the center comes out clean. Cool completely. Serve with whipped cream if desired. Store pie in the refrigerator.

1 piece: 391 cal., 18g fat (10g sat. fat), 88mg chol., 307mg sod., 51g carb. (28g sugars, 2g fiber), 5g pro.

SNICKERDOODLES

The history of these whimsically named treats is widely disputed, but their popularity is undeniable! Help yourself to one of our soft cinnamon-sugared cookies and see for yourself.
—*Taste of Home* Test Kitchen

PREP: 20 min. • **BAKE:** 10 min./batch
MAKES: 2½ dozen

- ½ cup butter, softened
- 1 cup plus 2 Tbsp. sugar, divided
- 1 large egg, room temperature
- ½ tsp. vanilla extract
- 1½ cups all-purpose flour
- ¼ tsp. baking soda
- ¼ tsp. cream of tartar
- 1 tsp. ground cinnamon

1. Preheat oven to 375°. Cream butter and 1 cup sugar until light and fluffy; beat in egg and vanilla. In another bowl, whisk together flour, baking soda and cream of tartar; gradually beat dry ingredients into the creamed mixture.

2. In a small bowl, mix cinnamon and the remaining sugar. Shape dough into 1-in. balls; roll balls in cinnamon sugar. Place 2 in. apart on ungreased baking sheets.

3. Bake until light brown, 10-12 minutes. Remove from pans to wire racks to cool.

1 cookie: 81 cal., 3g fat (2g sat. fat), 15mg chol., 44mg sod., 12g carb. (7g sugars, 0 fiber), 1g pro.

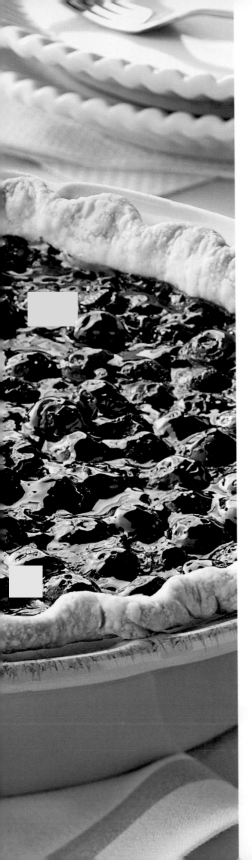

CONTEST-WINNING FRESH BLUEBERRY PIE

Blueberries are readily available in Michigan, and I've been making this dessert for decades. Nothing says summer like fresh blueberry pie!
—Linda Kernan, Mason, MI

PREP: 15 min. + cooling • **MAKES:** 8 servings

¾ cup sugar
3 Tbsp. cornstarch
⅛ tsp. salt
¼ cup cold water
5 cups fresh blueberries, divided
1 Tbsp. butter
1 Tbsp. lemon juice
1 refrigerated pie crust (9 in.), baked

1. In a saucepan over medium heat, combine sugar, cornstarch, salt and water until smooth. Add 3 cups of blueberries. Bring to a boil; cook and stir for 2 minutes or until thickened and bubbly.

2. Remove from the heat. Add butter, lemon juice and the remaining berries; stir until the butter is melted. Cool. Pour into pastry shell. Refrigerate until set and ready to serve.

1 piece: 269 cal., 9g fat (4g sat. fat), 9mg chol., 150mg sod., 48g carb. (29g sugars, 2g fiber), 2g pro.

"Definitely a keeper! I love that it uses fresh blueberries instead of canned. The texture of the berries is so nice since only some of them are cooked first."
—TNBLUFFBAKER, TASTEOFHOME.COM

GRANDMA'S RED VELVET CAKE

No one believes it's Christmas at our house until this jolly cake appears. The extraordinary icing is as light as snow.
—Kathryn Davison, Charlotte, NC

PREP: 30 min. • **BAKE:** 20 min. + cooling
MAKES: 14 servings

- ½ cup butter, softened
- 1½ cups sugar
- 2 large eggs, room temperature
- 2 bottles (1 oz. each) red food coloring
- 1 Tbsp. white vinegar
- 1 tsp. vanilla extract
- 2¼ cups cake flour
- 2 Tbsp. baking cocoa
- 1 tsp. baking soda
- 1 tsp. salt
- 1 cup buttermilk

FROSTING
- 1 Tbsp. cornstarch
- ½ cup cold water
- 2 cups butter, softened
- 2 tsp. vanilla extract
- 3½ cups confectioners' sugar
  Additional confectioners' sugar, optional

1. Preheat oven to 350°. Cream butter and granulated sugar until light and fluffy. Add eggs, one at a time, beating well after each addition. Beat in the food coloring, vinegar and vanilla. In another bowl, whisk together the flour, cocoa, baking soda and salt; add to the creamed mixture alternately with buttermilk, beating well after each addition.

2. Pour into two greased and floured 9-in. round baking pans. Bake until a toothpick inserted in the center comes out clean, 20-25 minutes. Cool layers 10 minutes before removing from pans to wire racks to cool completely.

3. For the frosting, combine water and cornstarch in a small saucepan over medium heat. Stir until thickened and opaque, 2-3 minutes. Cool to room temperature. Beat butter and vanilla until light and fluffy. Beat in cornstarch mixture. Gradually add confectioners' sugar; beat until light and fluffy. Spread between the layers and over top and sides of cake. If desired, sprinkle with additional confectioners' sugar.

1 slice: 595 cal., 34g fat (21g sat. fat), 115mg chol., 564mg sod., 71g carb. (52g sugars, 1g fiber), 4g pro.

TOP TIP

To avoid getting red crumbs in your white frosting, make sure the cake is completely cool before you frost it. Brush off stray crumbs with a pastry brush. Apply a very thin layer of frosting (a "crumb coat") and then refrigerate for 10-15 minutes. When set, apply the final coat of frosting.

EASY FRESH STRAWBERRY PIE

For my mother's 70th birthday and Mother's Day, I made two of these strawberry pies instead of a cake. Since it was mid-May in Texas, the berries were absolutely perfect. It was a memorable occasion for the whole family.
—Josh Carter, Birmingham, AL

PREP: 20 min. + cooling
BAKE: 15 min. + chilling • **MAKES:** 8 servings

- 1 **pie shell, unbaked (9 in.)**
- ¾ **cup sugar**
- 2 **Tbsp. cornstarch**
- 1 **cup water**
- 1 **pkg. (3 oz.) strawberry gelatin**
- 4 **cups sliced fresh strawberries**
  Whipped cream, optional

1. Preheat oven to 450°. Line unpricked pie shell with a double thickness of heavy-duty foil. Bake for 8 minutes. Remove foil; bake 5 minutes longer. Cool on a wire rack.
2. In a small saucepan, combine sugar, cornstarch and water until smooth. Bring to a boil; cook and stir for 2 minutes or until thickened. Remove from the heat; stir in gelatin until dissolved. Refrigerate for 15-20 minutes or until slightly cooled.
3. Meanwhile, arrange strawberries in the crust. Pour the gelatin mixture over the berries. Refrigerate until set. Serve with whipped cream if desired.
1 slice: 264 cal., 7g fat (3g sat. fat), 5mg chol., 125mg sod., 49g carb. (32g sugars, 2g fiber), 2g pro.

BIG & BUTTERY CHOCOLATE CHIP COOKIES

My take on the classic cookie is inspired by a bakery in California called Hungry Bear. It's big, thick and chewy—truly the best chocolate chip cookie recipe.
—Irene Yeh, Mequon, WI

PREP: 35 min. + chilling • **BAKE:** 10 min./batch
MAKES: about 2 dozen

- 1 **cup butter, softened**
- 1 **cup packed brown sugar**
- ¾ **cup sugar**
- 2 **large eggs, room temperature**
- 1½ **tsp. vanilla extract**
- 2⅔ **cups all-purpose flour**
- 1¼ **tsp. baking soda**
- 1 **tsp. salt**
- 1 **pkg. (12 oz.) semisweet chocolate chips**
- 2 **cups coarsely chopped walnuts, toasted**

1. In a large bowl, beat butter and sugars until blended. Beat in eggs and vanilla. In a small bowl, whisk the flour, baking soda and salt; gradually beat into the butter mixture. Stir in the chocolate chips and walnuts.
2. Shape ¼ cupfuls of dough into balls. Flatten each to ¾-in. thickness (2½-in. diameter), smoothing edges as necessary. Place in an airtight container, separating layers with waxed or parchment paper; refrigerate, covered, overnight.
3. To bake, place cookies 2 in. apart on parchment-lined baking sheets; let stand at room temperature for 30 minutes before baking. Preheat oven to 400°.
4. Bake until the edges are golden brown (the centers will be light), 10-12 minutes. Cool on pans 2 minutes, then remove to wire racks to cool completely.
Note: To toast nuts, bake in a shallow pan in a 350° oven for 5-10 minutes or cook in a skillet over low heat until lightly browned, stirring occasionally.
1 cookie: 311 cal., 19g fat (8g sat. fat), 38mg chol., 229mg sod., 35g carb. (23g sugars, 2g fiber), 4g pro.

GIANT MOLASSES COOKIES

My family always requests these soft, deliciously chewy cookies. They are also great for shipping as holiday gifts for family, friends or troops overseas.
—Kristine Chayes, Smithtown, NY

PREP: 30 min. • **BAKE:** 15 min./batch
MAKES: 2 dozen

- 1½ cups butter, softened
- 2 cups sugar
- 2 large eggs, room temperature
- ½ cup molasses
- 4½ cups all-purpose flour
- 4 tsp. ground ginger
- 2 tsp. baking soda
- 1½ tsp. ground cinnamon
- 1 tsp. ground cloves
- ¼ tsp. salt
- ¼ cup chopped pecans
- ¾ cup coarse sugar

1. Preheat oven to 350°. In a large bowl, cream butter and sugar until light and fluffy. Beat in the eggs and molasses. Combine the flour, ginger, baking soda, cinnamon, cloves and salt; gradually add to the creamed mixture and mix well. Fold in pecans.

2. Shape dough into 2-in. balls and roll in coarse sugar. Place 2½ in. apart on ungreased baking sheets. Bake for 13 15 minutes or until the tops are cracked. Remove to wire racks to cool.

1 cookie: 310 cal., 13g fat (7g sat. fat), 48mg chol., 219mg sod., 46g carb. (27g sugars, 1g fiber), 3g pro.

HOW TO SOFTEN BUTTER

Most recipes for cakes, cookies and other baked goods that contain butter will call for softened butter. Here are three quick ways to prep your butter.

1. Cut cold butter into cubes. Let it stand on the counter at room temperature for about 15 minutes before using.

2. Place butter between two sheets of waxed paper and roll out with a rolling pin.

3. Grate cold butter with a hand grater.

1.

2.

3.

FAMILY-FAVORITE CHEESECAKE

This fluffy, delicate cheesecake has been a family favorite for almost 20 years. I've even started baking it for our friends at Christmas instead of cookies. The recipe gets shared over and over.
—Esther Wappner, Mansfield, OH

PREP: 20 min. + cooling
BAKE: 1 hour + chilling
MAKES: 12 servings

- 2½ cups graham cracker crumbs
- ⅓ cup sugar
- ½ tsp. ground cinnamon
- ½ cup butter, melted

FILLING
- 3 pkg. (8 oz. each) cream cheese, softened
- 1½ cups sugar
- 1 tsp. vanilla extract
- 4 large eggs, separated, room temperature

TOPPING
- ½ cup sour cream
- 2 Tbsp. sugar
- ½ tsp. vanilla extract
- ½ cup heavy whipping cream, whipped

1. Preheat oven to 350°. In a small bowl, combine the cracker crumbs, sugar and cinnamon; stir in butter. Press onto the bottom and 2 in. up the sides of a greased 9-in. springform pan. Bake for 5 minutes. Cool on a wire rack. Reduce heat to 325°.
2. In a large bowl, beat the cream cheese, sugar and vanilla until smooth. Add egg yolks; beat on low just until combined.
3. In a small bowl, beat egg whites until soft peaks form; fold into cream cheese mixture. Pour over the rust.

4. Bake for 1 hour or until center is almost set. Cool on a wire rack for 10 minutes. Carefully run a knife around edge of pan to loosen; cool 1 hour longer. Refrigerate until completely cooled.
5. Combine the sour cream, sugar and vanilla; fold in whipped cream. Spread over cheesecake. Refrigerate overnight. Remove sides of pan.
1 slice: 414 cal., 23g fat (13g sat. fat), 132mg chol., 269mg sod., 47g carb. (36g sugars, 1g fiber), 5g pro.

BONUS: PUMPKIN CHEESECAKE WITH SOUR CREAM TOPPING

Instead of serving the traditional pumpkin pie, surprise your Thanksgiving guests with this delectable cheesecake. Trust me, there will be no complaints about the substitution!
—Dorothy Smith, El Dorado, AR

PREP: 15 min. + cooling
BAKE: 1 hour + chilling
MAKES: 14 servings

- 1½ cups graham cracker crumbs
- ¼ cup sugar
- ⅓ cup butter, melted

FILLING
- 3 pkg. (8 oz. each) cream cheese, softened
- 1 cup packed brown sugar
- 1 can (15 oz.) solid-pack pumpkin
- 1 can (5 oz.) evaporated milk
- 2 Tbsp. cornstarch
- 1¼ tsp. ground cinnamon
- ½ tsp. ground nutmeg
- 2 large eggs, room temperature, lightly beaten

SOUR CREAM LAYER

- 2 **cups sour cream**
- ⅓ **cup sugar**
- 1 **tsp. vanilla extract**
  Additional ground cinnamon
  Optional toppings: caramel sundae syrup, chocolate syrup, whipped cream, chocolate curls, ground cinnamon

1. Preheat oven to 350°. In a small bowl, combine crumbs and sugar; stir in butter. Press onto the bottom and 1½ in. up the sides of a greased 9-in. springform pan. Bake for 5-7 minutes or until set. Cool for 10 minutes. In a large bowl, beat cream cheese and brown sugar until smooth. Beat in the pumpkin, milk, cornstarch, cinnamon and nutmeg. Add eggs; beat on low speed just until combined. Pour into the crust.

2. Place pan on a baking sheet. Bake for 55-60 minutes or until the center is almost set.

3. In a small bowl, combine the sour cream, sugar and vanilla; spread over filling. Bake 5 minutes longer. Cool on a wire rack for 10 minutes. Carefully run a knife around edge of pan to loosen; cool 1 hour longer. Chill overnight.

4. Remove the sides of the pan. Let stand at room temperature for 30 minutes before slicing. If desired, serve with any of the suggested toppings.

1 slice: 329 cal., 18g fat (11g sat. fat), 85mg chol., 189mg sod., 37g carb. (28g sugars, 2g fiber), 5g pro.

ULTIMATE DOUBLE CHOCOLATE BROWNIES

As someone who grew up in the country, I love getting out in nature whenever I can. But I also love staying in and making home-style recipes, including these yummy brownies.
—Carol Prewett, Cheyenne, WY

PREP: 15 min. • **BAKE:** 35 min.
MAKES: 3 dozen

- ¾ cup baking cocoa
- ½ tsp. baking soda
- ⅔ cup butter, melted, divided
- ½ cup boiling water
- 2 cups sugar
- 2 large eggs, room temperature
- 1⅓ cups all-purpose flour
- 1 tsp. vanilla extract
- ¼ tsp. salt
- ½ cup coarsely chopped pecans
- 2 cups (12 oz.) semisweet chocolate chunks

1. Preheat oven to 350°. In a large bowl, combine cocoa and baking soda; blend in ⅓ cup melted butter. Add boiling water; stir until well blended. Stir in the sugar, eggs and the remaining butter. Add flour, vanilla and salt. Stir in pecans and chocolate chunks.
2. Pour into a greased 13x9-in. baking pan. Bake 35-40 minutes or until the brownies begin to pull away from sides of pan. Cool.
1 brownie: 159 cal., 8g fat (4g sat. fat), 21mg chol., 73mg sod., 22g carb. (17g sugars, 1g fiber), 2g pro.

FRESH CHERRY PIE

This ruby-red treat is just sweet enough, with a hint of almond flavor and a good level of cinnamon. The cherries peeking out of the lattice crust makes it so pretty.
—Josie Bochek, Sturgeon Bay, WI

PREP: 25 min. • **BAKE:** 55 min. + cooling
MAKES: 8 servings

- 1¼ cups sugar
- ⅓ cup cornstarch
- 1 cup cherry juice blend
- 4 cups fresh tart cherries, pitted or frozen pitted tart cherries, thawed
- ½ tsp. ground cinnamon
- ¼ tsp. ground nutmeg
- ¼ tsp. almond extract
PASTRY
- 2 cups all-purpose flour
- ½ tsp. salt
- ⅔ cup shortening
- 5 to 7 Tbsp. cold water

1. In a large saucepan, combine sugar and cornstarch; gradually stir in cherry juice until smooth. Bring to a boil; cook and stir for 2 minutes or until thickened. Remove from heat. Add the cherries, cinnamon, nutmeg and extract; set aside.
2. In a large bowl, combine flour and salt; cut in shortening until crumbly. Gradually add cold water, tossing with a fork until a ball forms. Divide dough in half so that one ball is slightly larger than the other.
3. On a lightly floured surface, roll out larger ball to fit a 9-in. pie plate. Transfer dough to pie plate; trim even with the edge of the plate. Add filling. Roll out the remaining dough; make a lattice crust. Trim, seal and flute edges.
4. Bake at 425° for 10 minutes. Reduce heat to 375°; bake 45-50 minutes longer or until crust is golden brown. Cool on a wire rack.
1 slice: 457 cal., 17g fat (4g sat. fat), 0 chol., 153mg sod., 73g carb. (40g sugars, 2g fiber), 4g pro.

BREAD PUDDING WITH NUTMEG

I always make this dessert for my dad on his birthday and holidays, and he says it tastes exactly like the bread pudding he enjoyed when he was a child.
—Donna Powell, Montgomery City, MO

PREP: 15 min. • **BAKE:** 40 min.
MAKES: 6 servings

- 2 **large eggs, room temperature**
- 2 **cups milk**
- ¼ **cup butter, cubed**
- ¾ **cup sugar**
- ¼ **tsp. salt**
- 1 **tsp. ground cinnamon**
- ½ **tsp. ground nutmeg**
- 1 **tsp. vanilla extract**
- 4½ to 5 **cups soft bread cubes (about 9 slices)**
- ½ **cup raisins, optional**

VANILLA SAUCE
- ⅓ **cup sugar**
- 2 **Tbsp. cornstarch**
- ¼ **tsp. salt**
- 1⅔ **cups cold water**
- 3 **Tbsp. butter**
- 2 **tsp. vanilla extract**
- ¼ **tsp. ground nutmeg**

1. Preheat oven to 350°. In a large bowl, lightly beat eggs. Combine the milk and butter; add to the eggs along with sugar, spices and vanilla. Add bread cubes and raisins if desired; stir gently.

2. Pour into a well-greased 11x7-in. baking dish. Bake for 40-45 minutes or until a knife inserted 1 in. from the edge comes out clean.

3. For the sauce, combine the sugar, cornstarch and salt in a saucepan. Stir in water until smooth. Bring to a boil over medium heat; cook and stir for 2 minutes or until thickened. Remove from the heat. Stir in the butter, vanilla and nutmeg. Serve with warm pudding.

1 serving: 419 cal., 19g fat (11g sat. fat), 118mg chol., 534mg sod., 56g carb. (40g sugars, 1g fiber), 7g pro.

"I thought the bread pudding my mother made in the '30s was wonderful, but I'll quit looking for that old recipe now—dessert can't get better than this."
—NELDA H. TILL, TASTEOFHOME.COM

FLOURLESS CHOCOLATE CAKE WITH ROSEMARY GANACHE

Moist, dense and chocolaty describes this rich cake. A silky bittersweet ganache infused with rosemary really takes the dessert over the top.
—Kelly Gardner, Alton, IL

PREP: 40 min. • **BAKE:** 30 min.
MAKES: 16 servings

- 1 **lb. semisweet chocolate, chopped**
- 1 **cup butter, cubed**
- ¼ **cup dry red wine**
- 8 **large eggs, room temperature**
- ½ **cup sugar**
- 1 **tsp. vanilla extract**

GANACHE

- 9 **oz. bittersweet chocolate, chopped**
- 1 **cup heavy whipping cream**
- 2 **fresh rosemary sprigs**

1. Preheat oven to 350°. Line the bottom of a greased 9-in. springform pan with parchment; grease the paper. Place on a double thickness of heavy-duty foil (about 18 in. square). Securely wrap foil around pan; set aside.

2. In a large heavy saucepan over low heat, add chocolate, butter and wine, stirring constantly while melting. Remove from heat; cool to room temperature.

3. Meanwhile, in a large bowl, beat the eggs, sugar and vanilla until frothy and doubled in volume, about 5 minutes. Gradually fold eggs into the chocolate mixture, one-third at a time, until well blended. Pour into the prepared pan. Place the springform pan in a larger baking pan; add 1 in. of hot water to the larger pan.

4. Bake for 28-32 minutes or until outer edges are set (the center will jiggle). Remove springform pan from water bath. Cool completely on a wire rack.

5. Run a knife around the edge of the pan to loosen; remove sides of pan. Invert onto a serving platter; remove parchment.

6. For the ganache, place chocolate in a small bowl. In a small saucepan, bring the cream and rosemary sprigs just to a boil. Remove from heat; discard rosemary. Pour the cream over the chocolate; whisk until smooth. Cool the ganache slightly, stirring occasionally. Pour over cake. Chill until set.

1 slice: 435 cal., 35g fat (20g sat. fat), 156mg chol., 121mg sod., 31g carb. (26g sugars, 3g fiber), 7g pro.

TOP TIP

Chopping chocolate before melting it helps to ensure that it melts evenly. When melted whole or in large, uneven pieces, some chocolate may burn before the larger pieces melt.

BANANA CREAM PIE

Made with our farm-fresh dairy products, this pie was a sensational creamy treat any time Mom served it. Her recipe is a real treasure, and I've never found one that tastes better!
—Bernice Morris, Marshfield, MO

PREP: 20 min. + cooling • **MAKES:** 8 servings

- ¾ cup sugar
- ⅓ cup all-purpose flour
- ¼ tsp. salt
- 2 cups milk
- 3 large egg yolks, room temperature, lightly beaten
- 2 Tbsp. butter
- 1 tsp. vanilla extract
- 3 medium, firm bananas
- 1 pastry shell (9 in.), baked
  Whipped cream and additional sliced bananas, optional

1. In a saucepan, combine sugar, flour and salt; stir in milk and mix well. Cook over medium-high heat until the mixture is thickened and bubbly. Cook and stir for 2 minutes longer. Remove from the heat. Stir a small amount into egg yolks; return all to saucepan. Bring to a gentle boil. Cook and stir for 2 minutes; remove from heat. Add butter and vanilla; cool slightly.
2. Slice the bananas into the pastry shell; pour filling over top. Cool on wire rack for 1 hour. Store in the refrigerator. If desired, before serving pie, garnish with whipped cream and more sliced bananas.
1 slice: 338 cal., 14g fat (7g sat. fat), 101mg chol., 236mg sod., 49g carb. (30g sugars, 1g fiber), 5g pro.

COOKIE JAR GINGERSNAPS

My grandma kept two cookie jars in her pantry. One, which I now have, always had these crisp and chewy gingersnaps in it. It's still my favorite cookie recipe!
—Deb Handy, Pomona, KS

PREP: 20 min. • **BAKE:** 15 min./batch
MAKES: 3 dozen

- ¾ cup shortening
- 1 cup plus 2 Tbsp. sugar, divided
- 1 large egg, room temperature
- ¼ cup molasses
- 2 cups all-purpose flour
- 2 tsp. baking soda
- 1½ tsp. ground ginger
- 1 tsp. ground cinnamon
- ½ tsp. salt

1. Preheat oven to 350°. Cream the shortening and 1 cup sugar until light and fluffy. Beat in egg and molasses. In another bowl, combine the next five ingredients; gradually add to the creamed mixture and mix well.
2. Shape level tablespoonfuls of dough into balls. Dip one side of each ball into the remaining sugar; place 2 in. apart, sugary side up, on greased baking sheets. Bake until lightly browned and crinkly, 12-15 minutes. Remove cookies to wire racks to cool.
1 cookie: 92 cal., 4g fat (1g sat. fat), 5mg chol., 106mg sod., 13g carb. (7g sugars, 0 fiber), 1g pro.

IVA'S PEACH COBBLER

My mother received this recipe from a friend of hers many years ago, and she shared it with me. We're fortunate to live right between two large fruit-producing areas in our state, so in summer, peaches are plentiful.
—Ruby Ewart, Boise, ID

PREP: 15 min. • **BAKE:** 45 min.
MAKES: 12 servings

6   to 8 large ripe peaches, peeled and sliced
2½ Tbsp. cornstarch
¾   to 1 cup sugar
CRUST
1   cup all-purpose flour
2   large egg yolks, room temperature
¼   cup butter, melted
1   tsp. baking powder
1   cup sugar
2   large egg whites, room temperature, stiffly beaten

Preheat oven to 375°. Combine peaches, cornstarch and sugar; place in a greased 13x9-in. baking dish. For crust, combine flour, egg yolks, butter, baking powder and sugar in a bowl. Gently fold in the egg whites. Spread over the peaches. Bake until the fruit is bubbling around the edges and the top is golden brown, about 45 minutes.
½ cup: 224 cal., 5g fat (3g sat. fat), 46mg chol., 83mg sod., 44g carb. (33g sugars, 1g fiber), 3g pro.

HOW TO MEASURE FLOUR

Scooping up a cup of flour can result in up to 20 percent too much flour in your recipe, which can produce dry, heavy desserts. Use this technique to measure flour in a measuring cup.

1. Flour settles as it sits in the container, so first use a spoon or whisk to fluff it back up, then spoon it into a dry measuring cup.

2. Drag the flat side of a knife across the top of the measuring cup to level the cup and remove the extra flour.

1.

2.

RECIPE INDEX